100 THINGS
KANSAS FANS
SHOULD KNOW & DO
BEFORE THEY DIE

Ken Davis

TRIUMPH
BOOKS

Library of Congress Cataloging-in-Publication Data

Davis, Ken, 1958-
  100 things Kansas fans should know & do before they die / Ken Davis ; [foreword by] Bill Self.
       pages cm.—(100 things...fans should know)
       ISBN 978-1-60078-817-8 (pbk.)
    1.   University of Kansas--Basketball—History. 2.   Kansas Jayhawks (Basketball team)—History. 3.   Kansas Jayhawks (Basketball team)— Miscellanea. I. Title. II. Title: One hundred things Kansas fans should know and do before they die.
  GV885.43.U52D37 2013
  796.323'630978165—dc23
                                        2013028903

This book is available in quantity at special discounts for your group or organization. For further information, contact:
    Triumph Books LLC
    814 North Franklin Street
    Chicago, Illinois 60610
    (312) 337-0747
    www.triumphbooks.com

Printed in U.S.A.
ISBN: 978-1-60078-817-8
Design by Patricia Frey
Photos courtesy of AP Images unless otherwise indicated

To my wife, Nancy, and our sons, Patrick and Joseph— my personal Jayhawk team. I hope you understand you are always No. 1 in my rankings.

Contents

Foreword

The day I was introduced as the eighth head coach in Kansas basketball history, I talked about the thrill of driving up Naismith Drive to my new office. It was something I had thought about for quite some time and it was important to take that route to work on my first day. I think any basketball coach would tell you it's pretty cool to head to work every day on Naismith Drive.

And there's only one place where you can do that.

Now I've had the pleasure of working at Allen Fieldhouse for 10 years and I'm reminded every day that the University of Kansas is a special place. That road is named for Dr. James Naismith, the first basketball coach at Kansas and the man who invented the sport. One of Naismith's students was Forrest C. Allen, better known around here as "Phog" or "Doc." Even though Naismith told Allen, "You can't coach basketball; you just play it," Dr. Allen had his own ideas and he ultimately became known as "the father of basketball coaching," winning 590 games in 39 seasons as KU's coach.

You could stop right there and clearly understand how much basketball means to the Jayhawks and all of our fans. But Kansas basketball has never stopped, has never taken a day off, and has never backed down from the challenge of trying to win every game and every championship. From Adolph Rupp to Dean Smith to Clyde Lovellette to Jo Jo White to Bud Stallworth to Danny Manning and on to Mario Chalmers and the rest of the players I've been lucky enough to coach, the tradition and the pride of wearing "KANSAS" across the front of the jersey has always been the most important thing.

In April 2003, I had just completed my third season at Illinois and I thought I had a pretty good thing going. There wasn't a thought in my head about leaving that job until I got a message to call the University of Kansas while I was on vacation in Florida. During the 1985–86 season, I had learned what it meant to be a Jayhawk when I was a graduate assistant coach on coach Larry Brown's staff. Coach Brown once said of Kansas that, "There's no better place to coach. There's no better place to go to school. There's no better place to play." Coach Brown was honored to coach at a place that understands the value of history, tradition, and sportsmanship. If I learned anything during that one season under Coach Brown, it was the importance of respecting the history at Kansas. That's why I had to respond when that message arrived from KU.

I knew it wouldn't be easy following Roy Williams, who had tremendous success in his 15 seasons at Kansas. Coach Williams, just like Coach Brown, was a product of North Carolina. Both had immersed themselves in the lessons of Tar Heels coach Dean Smith, who learned the game from Phog Allen during his days in a Jayhawks uniform. And both worked hard to uphold the tradition of Kansas basketball. They knew the importance of having every seat filled in Allen Fieldhouse, having that energy and passion in the building that gives our players such an advantage.

Every new season at Kansas starts with pressure and expectations. Without that passion, Kansas would have an ordinary basketball program instead of, in my opinion, the best in college basketball. I cherish the atmosphere at Allen Fieldhouse; it is an honor to be part of that gameday experience with fans who appreciate the home team's effort and focus. That's the way it is every time we take the floor. We can feel that excitement building in the locker room before the game and during warm-ups. When the door opens and it's time to walk through that tunnel, the adrenaline is pumping. That never gets old. Every time that happens, I remind myself of how lucky I am to be the basketball coach at Kansas.

There's so much to know about Kansas basketball, so many great stories behind the wins, the losses, the coaches, the players, and the fans. KU has the best fans and the best traditions—from the Rock Chalk Chant to the "Crimson and the Blue," from "I'm A Jayhawk" to Fighting Jayhawk to the waving of the wheat, and everything else that is part of the gameday experience. There is no better setting in college basketball than a Saturday afternoon game with the sunshine streaming through the Allen Fieldhouse windows.

That's what this book is all about. *100 Things Kansas Fans Should Know & Do Before They Die* is a handbook that reminds us of all the things that make this program special. Author Ken Davis started following Kansas basketball as a youngster when Jo Jo White was playing for coach Ted Owens. As a student at Kansas, Ken was a classmate of Jayhawk greats such as Darnell Valentine, Paul Mokeski, and Ken Koenigs. He began his reporting career in Lawrence and while covering the national college basketball scene he also has studied KU basketball history. Ken has witnessed every KU Final Four appearance since that 1985–86 season when I was a graduate assistant with Coach Brown. He was there when Danny and the Miracles won the national championship in 1988. And he had a terrific view of Mario's Miracle in San Antonio in 2008.

Kansas has 114 years of great basketball memories. Our program keeps moving forward, but it is so important to keep all of these stories alive. Enjoy this great book and then come back home to Allen Fieldhouse for more memories. We'll be there to greet you, waiting to add another layer of goose bumps to the ones you already have.

—Bill Self

Introduction

Over the years, I've lost count how many times I've had to answer these questions. "Why didn't you study journalism at the University of Missouri? Doesn't MU have the best journalism school?" My first response always has been, "I never gave it a thought." That's just me being honest.

I never had serious thoughts of attending any school other than the University of Kansas. First, the William Allen White School of Journalism at KU takes a backseat to no other university. Yes, I am biased, but the faculty at KU was terrific when I was in school and remains so today. Second, I was brought up on Kansas basketball. My first memories of college basketball involve the Big 8 holiday tournament in Kansas City, Jo Jo White, Ted Owens, and the Jayhawks. The history and the tradition of the program became important to me at an early age. By the time 1971 rolled around, I was hooked. That's the year Dave Robisch, Bud Stallworth, Roger Brown, Pierre Russell, and Aubrey Nash took KU to the Final Four.

And that brings me to the final reason: Who wants to attend a school that has never reached the Final Four? Poor Mizzou.

Back in 1976–77 during my freshman season as a KU student, the headline on the game programs declared: "Kansas: The Basketball School." In small print below that headline were the names of great KU players and seasons, conference championships, NCAA finishes, and so on.

The Basketball School. It's a bold statement. But the Jayhawks back it up. Kansas has the second most victories (2,101) in NCAA Division I men's history and the most regular season conference championships (56) in Division I (including a current streak of nine in a row). The Jayhawks won 197 games from 2006–07 to 2011–12 to set the Division I record in a six-year span and have won 23 or more games in each of the past 24 seasons. Kansas has been to the NCAA tournament 42 times and holds the longest active streak in the nation with 24 consecutive appearances. KU has reached the Sweet 16 on 30 occasions and appeared in the Final Four 14 times. The Jayhawks have won the NCAA tournament three times—in 1952, 1988, and 2008.

Many consider Allen Fieldhouse the most historic arena in college basketball and the best place to watch a game. No argument there. My idea of a perfect day would be a KU game in the afternoon and a Bruce Springsteen concert that night—both in Allen Fieldhouse.

The Jayhawks have played in front of 197 consecutive sellout crowds in "the Phog" dating back to 2001–02. It's not just the building, it's not the attendance figure, it's the fans—especially the students—who make Allen Fieldhouse special. What a great atmosphere. Opponents are warned upon entrance to "Beware of the Phog," and that has been so true the past 10 years when coach Bill Self has compiled a 161–8 record in Allen Fieldhouse. The numbers are awesome, but this book goes way beyond the stats to delve into the people, events, and traditions. Kansas basketball is all about the players, the coaches, the people, and their stories—the stories behind those incredible numbers.

My career as a sportswriter shipped me to the East Coast in 1981. Since that time I've covered some of the top basketball programs in the country as a beat writer for Syracuse, Maryland, and Connecticut. Each school has its colorful stories and a history to tell. But the tradition at Kansas is unmatched.

The arrival of Andrew Wiggins is the most important thing for KU in 2013. Readers of this book will find this spectacular, athletic freshman in more than one chapter. But when it came to ranking the 100 things to know and do for Kansas fans, No. 1 was a no-brainer. Dr. James Naismith invented the game of basketball and brought it to KU. He was the first coach of the Jayhawks (and the only coach with a losing record).

That beginning back in 1898 might not sound too interesting until you learn more about Naismith. Without Naismith the Kansas story would be totally different. So we start there and move next to Phog Allen. Maybe you've seen Allen's statue and you know Allen Fieldhouse is named for him. Do you know Allen is considered "the father of basketball coaching," that he spent 39 seasons at Kansas, that he was an inventor and an innovator, got basketball into the Olympics, and was way ahead of his time?

Bill Self is only the eighth coach in Kansas history. Four of those coaches are in the Basketball Hall of Fame, which is named in honor of Naismith. Self is well on his way to becoming the fifth. There are 17 former Jayhawks—including women's basketball standout Lynette Woodard—in the Hall of Fame. That's more than any other Division I school. One of the things we suggest to do in this book is visit the Hall of Fame in Springfield, Massachusetts. You will leave as a proud Jayhawk.

All the great KU players—Wilt, Danny, Clyde, Jo Jo, Jacque, Mario, and the rest—are in the book. The big wins and the big plays are here. But so are the shocking, depressing defeats that are so much a part of the KU story. Ignoring those heartbreaking losses to Arizona, Texas Western, VCU, the Killer Bs, Syracuse, and Kentucky would make the story incomplete.

This is the second book I've written about Kansas basketball. The first was a complete history from 1898 through 2008. Talk about a great ending. Mario and the Jayhawks wrote a perfect final chapter for that edition. History is here, too, but I view this book as a collection of short essays. From Naismith to Wiggins, the final 10 chapters were just as enjoyable to write as the first 10.

If Kansas sparked your passion for college basketball, you already know there's no place like home. Maybe you will learn something, maybe you will laugh, or maybe you will cry. Kansas basketball packs a lot of emotion. Enjoy the book. And, as Wilt said, "Rock Chalk Jayhawk."

—Ken Davis

1 James Naismith

University of Kansas chancellor Francis Snow needed a physical education director and someone to lead daily chapel services when he contacted University of Chicago chancellor William Harper in 1898 and asked for a recommendation. Harper immediately sought the advice of his football coach, the renowned Amos Alonzo Stagg.

Stagg fired off a telegram to Snow that read, "Recommend James Naismith, inventor of basketball, medical doctor, Presbyterian minister, tee-totaler, all-around athlete, non-smoker, and owner of vocabulary without cuss words. Address Y.M.C.A., Denver, Colorado."

Stagg had met Naismith at YMCA Training School in Springfield, Massachusetts, in 1890, a little more than one year before Naismith invented the game of basketball. They became good friends and admired one another but had gone their separate ways. Snow took Stagg's recommendation under consideration and wasted little time offering Naismith the job.

Naismith accepted. He was bound for Lawrence, and that brings us to the most important thing fans should know about Kansas basketball before they die. James Naismith did not invent the game of basketball while at KU, but his arrival at the university marks the beginning of the school's basketball timeline.

Naismith wasn't even thinking about Kansas basketball when he took the job in Lawrence. Coaching basketball wasn't part of the job description because Kansas didn't have an intercollegiate basketball team. His initial salary was $1,300 a year—or about $25 a week. He often said the only reason he was offered the job was that he knew how to pray.

But Naismith did become the first basketball coach at Kansas, taking that position in 1899. Without even trying, he laid a foundation for the sport that has given the university its athletic identity for more than a hundred years. In the process he became a treasured member of the faculty and the community, remaining in Lawrence until his death in November 1939.

Naismith, born November 6, 1861 in Almonte, Ontario, was orphaned and experienced a difficult childhood before moving to the U.S. in 1890. In December 1891 he was placed in charge of 18 "incorrigible" young men at the YMCA Training School (which later became Springfield College). Dr. Luther Gulick, dean of the physical education department, told Naismith to keep the men from being bored and was given 14 days to discover a cure for their "cabin fever."

In addition to inventing a new game, Naismith felt he had the toughest teaching assignment in the school. In a biography of Naismith written with Naismith's granddaughter, Helen Carpenter, author Rob Rains points out that Naismith considered it an "imposition." "If I ever tried to back out of anything, I did then," Naismith is quoted as saying in that book, *James Naismith, The Man Who Invented Basketball.* "I did not want to do it." But later, Naismith had to admit it worked out for the "ultimate good."

He borrowed a little from lacrosse, soccer, rugby—and a game popular with Canadian children known as duck-on-a-rock—and basketball was born. The school janitor had no boxes, so Naismith nailed a pair of peach baskets to the balcony, which just happened to be 10 feet above the floor. It took almost all the 14 days he had been allotted but Naismith still had an hour to write down the game's 13 original rules. Naismith chose a player from each team, and the first center jump was held.

The game was starting to gain popularity across the nation when Naismith arrived at KU. Women had played basketball in Lawrence, but the sport had not caught on. Naismith's presence

James Naismith, the game's inventor, is the only KU basketball head coach in the school's history to finish with a losing record.

did create more interest in the formation of a school team. The record shows that KU lost its first game 16–5 against the Kansas City YMCA on February 3, 1899 in Kansas City, Missouri. Naismith's first team then won six in a row and finished 7–4 in that initial season.

It is often pointed out that Naismith remains the only losing coach in Kansas history. That is true, but Naismith gave no thought to statistics. He won 55 games and lost 60 before handing the coaching duties to one of his students, Forrest C. "Phog" Allen, after a 7–8 season in 1907. In Naismith's mind, basketball was nothing more than a way to pass time between football and outdoor spring sports. Naismith didn't think the game needed to be coached and due to his other campus duties he often didn't travel to away games. He also was known to serve as referee at many games, including that first one in Kansas City.

An article written in 1937 by *The Arkansas Gazette* said, "Games in which [Naismith] officiated generally went off smoothly for he knew the game and players took his word as final." Apparently the men from the Kansas City YMCA didn't see it that way in the first game. Naismith was frustrated that the Kansas City players went after the ball "without respect to the rule that a player was entitled to his place on the court." "On calling fouls I was informed that no foul had been committed, and it was impossible to convey the idea of it being a foul," Naismith later wrote. "My idea of sportsmanship was to play the rules as written, and I kept trying to overcome this handicap with skill, but we were defeated."

Naismith didn't walk away from basketball completely in 1907, but he was more than content staying in Lawrence as a Presbyterian minister and a member of the KU physical education department. He played a key role in the construction of Robinson Gymnasium, but his main interest was teaching sports physiology and clean living.

There aren't many people still alive who can offer first hand accounts of connecting with Naismith. One is Fred Bosilevac, who played for Allen from 1936–37. At age 96 Bosilevac returned to Allen Fieldhouse in 2013 for the 115th anniversary of KU basketball. He remembers taking two physical education courses from Naismith, who led a quiet, ordinary life in Lawrence—not a life of celebrity. "He had an office in Robinson Gymnasium," Bosilevac said during a 2008 interview. "Once in a while, he'd come over and watch the boys practice but very few times. People had a lot of respect for him—maybe because he was a preacher, but not because he was the inventor of basketball. He was not an outstanding personality. He was a preacher, a good man, and an honest man. That's what he tried to impart in those two classes I was in."

Upon Naismith's death, Phog Allen made sure his mentor's contribution wouldn't be forgotten. Allen wrote: "This game, the only international game that is the product of one man's brain, stamps Dr. Naismith as a great educator, a kindly humanitarian, and a model Christian."

Phog Allen

Imagine the college coaching profession today with Dr. Forrest C. "Phog" Allen as its star personality. Allen became known as "the father of basketball coaching" during his 39 remarkable seasons at Kansas, but he was much more than a coach. He was the game's best friend.

Sports Illustrated noted that if Dr. James Naismith invented the game of basketball, Phog Allen "invented the spectacle of it, literally taking the sport from the cramped gymnasiums of its birth to the far corners of the world." That certainly is true, but as Allen became the global caretaker of the sport, he was evolving as the most dominant figure in Kansas basketball history. "The tradition of Kansas basketball started with Phog Allen," says Jerry Waugh, who played for Allen from 1948–51 and later was an assistant coach and administrator at KU.

There are hundreds, if not thousands, of examples to support Waugh's statement. Anyone who has ever walked to Allen Fieldhouse on a snowy winter night must have a sense of what the man meant to Jayhawks basketball. When the building named for him is full of rowdy fans, joining together in the Rock Chalk Chant or waving the wheat, his spirit is in the air. When opponents look up to that foreboding banner that reads, Pay Heed, All Who Enter: BEWARE OF "THE PHOG" his power and his presence is felt beyond all doubt.

Allen often told the story of a conversation with Dr. Naismith that took place in 1905, when Baker University was interested in hiring Allen as a basketball coach. "I've got a good joke on you, you bloody beggar," Naismith said to Allen. "They wanted you to coach basketball down at Baker."

Allen replied: "What's so funny about that?"

"Why, you can't coach basketball. You just play it," the game's inventor said. "Well, you certainly can coach free throw shooting," Allen said. "And you can teach the boys to pass at angles and run in curves. You can show them how to arch their shots. And pivot toward the sideline instead of into the court where a guard can get the ball." That may not have immediately changed Naismith's mind, but KU's first coach later presented his prize pupil with a portrait bearing the inscription: "From the Father of Basketball to the Father of Basketball Coaching."

Allen, who did coach at Baker for three years, was a decent high school player in Independence, Missouri, and later at KU.

In 1906, the *Kansas University Weekly* referred to Allen as "the best goal-thrower in the world." But by December 1907, he had embarked on the first of two stints as Kansas coach—an assignment that would ultimately total 39 historic seasons.

Allen was an innovator and an inventor, a promoter, and a publicist. His favorite hobby was promoting causes or rule changes that he believed would help the game. When the NCAA tournament got off to a shaky start, he promised to make the event popular and a financial success. Allen worked hard to get basketball approved as an Olympic sport, allowing Naismith to see competition in his sport at the 1936 Games. Allen also formed the National Association of Basketball Coaches.

Allen loved to write letters, many of them still on file in the archives of KU's library and museum system. In August of 1950, he wrote to his "Jayhawk Basketeers" about their physical condition and warned them to lose any "excess poundage" before arriving back in Lawrence. "We have got to learn to do the things we did last year, snappier," Allen wrote. "We must execute those fundamentals with a surer, more deft reaction. And all of these must be favorable."

Legend has it that he drank between four and eight quarts of water on the bench during games. He had his own sneaker made by the brand Servus, and that "Phog" Allen Basketball Shoe was designed for fast, sure footwork. He was an actual doctor, studying osteopathy in medical school, so he often served as trainer to his own players. He was a supporter of the Lang Foot and Arch Normalizer device and kept one in the KU locker room, encouraging his players to use it. "It was just a rolling pin," All-American center Clyde Lovellette said. "He made us get up there and roll your foot with the arch. And it was painful. I don't know what that did for you. All I can remember was a lot of pain with that. But we all did it because Phog said it would be good for us."

Allen used to describe Lovellette as "a big turkey gobbling up all the grain." Outrageous statements were another part of his persona. He didn't care for New Yorkers in general and especially disliked Eastern sportswriters. Once he referred to a New Yorker as "so provincial that when he gets as far as Philadelphia he thinks he's on the Lewis and Clark expedition."

New York Post columnist Milton Gross shot back with a reference to Allen's nickname, a shortened version of a foghorn. Gross noted it is "an instrument, which operates on hot air and indicates the one blowing the whistle has more or less lost his way."

Allen didn't lose his way too often. He won 590 games at Kansas and lost 219. In his entire coaching career, Allen won 746 games, and that stood as the record until one of his pupils, Adolph Rupp at Kentucky, broke it. Allen won 24 conference championships and the 1952 NCAA championship. Forced to retire at age 70 by Kansas law, Allen never got to coach Wilt Chamberlain on a varsity squad. But he did witness the opening of Allen Fieldhouse, still the home of the Jayhawks after 58 years. On the east side at the entrance to the Booth Family Hall of Athletics, there is a bronze statue of Allen.

The Naismith Basketball Hall of Fame, named for his mentor and the inventor of the game, is home to many of his protégés. Allen died on September 16, 1974, at age 88, and many of those protégés attended his funeral at Plymouth Congregational Church in Lawrence. "He'll go down in history," Adolph Rupp said, "as the greatest basketball coach of all time."

3 Allen Fieldhouse

Fifty-eight years after Allen Fieldhouse was dedicated with a 77–67 victory against Kansas State, it's hard to imagine this magnificent basketball facility was a product of envy, and Phog Allen's desire to keep up with Kansas State and Missouri. But that is the truth. Call it the "Monarch of the Midland," but it is not "The House That Wilt Built." The home of the Jayhawks was—and always has been—a tribute to the illustrious career of Dr. Forrest C. "Phog" Allen.

The distinctive limestone structure has needed extensive sprucing up from time to time. Construction required 2,700 tons of structural steel, 700,000 bricks, 1,625 tons of stone, 52,000 haydite blocks, 4,500 gallons of paint, and 245,000 board feet of lumber for the roof. The price tag was $2,613,167. Just imagine what it would cost today.

None of that was as impressive as the giant smile on Allen's face the day the building was completed. And none of that is as important as the basketball memories created inside those walls, moments that link generations and eras through the stories of great coaches and great players who called Allen Fieldhouse home.

Allen battled long and hard for a building worthy of the tradition he had built at Kansas. While the Jayhawks played in front of a stage in the cramped confines of Hoch Auditorium, the state of Kansas had approved construction of Ahearn Fieldhouse in Manhattan. Missouri had Brewer Fieldhouse. From the first site studies to the completion of construction, the process took nine long years. It wasn't until December of 1954 that the decision to name the building after Allen was approved.

Words of Praise for Allen Fieldhouse

Kansas celebrated the 50th anniversary of Allen Fieldhouse in 2005 with a series of reunions and special events. The *Lawrence Journal-World* published a "Fieldhouse at 50" special section. With a tip of the hand to the *Journal-World*, here's a sampling of comments from that section.

"I remember the first time I ever saw Allen Fieldhouse. I was awestruck. I had never seen so many fans for a basketball game in my life. The layout of the place, the bleachers on the floor and the seats above, the color combinations of the old gray walls, the windows from another generation, and the banners suspended from the ceiling, all combined to make it a special place. There is no place I could imagine being better."

—Former KU player Jeff Boschee

"It is a place very special to me and all members of the Kansas basketball family. There is no better venue for basketball than Allen Fieldhouse."

—Former KU player and assistant coach Danny Manning

"The pep band is the best. It is the best tradition. Our fans are so knowledgeable. Some places the fans boo everything. Not at the fieldhouse. I think I had the privilege of coaching more games in Allen Fieldhouse than any other coach. On the other hand, Roy Williams won a lot more than I did."

—Former KU coach Ted Owens

"For me, coaching in Allen Fieldhouse is almost a childhood dream. To go to Kansas, where basketball was born to Allen Fieldhouse...I think the problem with this profession is that it has become more of a business, and this was my turn to be a kid."

—Michigan State coach Tom Izzo

"At Kansas the student body is great. The kids sit out there waiting weeks sometimes. I think it's good for players' morale, knowing their fellow students really do care that much about it."

—North Carolina coach and former KU coach Roy Williams

"This crowd is the best I've seen anywhere in terms of organization and how they go through warm-ups with the team. Whoever started it here had done a great job with the tradition."
—Former Arizona coach Lute Olson

"Allen Fieldhouse is the Wrigley Field of college basketball. This building speaks to you. It is one of the gems of college basketball. I think if you asked anybody in all the different places, they'd say the same thing."
—ESPN analyst Jay Bilas

Allen told Bill Mayer of the *Lawrence Journal-World* that, "No man could get such an honor and not be mighty jolted but in a mighty pleasant way. You know, it's hard to realize that anything that big and grand will bear my name...I've received a lot of honors at various times, but this means more than all because it comes to me at my home state."

The official dedication came on March 1, 1955. The game program cost 25 cents. Every former Kansas player that could be found was invited back. Allen turned over that night's coaching duties to assistant coach Dick Harp, who told the players they had to win one for Phog. The ceremony took place at halftime, which was extended from 15 minutes to 35. Allen declared the building's capacity to be 17,000 before anyone could count the seats. That number has been revised from time to time and is now set at 16,300.

The combination of history, tradition, the noise from a student section of 4,000, the home-court advantage, and all the winning has led many prominent coaches, writers, and broadcasters to say Allen Fieldhouse is the best place to watch college basketball. Where else do you find a fanbase that fills almost every seat some 20 minutes before tipoff—just to witness the pregame festivities? From Fighting Jayhawk, to the national anthem, to the alma mater, the Rock Chalk Chant, "I'm a Jayhawk," the player introductions, and the recent addition of Rock Chalk Video's spellbinding intro videos, there is no other pregame show that produces as many goose bumps for its patrons.

KU basketball has enjoyed 18 undefeated seasons at Allen Fieldhouse, including five under coach Bill Self, who has won 95.3 percent (for a 161–8 record) of his games in the Phog in his first 10 seasons. "There are some great places in America to play, but I don't know if there's any better than this one," Self said. "This building rocks."

Kansas has led its conference in attendance 27 years, dating back to 1986–87. There have been 197 consecutive sellouts from 2001–02 to 2012–13. There is not a more unique setting in all of college athletics. The very best moments are those Saturday afternoon games during the conference season when sunshine streams into the gym through those old fashioned windows at each end of the building. In those instances the presence of Phog Allen can be felt as he smiles down on the building that bears his name. "The ghost of Phog Allen oversees all the games here," KU legend Bud Stallworth said. "We think we have a distinct advantage. If things get down to being really close, supernatural things happen to the other team."

Tear it down and build another? Don't even think about it. Self says it won't happen on his watch. "Hopefully the Jayhawks will play here forever," Danny Manning said.

Bill Self

Ten seasons with the same coach has provided a photo album full of indelible pictures. Bill Self isn't one to hide his emotions, and the images are embedded in the souls of Kansas fans. We've seen Self climb ladders, snip away pieces of net, and flash that bright, beaming smile at Jayhawk Nation. We've seen him hoist championship trophies, deliver memorable pregame talks, dance with his players in the locker room, and shake hands with a president at the White House.

There's an iconic photo of Self pumping his fist and letting out a mighty roar after the Jayhawks defeated Missouri 87–86 in overtime on February 25, 2012. That game, as far as we know, will stand as the final battle in the long and bitter rivalry known as the Border War. And that photo captures exactly how much it meant to the KU coach to win that game. No one will ever forget the confetti shower in the Alamodome and Self hugging his players one-by-one after the amazing comeback that produced a championship in 2008. But there is another image from that NCAA tournament that represents his personal journey better than any other.

On March 30, 2008 in Detroit, Bill Self watched Davidson's final shot in an Elite Eight game down on both knees. With the Jayhawks leading by two at Ford Field, there were 16 seconds remaining to decide who would advance to the Final Four and who would go home disappointed. Self had traveled down the disappointment track too many times before. It was his fifth trip to a regional final with no Final Four appearance to show. In his first season at Kansas, trying to mold a group of Roy Williams recruits into his own image, Georgia Tech blocked the way. Then came those first-round disasters: Bucknell in 2005 and Bradley in

2006. Another Elite Eight came in 2007, but Brandon Rush, Mario Chalmers, Julian Wright, Darrell Arthur, and Sherron Collins couldn't handle UCLA. Those are the results that bring a coach to his knees. "It's something that I think about all the time," Self said in 2008 just weeks after winning it all, "and a lot of times, many times a day."

Davidson, a No. 10 seed, had become the Cinderella team of 2008. *Sixteen seconds.* Tournament sensation Stephen Curry had that much time to hit a three that would create one more bad memory for KU. Memphis, UCLA, and North Carolina—the tournament's other No. 1 seeds—had already won their regional finals. Would Kansas fail or would the Jayhawks complete the first Final Four field composed of all No. 1 seeds?

Racing to 500

When the Jayhawks won 108–96 in overtime at Iowa State on February 25, 2013, it was career victory No. 500 for coach Bill Self. He became the ninth fastest coach in Division I history to reach that milestone, tying John Chaney (Cheyney State and Temple). Both coaches accomplished it in 662 games. Self's win total includes his games at Oral Roberts, Tulsa, Illinois, and Kansas.

Self is one of only four coaches to reach the milestone in his 20th season or sooner, joining former KU coach Roy Williams—who did it in his 19th season—Jerry Tarkanian (20th), and former KU assistant John Calipari (20th). Of the 12 fastest coaches to 500, six of them have ties to Kansas basketball. Kentucky's Adolph Rupp, who played at Kansas under Phog Allen, tops the list, having won 500 in just his 583rd contest. The others are Williams (627), Allen (646), Calipari (652), Dean Smith (653), and Self.

On March 24, 2013, Self picked up his 300th victory at Kansas when the Jayhawks defeated North Carolina in the NCAA tournament. Four of the eight coaches in KU history have 300 wins. Self got there the fastest, needing only 358 games. Williams was next at 370 followed by Allen (387) and Ted Owens (443).

Self had just told his players not to let Curry shoot a three under any circumstance. Russell Robinson dogged Curry up the floor. Curry pump-faked but had no open shot. He passed to Jason Richards, who heaved a three-pointer with Jayhawks flying out at him. The shot came off the backboard and bounced away. The buzzer sounded, and KU was headed to San Antonio. Self watched from his knees. Then he dropped his head and slapped the floor with his hand. He had finally broken through.

A reporter asked Self whether he felt as if an 800-pound gorilla had been removed from his shoulder. "I thought it was 1,200 pounds," he replied.

That was Self's moment of truth at Kansas. The Jayhawks played timid against Davidson, and Self prides himself on the way his teams attack. Fair or not, another loss at that stage would have raised many doubts about KU hiring Self. Instead, the Jayhawks relaxed after beating Davidson and beat North Carolina and Memphis to win the national championship for the first time in 20 years.

Kansas basketball has enjoyed 26 remarkable seasons from 1987–88 to 2012–13. Coach Larry Brown led the Jayhawks to the national championship in 1988. Roy Williams followed that with 418 victories and four Final Four appearances over the next 15 seasons. Self now has 300 wins, nine consecutive Big 12 regular season championships, two Final Fours, and a national championship during the past 10 seasons.

Anyone who thought Kansas was finished in 2003 owes Bill Self an apology. Trying to fill Williams' shoes was no easy task. Self might not admit it, but there were a lot of ghosts following him around Allen Fieldhouse in those first few years. Self has sent them packing. It is time for Kansas fans to admit the truth: The KU program is in better hands than it ever has been. Self is a fierce competitor and he's a winner. He has emerged as one of the top recruiters in college basketball as evidenced by 2013 signee and consensus No.1 recruit Andrew Wiggins.

Self is personable, has embraced the school's basketball history, and has a tremendous relationship with the media. He also has a contract that extends his agreement with KU through the 2021–22 season and would pay him over $52 million. "I believe in rewarding great coaches," athletic director Sheahon Zenger said, "before others try and take them away."

5 Wilt the Stilt

He may have been the most dominant player in the history of basketball. But Wilt Chamberlain wasn't sure how he would be received when he returned to Allen Fieldhouse on January 17, 1998 to have his jersey retired during the 100th anniversary of basketball at Kansas. Before he stepped onto the court for his ceremony, he asked a few people if they thought he would be booed.

Wilt was told to brace himself—that he was in for a big surprise. The cheers and the applause that greeted Chamberlain obviously touched him deeply. In return his emotional speech to the crowd punctuated by his "Rock Chalk Jayhawk" was one of the greatest gifts a former KU athlete ever presented to the fans.

When the 50th anniversary of Allen Fieldhouse was celebrated in 2005, voters at *KUSports.com* ranked Chamberlain's return the third most memorable moment in the building's history. Wilt commanded the No. 1 spot as well, but that event was from a different generation when he made his varsity debut with 52 points and 31 rebounds in an 87–69 victory against Northwestern on December 3, 1956. Allen Fieldhouse had just opened in 1955, and the building was oversold the night of that historic Northwestern game. The athletic seven-footer made 20-of-29 shots from the floor and hit 12 free throws. He broke Clyde Lovellette's scoring record of 44 points with 5:48 remaining in the game. Both statistics were Kansas single-game records. The point total still stands. Jerry Waugh, an assistant to head coach Dick Harp on that team, remembers that each time Chamberlain dunked, the cables holding up the basket would shake ferociously. Teammate Ron Loneski recalls seeing a photo from that debut that shows Northwestern defenders cowering under the basket, trying to protect themselves as Chamberlain landed after every dunk.

Chamberlain broke his own rebounding record with 36 against Iowa State on February 15, 1958. "He was an attraction," teammate and future Kansas athletic director Monte Johnson told the *Lawrence Journal-World* in 2010. "We've had so many good players over the years, but you haven't had many like that. He was an absolute magical person to watch."

That was the certainly the case when Chamberlain made his spectacular debut. On November 18, 1955, Chamberlain led the freshman team to an 81–71 victory against the varsity with 42 points and 29 rebounds. A crowd of 14,000 had shown up for that glorified scrimmage that took place on Phog Allen's 70th birthday. It was after that game that Allen boasted that KU could win the 1957 national championship with "Wilt, two Phi Beta Kappas, and two aggressive coeds."

Allen's 70th birthday was significant because that was the mandatory retirement age in Kansas. As hard as Phog battled for a chance to coach the Big Dipper, he was denied. Harp took over as head coach and was forced to deal with the pressure from Phog's championship statement. After an epic recruiting process and landing Chamberlain to come to Kansas from Philadelphia, Allen was very upset by the forced retirement. "Dad was more or less promised by the chancellor that he could have one [varsity] season with Wilt," Allen's son, Bob, told *The Sporting News* in 1988. "Then someone harangued against it in the state legislature, and the chancellor caved in."

Chamberlain was deeply disappointed, too. "He was the coach of the era," Chamberlain once told Kansas broadcaster Max Falkenstien. "He was the coach—maybe of all time. While working with him during my freshman year on things he was teaching me, I looked forward to being under him."

Word spread through college basketball regarding Chamberlain's debut against Northwestern. Teams started sagging their defenses, never trying to guard him one-on-one. Some used as many as four players in an effort to stop him. And sending him to the foul line was not a solution. "At the time the rule for free throws was that you had to release the ball before your foot hit the ground [in the lane]," Bob Allen said. "So Dad had Wilt take a two-step start and then extend his arm. It was almost a dunk, and he shot 100 percent. He also practiced throwing the inbounds pass over the backboard where nobody could stop Wilt."

Those were just two reasons why several college rules had to be changed because of the impact he had on the game. Chamberlain stayed at Kansas only two years, leaving after his junior year. The Harlem Globetrotters paid him $50,000 to tour one year before he could begin his legendary NBA career.

But in his short stay in Lawrence, Chamberlain was a leader on campus and in his 1973 autobiography he bragged of "single-handedly integrating the whole [Lawrence] area." It was a remarkable process that changed Kansas and KU basketball. But along with the disappointment of not being coached by Allen, Chamberlain also never won that national championship. The Jayhawks went all the way to the 1957 title game in Kansas City but lost to North Carolina in an epic triple-overtime game.

It turned out Wilt carried that burden with him his entire life. That's why he didn't return sooner. And that's why he thought he would be booed when he returned to have his number 13 was retired. It was good that he had been convinced to return. Chamberlain died 21 months later, on October 12, 1999, of heart failure.

Everyone at Kansas was glad they had one last chance to connect with the Big Dipper. "He signed autographs for about three hours [that day]," said Johnson, who remained close to Chamberlain after their playing days together at KU. "But that's the way I remember him. I never had a problem that he didn't come back earlier. His schedule was crazy. And I don't know if anyone every really knew the talents Wilt had. He could run like a deer. He could jump. From the waist up, he looked like a weightlifter. He was super-human. He was so sick [that last trip], and people didn't know it. We were with him three days, and he didn't say a thing. But before he left he told us it was one of the most—if not the most—meaningful day of his life."

6 Danny Manning

One championship effort came in KU blue with that trademark No. 25 on his jersey, and the fans in Kansas City were absolutely delirious. Twenty years later his championship role required a suit and tie, and the result prompted a party along San Antonio's Riverwalk, where the Rock Chalk Chant could be heard into the wee hours of the following morning. Danny Manning's legendary status at Kansas was secured long ago. These days, it's just twice as nice.

In 1988 he capped his senior season in that No. 25 jersey by putting his teammates on his back and carrying KU to the national title with a victory against Oklahoma. In 2008 Manning was an assistant coach on Bill Self's staff as the Jayhawks staged one of the most incredible championship rallies in NCAA history to defeat Memphis. On both occasions Manning handled himself with the dignity and humility that Kansas fans have come to expect from their All-American hero. He is a quiet man who rarely speaks about himself. But when actions speak louder than words, people get the message. "For me it was a very overwhelming feeling of joy as a coach," Manning said when asked to compare the two experiences. "When I say overwhelming, I mean as a former player and an alumnus. There's a sense of passion and pride to see your school do well. It's my school. It's our school. It's our program. To see so many former players there that night [in the Alamodome] and see how happy they were, it was just overwhelming."

And for Kansas fans, it was enthralling to see Manning part of the celebration once again. After retiring from the NBA, he returned to Lawrence in 2003 when Self offered him an administrative position on the coaching staff. With his two children still in high school, Manning held that spot until he was promoted to full-time assistant in March 2007. "I always thought he'd be an excellent teacher," Self said of Manning, a two-time All-Star who managed 12,367 points in the NBA despite reconstructive surgeries on both knees. And it turned out he was just that, playing a major role in the development of players such as Darrell Arthur, Sasha Kaun, Cole Aldrich, Jeff Withey, the Morris twins, and Darnell Jackson. "The things he showed me, the things he told me, they all worked," said Jackson, who averaged 11.2 points and 6.7 rebounds on the 2008 national champions. "It was like he was putting his identity into all of us."

And what a tremendous identity Manning had as a player. It was that way even in high school. "Danny was the leading scorer, second-leading assist man, and leading rebounder on a 26–0 team that won the state title," Mac Morris, Manning's coach at Page

High in Greensboro, North Carolina, told *Sports Illustrated* in 1983. "He's 6'10" and he has the agility to be a point guard."

Yeah, Manning's inner-Magic Johnson was displayed from time to time during his KU days. He could do it all, and the all-time career rankings at KU bear that out. It is unlikely any player will ever come close to his 2,951 career points. Nick Collison is second at 2,097. He stands No. 1 in rebounding as well with 1,187. He is fourth in steals (250), 18th in assists (342), seventh in blocked shots (200), and first in games played (147).

Manning took a major career step in 2012, accepting the head coaching job at Tulsa just as the Jayhawks were about to depart for the Final Four in New Orleans. He was 17–16 in his first season at Tulsa, but the Manning presence remains at KU. Danny's son, Evan, was an invited walk-on freshman during the 2012–13 season. He played in 12 games, scoring eight points in 34 minutes. "He grew up a Jayhawk and always wanted to be a part of that," Danny said of Evan. "I'm happy for him and I know he's extremely happy and fortunate that Coach Self is giving him an opportunity."

Through it all, the Manning family has become part of the community, and Lawrence has become home. Danny first arrived in 1983, amidst a bit of controversy shortly after Larry Brown was named coach of the Jayhawks. Two days after Brown hired Danny's father, Ed Manning, as an assistant coach, Danny told a press conference he was going to sign with KU. "If I was still living back East, I probably would be going to North Carolina, but my home is here in Lawrence now, and I want to be close to my parents," Danny said. Fans in North Carolina cried foul. At Page High, a candidate for sophomore class president built his platform around the slogan *Bring Danny Manning Back To North Carolina* and boycotted grocery products using Kansas wheat.

But Manning never went back. He enrolled at Lawrence High School, where he became Kansas Player of the Year in 1984 and then permanently upgraded the KU basketball program by reaching the Final Four in 1986 and 1988. When everything was falling apart around him during that 1988 season, he rose to the occasion and led a team with 11 losses to the promised land. Manning's 31 points and 18 rebounds that led "Danny and the Miracles" to an 83–79 victory against Oklahoma remains one of the all-time great championship game performances by an individual player. "The bottom line is that we asked so much, and he handled it so well," Brown said.

Twenty-five years later in Atlanta, the NCAA celebrated the 75th anniversary of the tournament, and Manning was named one of the 15 top players in the history of the event. "It was a very special time," Manning said in Atlanta. "I had a great coach in Larry Brown. And we must talk about the impact that our teammates had on our careers, how unselfish they were, and the different situations they put us in so that we could receive a little bit more notoriety than some of them."

7 Mario's Miracle

Imagine little Mario Chalmers as a four-year-old, hanging out in the basement of his parents' home in Anchorage, Alaska. His father, Ronnie, would move the furniture around, place a Nerf basketball goal at each end of a makeshift arena, and use couches as the team benches. Every game they played was for the championship. This was the real deal or at least it was to a four year old. Mario would have his mother, Almarie, perform "The Star-Spangled Banner." After all, you can't have a national championship game without the national anthem. Then Ronnie and Mario would play. If there was

Mario Chalmers' three-point shot over Derrick Rose (23) and Robert Dozier (2) with 2.1 seconds left sends the 2008 national championship game into overtime. (Getty Images)

an actual game clock, young Mario was prone to ignoring it. He would just skip ahead to the final seconds and start counting down.

Three…two…one…Mario Chalmers with the shot…Good!

Fast forward to 2004. Ronnie Chalmers, KU director of basketball operations, is sitting in the Alamodome with his son, watching Connecticut beat Georgia Tech for the national championship. Mario looks at his father and says, "One day, I'm going to be there winning the national championship."

Now it's 2008. Chalmers is on the court at the Alamodome in San Antonio, wearing the uniform of the Kansas Jayhawks. With 2:12 to play, Memphis leads KU 60–51 in the national championship game. But good things start happening for the Jayhawks. With 10.8 seconds to go in regulation, Memphis freshman Derrick Rose has two free throws with the Tigers now leading 62–60. Rose misses the first and makes the second. Kansas is down three with the ball.

Everyone in the building knows the Jayhawks have a chance to force overtime. Kansas coach Bill Self calls the "chop" play. Sherron Collins takes the inbound pass and waits two seconds for Darnell Jackson to clear out of the way. Collins brings the ball up, gets past Rose but then loses his balance and starts to fall. Rose is forced to guard Collins just a little longer. Instead of handing the ball to Chalmers, Collins has to shovel a pass about three feet to his teammate. "That split second of hesitation gave Mario space," Coach Self said. "And then he could get his feet set."

Now the clock is ticking. Chalmers doesn't have to count it down himself. There's a clock straight ahead in his line of vision. This ball isn't a Nerf ball. This is a regulation job with the pebbled surface, and NCAA stamped on it. At the pinnacle of his jump, his left hand is providing fingertip guidance and starting to come off the ball, but his right hand is spread across the ribs, ready to provide the proper orbit. The clock is at 3.9 seconds as Chalmers releases his three-pointer. Rose tries to leap at Chalmers, but the ball is in the air. It seems to hang there forever. Even from the Kansas bench, it seemed that live action switched to slow motion and then back again. Mario's beautiful rainbow projection fell through the net with 2.1 seconds left. The game was tied 63–63.

Twenty years after Danny and the Miracles, Jayhawks fans everywhere had something new to marvel at: Mario's Miracle. "As soon as it left my hand, it felt good, and I knew it was going in," Chalmers said. "I just waited for it to hit the net."

Memphis coach John Calipari said he wanted his team to foul before the shot. The Tigers didn't get it done. The KU players didn't get caught up during the excitement. They got back on defense and prevented Memphis from getting a winning shot.

Kansas had the momentum and dominated overtime. As Collins dribbled out the final seconds of the game, CBS announcer Jim Nantz declared a "Rock Chalk championship." The confetti shower began, and Kansas had put together a comeback for the ages to win the national championship game 75–68. "He lives for those type of moments and those type of games," Ronnie Chalmers said of his son. "It was a sensational moment. When the game was over, he came to me on the court, and we embraced. And then he said, 'Dad, we did it.'" Mario raced to his mother and hugged her tightly. "My son: his heart, his guts—It's unbelievable," Almarie Chalmers said.

"It will probably be the biggest shot ever made in Kansas history," Self said. "You know, Mario has no memory. The next thing that happens is the only thing that he's ever thinking about. It's just remarkable that a guy can have that much poise when the pressure's on like that."

Down nine, Self said he didn't think the Jayhawks were dead. Even though the players and coaches kept their poise during time-outs and huddles, the Jayhawks actually weren't so sure. "I thought the game was over," said Darrell Arthur, who was sensational with 20 points and 10 rebounds. The key to this Kansas team all season had been balance, and that was true again. Chalmers, who joined Clyde Lovellette (1952), B.H. Born (1953), Wilt Chamberlain (1957), and Danny Manning (1988) as Jayhawks to be named Most Outstanding Player in the Final Four, had 18 points. Brandon Rush (12), Collins (11), Jackson (eight), Sasha Kaun (four), and Russell Robinson (two) all contributed to the comeback and overtime. "We kept saying, 'Believe. There's a lot of time on the clock,'" Jackson said. "Coach did a great job of making us focused."

Self laid to rest any question about his ability to win the big game. And the victory put an end to all those Rock "Choke" Jayhawk headlines that publications enjoyed over a 20-year period without a championship. In Self's book, *At Home in the Phog*, he wrote about seeing former Kansas players Scot Pollard, Greg Gurley, and Ryan Robertson in his hotel suite after the game and talking to Wayne Simien on the telephone. He told them he wished they could have experienced a championship themselves. Self said Pollard and Simien responded the same way. "We did win the championship. We won it tonight with your team."

That had been Self's message to his players before the game. "I told our guys last night and I told them again today that Kansas basketball is Dr. Naismith, Rupp and Allen, Owens and Brown, and Williams and Wilt," Self said after the game. "You can go on and on and on. There are so many great teams. This is the winningest team [37–3] ever in the history of the program. And I told them [before the game], they'll be remembered as the best team ever in the history of the program if we take care of business. That to me is very humbling. This one will go down as the best ever."

8 What's a Jayhawk?

For many people, especially the avid sports fan, the first exposure to a university comes through an athletic event. It might be at the stadium or an arena. It might be on television. And for that reason, many university administrators consider athletics to be the front porch of a university.

If that's the case, then there should be a familiar face waiting on that porch at all times. For most schools that face belongs to the mascot. And that's especially true at Kansas, where the Jayhawk is at the center of everything associated with the university. There are dogs and cats and birds of every feather that represent schools across the country, but few are as beloved or as acclaimed as the Jayhawk.

But what is a Jayhawk?

If you attended KU, graduated from Kansas, or you're just a fan of the Jayhawks, there's no doubt someone you know has asked that question. What did you tell them? Did you take them to a game and point out Big Jay and Baby Jay? Or, did you just tell them the Jayhawk is a mythical bird?

The mythical part is important because it's obvious that character on the front porch—the one with the red head, the big yellow beak, and those gorgeous blue eyes—isn't a real bird.

But there's so much more to the story and so much more to the answer. The origin of the Jayhawk is rooted in the early days of Kansas' settlers and the historic struggles they faced. It isn't known where the use of the term "Jayhawk" actually began. The best guess is that the term was coined around 1848. A group of pioneers crossing the territory now known as Nebraska called themselves

"The Jayhawkers of '49." And the term was known from Illinois to Texas.

The name itself combines the characteristics of two birds that are certainly real—not mythical. The Jayhawk is a merger of the blue jay and the sparrow hawk. In December 1926, Dr. F.W. Blackmar addressed the origin of the "Jayhawk." From 1889 to 1929, Blackmar was the first dean of the graduate school and delivered his thoughts on the annual KU Radio Nite Program on December 17 of that year. "It is neither beast, fish, nor fowl," Blackmar said of the Jayhawk. "The myth had its rise in the characters of two birds that frequent the Missouri Valley, namely the blue jay—a noisy quarrelsome robber that takes delight in pouncing upon small birds and robbing their nests of eggs and young birds—and the sparrow hawk—a genteel killer of birds, rats, mice, and rabbits and when necessary a courageous and cautious fighter. Just when, where, and by whom the names of the two birds were joined in 'Jayhawk' and applied to human beings, no one knows. However, it is known that the term 'Jayhawk' originated in the home territory of these birds somewhere between Texas and Nebraska. It is known that it was applied to an overland company of gold seekers on their way through Nebraska to California. It was applied to Jennison's band of free-booters, to Montgomery's rangers, to Missouri guerrilla bands of border ruffians, and finally in a general way to the free-soilers of Kansas."

This was the basic message: Don't turn your back on this bird. These were the early days of government, and there was a bold sense of purpose. "Jayhawking" became a general term used to express marauding or plundering. One of the most famous Jayhawkers was John Brown, who fought for the abolition of slavery in Kansas in the 1850s. Brown was involved in the Battle of Black Jack, considered by some to be the unofficial start of the Civil War.

The Kansas Territory became a battleground between those who wanted slavery to be legal and the abolitionists, like Brown, who were committed to a free state. Eventually the Jayhawkers name stuck to the so-called free staters when Kansas was admitted as a state in 1861. And Lawrence, where the University of Kansas was founded in 1865, was a stronghold for those free staters.

During the Civil War, the Jayhawk image evolved away from the ruffians known for looting, sacking, and attacks on settlements. The symbol became more patriotic as Kansas Governor Charles Robinson raised a regiment known as the Independent Mounted Jayhawks. Later it was officially known as the First Kansas Calvary and then the Seventh Kansas Regiment. By the end of the Civil War the term Jayhawk was associated with the impassioned people and the courageous fighting qualities that kept Kansas a free state, according to historical accounts.

By 1886 the university had adopted the mythical bird as part of the school yell—the now famous Rock Chalk Chant. And when the first football team took the field in 1890, "it seemed only natural" to call them Jayhawkers, the school's athletic media guides now note.

So yes, the Jayhawk is a mythical bird. But he's so much more than that. When that Jayhawk greets you on the front porch to KU, realize this is a mascot who symbolizes the struggles of the people who founded a state and a school.

9 Roy Williams

Roy Williams has never hesitated to poke fun at himself. He tells people all the time that he's "corny" and then uses words like "dadgum" and "doggone" when other coaches would just let fly with another expletive. He describes himself as "half-Tar Heel,

Out of the Outhouse

The Downtown Barbershop in Lawrence has always monitored the pulse of Kansas athletics. So in 2003 when Roy Williams left the Jayhawks for North Carolina, the barbershop relegated a sketch of Williams to the men's restroom.

But on April 14, 2008, just after KU beat Williams' Tar Heels in the national semifinals and went on to win the national championship, the Associated Press reported that "Ol' Roy" had been returned to a place of prominence—along with hundreds of other photos and memorabilia that make up a KU shrine in the front portion of the shop. Williams was restored to a spot between Jayhawk greats Clyde Lovellette and Wilt Chamberlain after five years of urinal exile.

"The hatchet is buried," shop owner Jon Amyx said. "I think most people would tell you that now." In addition "the Roy Room" became the men's room again. It still contains what the AP called "unflattering references to the hated archrival Missouri Tigers."

After Kansas defeated Roy Williams' North Carolina team in the 2008 Final Four, Jon Amyx, the owner of the Downtown Barbershop in Lawrence, removes a painting of the former KU coach from his shop's restroom.

half-Jayhawk" and enjoys some strange superstitions, such as spitting in rivers before big games.

More than anything else, Williams likes to remind anyone who will listen that nobody knew who he was until Kansas hired him as basketball coach in 1988. He even used that as a major punch line in his Hall of Fame acceptance speech in 2007. "Chancellor Gene Budig and Dr. Bob Frederick, my athletic director at Kansas, took a tremendous chance by hiring me," Williams said. "Kansas wanted a name coach—a successful and proven coach—and I was not a household name even in my own house. But Bob had a belief and gave me a chance. Even when his wife said, 'You're not going to hire that no-name guy from North Carolina, are you?'"

Frederick confirmed that story on more than one occasion. Margey Frederick did think Bob was crazy for hiring Williams. And so did thousands of Kansas basketball fans who asked the same question, "Roy who?"

Want to know the funny thing about that? Fifteen years later, some of the same people were calling Williams a traitor when he returned to his alma mater to coach the Tar Heels in 2003. That's where the half-and-half thing comes into play. Williams was fiercely loyal to UNC and his mentor, coach Dean Smith, but as Kansas grew on him, he also became deeply divided. The conflict meant Kansas fans viewed him as a flight risk for most of his tenure. As Williams became more popular, Jayhawk Nation became increasingly anxious about losing him. "I love [Kansas] so much," the UNC coach said in 2007. "If somebody says 'Rock Chalk Jayhawk' when I'm walking through an airport, I still say, 'Go KU.' I have no problem doing that because I truly loved my 15 years there. In fact it's probably the happiest 15 years of my life. I hope 20 years from now, I'm still not saying that."

Williams arrived at KU in 1988 and was asked to put together the pieces after recruiting violations by Larry Brown landed the Jayhawks in the penalty box, preventing them from defending their national championship. Williams immediately proved he could reach his players, which was necessary because he only had nine on scholarship. KU broke out of the box 11–1 and climbed to No. 16 in the Associated Press poll before injuries and bad breaks took their toll. After a 19–12 season, more people knew who Williams was. "Those guys gave me a chance," Williams said of his first team. Kansas hasn't missed the NCAA tournament since that probation year.

Determined to justify Frederick's belief and Smith's recommendation, Williams ran with his opportunity. In the second season, the Jayhawks finished 30–5 with Kevin Pritchard, Mark Randall, Ricky Calloway, Terry Brown, and Jeff Gueldner in the lineup but lost to UCLA 71–70 in the second round of the NCAAs. Good things were happening despite that disappointing tournament exit. "The tradition of Kansas basketball started with Phog Allen, and in fairness it was rekindled with Roy Williams," said Jerry Waugh, former KU player, assistant coach, and athletic administrator.

Over the next 13 seasons, the Jayhawks would average more than 28 victories, win or share nine conference championships, win four conference tournaments, advance to the Sweet 16 or better nine times, and reach the Final Four on four occasions. But there never was a national championship, and that became an important part of the story line as well.

With his first recruit, Adonis Jordan, taking over at the point guard, and Alonzo Jamison and Mike Maddox joining Brown and Randall in the starting lineup, Williams reached that first Final Four in just his third season at KU. The Jayhawks went 10–4 in the Big 8 and then rolled past New Orleans, Pittsburgh, Indiana, and Arkansas to reach the national semifinals against North Carolina. Coaching in just his second NCAA tournament, Williams won matches with Indiana's Bob Knight, Arkansas' Nolan Richardson, and Smith, his mentor at North Carolina. Beating Arkansas in Charlotte, North Carolina, was especially gratifying since Richardson had said before the game he wanted to play Indiana because a victory against the Hoosiers would earn some respect for his program. Down 12 at halftime, KU rallied to win 93–81. The magical 1991 run ended in the championship game in Indianapolis, where Duke's Christian Laettner, Bobby Hurley, and Grant Hill combined to beat Kansas 72–65 and give coach Mike Krzyzewski his first NCAA title in five trips to the Final Four.

Williams didn't get his first championship until 2005, after he had moved back to North Carolina. There was a 78–68 semifinal loss to Smith's Tar Heels in the 1993 Final Four in New Orleans and a 97–88 semifinal loss to Maryland in 2002. The only other appearance in a championship game came the next season again in New Orleans. This time Syracuse held off a late rally by the Jayhawks as Jim Boeheim won his first title with an 81–78 victory.

That was the last game Williams coached at Kansas. In 2000, when Bill Guthridge retired at North Carolina, Williams surprised most everyone by turning down an offer to return to Chapel Hill. Williams waffled for a week and then held a press conference to say, "I'm staying." More than 15,000 fans watching on the Jumbotron at KU's Memorial Stadium cheered the decision. "If we have another press conference like this, it will be either when I'm retiring or dying," Williams said.

Kansas fans believed him.

But faced with the decision again after Matt Doherty was forced to resign just before the 2003 Final Four, Williams couldn't say no again. One week after losing to Syracuse, he bid a teary-eyed good-bye to KU. After a magnificent 15-year run, many Kansas fans could only focus on the end. They felt Williams had not kept his promise. And Williams could only admit that he regretted his own words. "Some people feel like I lied," he said. "If you look at it word by word, it is a lie. But when I said that, I thought it was the truth."

10 Danny and the Miracles

The April 11, 1988 issue of *Sports Illustrated* was a real keeper—especially if you happen to be a Kansas basketball fan. When the mail arrived in Oklahoma, Sooner fans might have tossed the magazine in the trash before they got past the front cover. The cover boy was KU's Danny Manning, and he was photographed during the national championship game in Kansas City, Missouri. The power and grace reflected by this one-of-a-kind player is mesmerizing. The magazine's headline was: "OH DANNY BOY! Danny Manning Leads Kansas To The NCAA Title." But the photo of Manning's isolated figure on the Kemper Arena floor tells all you need to know. There's not an Oklahoma player near him. Manning seems capable of doing whatever he wants as the basketball comes off his right hand. So you wonder—is that how Manning looked to Oklahoma all night long?

Probably. He scored 31 points and grabbed 18 rebounds to lead the Jayhawks to their 83–79 victory against Oklahoma in the first all-Big 8 Conference national championship game ever. Manning made 13-of-24 shots from the field and hit 5-of-7 free throw attempts to earn Most Outstanding Player honors for the NCAA tournament. And then Manning sat down at the postgame press conference and issued a message to all the non-believers. "To anybody who's ever involved in any type of competition, keep your head up and work hard; who knows what can happen," Manning said. "To all the people who said it couldn't be done, that we were finished: We're No. 1. How do you like us now?"

The Jayhawks did have their doubters after a 12–8 start to the season. They did finish the season with a 27–11 record, setting the NCAA record for most losses by a national championship team.

After overcoming so much adversity following injuries, suspensions, and academic casualties, these champions were given the nickname "Danny and the Miracles."

After all these years, Manning is the only one who begs to differ. "Danny's unbelievably humble. He's the only one who complains about the name, 'Danny and the Miracles,'" reserve guard Scooter Barry told the *Lawrence Journal-World* when the champions gathered for a 25th anniversary in 2013. "Everybody else says it's a perfect name. Danny always says, 'It wasn't me. It was all of us.' Everybody knows he and Coach [Larry] Brown carried the weight of the team. With their experience and ability to communicate and take over games…it gave us the opportunity to be in position to win."

Manning was a classic big man with point guard skills. He was often compared to Magic Johnson, but after the championship was won, John Feinstein of *The Washington Post* likened him to Larry Bird. "That's pretty fair company especially when one considers this: Manning did what Bird could not do. He took an ordinary team and made it into a national champion," Feinstein wrote.

KU opened the season as a championship contender in large part because of Manning. But the walls around him started tumbling down during the season. Forward Archie Marshall, who tore the anterior cruciate ligament in his right knee against Duke in the 1986 Final Four, tore his left ACL against St. John's on December 30, 1987. He had surgery, and his college career was over. Forward Marvin Branch was declared academically ineligible after 12 games. Forwards Sean Alvarado (academics) and Mark Randall (medical) were redshirted. Otis Livingston and Mike Masucci were suspended from the team in March.

The Jayhawks suffered four consecutive losses, including a 72–61 setback to Kansas State that ended a 55-game winning streak at Allen Fieldhouse. There was talk in the KU athletic department of planning for a home game in the NIT. Brown

Sunflower Series Shifts to Silverdome

With a 21–11 record in 1988, Kansas received the No. 6 seed in the Midwest Regional and was sent to Lincoln, Nebraska, for the opening round, where the Jayhawks defeated No. 11-seed Xavier and escaped a scare from No. 14-seed Murray State. Suddenly the bracket was opening up in KU's favor. Vanderbilt beat No. 2 Pittsburgh, setting up a Sweet 16 game with Kansas in Pontiac, Michigan.

When the Jayhawks won their third game, there was a familiar foe waiting in the regional championship. Kansas State, seeded fourth, had knocked off No. 1-seed Purdue. That meant the Jayhawks and Wildcats, who had beaten KU twice already, would meet for the fourth time that season—with a Final Four bid at stake.

The most important game ever in the Sunflower State rivalry would be played in the Silverdome. Danny Manning and Milt Newton combined for 38 points, Scooter Barry chipped in 15 more, and Newton turned in another defensive gem, limiting K-State star Mitch Richmond to 11 points on 4-for-14 shooting during the 71–58 victory, sending Kansas to the Final Four. "There was a lot of pressure on K-State," coach Larry Brown said. "They're supposed to beat us. They were convinced they could beat us."

On the KU radio network as Bob Davis and Max Falkenstien called the final seconds of the game, Falkenstien broke into a chorus of "Goin' To Kansas City."

added Clint Normore and Marvin Mattox from the football team. Forward Chris Piper, playing with a nagging groin injury, moved into Branch's starting spot. Kevin Pritchard moved to point guard, Jeff Gueldner became a starter, and Milt Newton was asked to score more. Brown told Manning he had to play as if the end was near— because it was. "As a player you never give up hope," Manning said. "People were saying things, but it just doesn't register. Coach Brown changed things quite a bit. He devised a way. That's part of his coaching genius."

Kansas was seeded No. 6 in the Midwest Regional and defeated No. 11 Xavier, No. 14 Murray State, and No. 7 Vanderbilt to reach

Chris Piper (24) and Danny Manning celebrate after defeating rival Kansas State 71–58 to advance to the 1988 Final Four in Kansas City, Missouri.

the regional final against Kansas State in Pontiac, Michigan. By avenging regular season losses to K-State and Duke, the Jayhawks advanced to the title game against Oklahoma.

The Sooners—led by Mookie Blaylock, Stacey King, and Harvey Grant—had already defeated KU twice. They were athletic and averaged 104 points a game. Brown's final words to his staring lineup were a warning: "If we run with them, we're playing into their hands." Newton then remembers Manning calling his own huddle. "Danny gathered us together and said, 'Guys, forget that.' But he used some other f-words. 'Forget that. Let's run with them. Let's show them that we're not afraid of them.'"

The Jayhawks did run. And the first half was unlike anything the NCAA tournament had ever seen. KU shot 71 percent. Oklahoma hit seven three-pointers. No one took a breath. The score was tied 50–50 at halftime. Brown convinced the Jayhawks to return to a more controlled game in the second half. Newton scored 15, Pritchard had 13, and Piper had eight. Normore even had seven huge points off the bench. Manning hit both ends of a one-and-one with five seconds left, and the Rock Chalk Chant filled Kemper Arena. "I was thinking, *It's over*—before the free throws," Manning said. Said Brown, "I wish you had told me that." The nomadic coach, who settled into Lawrence for five seasons, seemed dazed by the victory. "I have never been through anything like this. I don't know how I feel. I can't even say, 'national championship.' It'll feel great tomorrow, I know that."

As Brown spoke, parties were beginning in Kansas City's Country Club Plaza. Back in Lawrence, at least 10,000 students spilled onto Jayhawk Boulevard. They climbed trees and statues. Fireworks shot into the air. There was drinking and high-fiving. People acted as if they had just witnessed a miracle. Just don't tell that to Manning. "This was no gift," Manning said. "Some people might say we're lucky, but what's luck? Luck presents an opportunity, and we were prepared for that opportunity."

11 Larry Brown

The late Bob Frederick, athletic director when Kansas won the 1988 national championship, saw a little bit of everything during his time a basketball player, assistant coach, administrator, and professor at KU. But no one left Frederick more puzzled than coach Larry Brown.

Basketball's ultimate nomad pulled into Lawrence in 1983 as successor to Ted Owens and the sixth coach in KU history. He stayed five seasons, won 135 games, made two Final Four trips, and delivered the first national championship to Kansas since 1952. Then it was off to the next challenge—gone as quickly as he had arrived. "I'm not sure [why he moved from job to job] and I've thought about that ever since 1988," Frederick said in a 2005 interview. "He's really an interesting person in the sense that each time that he moved, right away he was talking about how good the last job was. And then when he gets in that job, he's thinking about how good the next job is going to be. I've never been able to figure it out."

Those five seasons Brown spent at KU qualified as his longest stint in one place until he coached the Philadelphia 76ers from 1997–2003—and the shortest tenure ever for any KU coach. Before he arrived in Lawrence, he had coached in the ABA, the NBA, and at UCLA, where he took the Bruins to the 1980 national championship game before losing to Louisville. Brown is the only coach ever to win a NCAA championship and an NBA championship, taking home the latter trophy in 2004 with the Detroit Pistons. In 2012, he returned to college coaching at Southern Methodist University, the 14th stop in a coaching career that began as an assistant at North Carolina, his alma mater, in 1965.

Monte Johnson had been AD at Kansas for four months when he decided to fire Ted Owens and begin the search for a new coach. Johnson offered the job to North Carolina coach and KU grad Dean Smith, who turned down the invitation. Johnson then asked Smith for a rundown on Brown, who had been an honorable mention All-America guard at UNC. "He's a good coach, but you'd better find out why he doesn't stay any place," Smith said. Said Johnson, "It wasn't what you would call a ringing endorsement."

Brown would not be crossed off the list of candidates for the simple reason that all of his teams had won. Johnson narrowed his choices to Brown and Arkansas coach Eddie Sutton, who dragged his feet on a decision, and that opened the door to Brown.

The first controversy of the Brown era came when he decided not to retain KU legend Jo Jo White as an assistant coach. Brown replaced White with Ed Manning, a truck driver from Greensboro, North Carolina, and one of Brown's former ABA players. Manning also just happened to be the father of the most heavily pursued prospect in the nation, and two days later Danny Manning announced he would be playing for the Jayhawks.

With the players Owens had left behind, Brown won 22 games and made the first of five NCAA tournament appearances in 1984. There were 26 victories in Manning's freshman season, and a 35–4 record in 1986 took the Jayhawks to the Final Four in Dallas before losing a national semifinal game to Duke.

Brown was the most colorful coach at Kansas since Phog Allen. He had superstitions about everything, from not shaving on game-days, to the style of ties his coaching staff wore, to hiring the same Detroit bus driver from KU's regional title run in 1988 to drive the Jayhawks around Kansas City at the Final Four.

The buildup to Manning's senior season in 1987–88 was incredible. But Brown's task became more difficult when injuries, suspensions, and academic issues left the coach with a shortage of players and a 12–8 record. KU's 55-game winning streak at Allen Fieldhouse was snapped, and Brown was forced into a series of adjustments. "He devised a way," Danny Manning said. "That's part of his coaching genius."

Just when the KU athletic department was pondering the notion of NIT home games, the Jayhawks built up a head of steam and rolled into the NCAA tournament. Manning and his teammates defeated Kansas State in the Midwest Regional final and headed to Kansas City's Kemper Arena to celebrate the 50th anniversary of the Final Four. The Jayhawks were 27–11 after beating Duke and Oklahoma, but Brown and Manning had brought another championship to Kansas.

Four days after winning it all, the Naismith Coach of the Year agreed to return to UCLA. But on the trip back to Lawrence, he changed his mind and even surprised himself when he announced at a press conference that he was staying. His stay lasted two more months. On June 13, Brown said yes to a "once-in-a-lifetime" opportunity to coach the San Antonio Spurs. "I have the greatest respect for him and his coaching ability," Frederick said. "But he's always looking for a fresh start."

12 Rock Chalk Jayhawk

It was 1986, and Jim Valvano, the late, great coach of North Carolina State, was not happy about the path his team would have to travel if it wanted to reach the Final Four in Dallas. The Wolfpack had been bracketed into the Midwest Regional with an Elite Eight contest slated for Kemper Arena in Kansas City, Missouri, just 40 minutes away from the Kansas campus in Lawrence.

NCAA rules have since changed, but in 1986 there was nothing stopping the Jayhawks from playing regional semifinals and finals in the building that bitter N.C. State fans still describe as "Allen Fieldhouse East." Valvano knew it would be hard enough to deal with a No. 2-ranked Kansas team that featured Danny Manning, Cedric Hunter, Calvin Thompson, Greg Dreiling, Ron Kellogg, and Archie Marshall.

But the battle wasn't confined to the Jayhawks on the court. A hometown, Kansas-biased crowd of almost 17,000 supported the Jayhawks when they needed it most and created, in Valvano's words, "a drop in our sense of safety. Clapping, stomping, waving the wheat, singing that Rock Chalk—whatever the hell that is—I thought I was in the middle of Farm Aid."

Singing that Rock Chalk—whatever the hell that is. Valvano had a wonderful sense of humor, and Kansas fans had to laugh when they heard that. Over the past 100 years or so, how many coaches and opponents have heard the haunting Rock Chalk Chant and wondered the same thing?

Thanks to the enormous exposure provided by the men's basketball program, the Rock Chalk Chant is one of the most recognized traditions in college athletics. A long list of coaches and teams have been intimidated by Kansas battle cry either during pregame ceremonies at Allen Fieldhouse or in the final seconds of a Jayhawks victory—at home or on the road.

Those flustered by the chant would be surprised to know it was a KU professor of chemistry who got the whole thing started. Legend has it that E.H.S. Bailey wanted a cheer for his KU science club. Bailey and some of his associates were returning from a convention in Wichita, Kansas, when they got the idea to pattern a yell after the "rhythmic cadence of their train rolling along the tracks." On May 21, 1886, Bailey presented the cheer to the science club.

Woo Is Not Me

Like all good things, the Rock Chalk Chant has been unable to avoid controversy in recent years. For whatever reason some students in attendance at Kansas games thought it would be wise to yell, "Woo!" between the long, slow repetitions of the chant.

Traditionalists did not appreciate this, arguing that it was disrespectful to the original Rock Chalk Chant, which has existed for so long. Opponents also believe this modernization diminishes the uniqueness of a chant intended to haunt opponents. Newspaper columns and message boards have debated the issue, and an overwhelming majority supported the traditional form without the "woo."

"Stop the Woo" T-shirts have been sold. One shirt featured a Jayhawk on the front with a slogan on the back that read, "Friends Don't Let Friends 'Woo' During the Rock Chalk Chant." Observers seem to think there has been diminished participation in the "woo!" For frequent updates, check the "There is no 'WHOOO' in the Rock Chalk Chant" page on Facebook.

The original chant was "Rah, Rah, Jay Hawk, K.U." with the words repeated three times. By the next year, the science club was using the cheer, and frequent references to "The Science Club Yell" appeared in the student newspaper. Then the chant started to evolve. It was popularly suggested that "Rock Chalk" would substitute for "Rah, Rah." Not only did the word rhyme with Jayhawk, but it also would be symbolic of the chalky limestone formations found on Mount Oread, where the campus is located. Bailey credited the geology department for that change; others cited an English professor.

The chant then was adopted as the "college yell" after the state oratorical contest in Topeka in 1886. The reason given was that KU student yells for the school's winning teams were enthusiastic but "unorganized." On November 4, 1887, the student newspaper reported that Rock Chalk Jayhawk was the official school yell. "Every college of importance in this country has a college cry," the newspaper reported. "In every town in which a college is situated, the midnight air resounds with the hideous yells of the student, symbolic of victory, defeat, or devilment. The students of the University of Kansas use their yell but little, and it is only amidst great victory that 'Rock-chalk-Jay-Hawk, K-U-U-U' floats through the midnight air reminding one of a band of Apache Indians."

Two years after it was adopted, the cheer was refined to its most popular form: a drawn out cadence repeated twice and followed by three faster and more staccato repetitions.

Teddy Roosevelt once said the Rock Chalk Chant was the best he had ever heard. Troops originating from Kansas have used the chant in the Philippine-American War, the Boxer Rebellion, and World War II. And during the 1920 Summer Olympics, Albert I of Belgium asked to hear a typical American college yell. The gathered U.S. athletes replied with the Rock Chalk Chant.

During pregame ceremonies today, the chant is preceded by the "Crimson and the Blue" alma mater and then followed by the fight song, "I'm a Jayhawk." And since the early 1980s, KU fans have carried out a constant, slow repetition of "Rock Chalk...Jay-Hawk...KU" at the end of games, but only when the Jayhawks have secured a safe lead, and victory is guaranteed. It would be considered improper and possibly perilous to begin that chant too soon.

As for Valvano's fears back in 1986, they all came true when Manning scored 12 straight points to rally the Jayhawks from a five-point deficit to a 75–67 victory that sent KU to the Final Four. The fans serenaded the Wolfpack home to Raleigh: "Rock... Chalk...Jay-hawk. K—UUUUUUUU."

"I thought we might be in a little trouble," Valvano said.

13 Clyde Lovellette

By the time the Kansas Jayhawks arrived in Seattle for the 1952 Final Four, big Clyde Lovellette was a major news item in college basketball. He was a consensus All-American in both 1951 and 1952 and clearly was the most valuable player in the game. Lovellette's scoring average was steadily rising at the end of the season, and there was great intrigue over this 6'9" mountain of a man with the natural scoring touch. In the first round of that NCAA tournament, Lovellette saved the day by scoring 31 points in a 68–64 victory against Texas Christian. The next day he scored an NCAA tournament-record 44 points as the Jayhawks advanced with a 74–55 win against St. Louis. It was only natural that *The Seattle Times* wanted to size up "Cumulus Clyde" as he arrived with the Final Four teams. "Clyde Lovellette looks like a Scandinavian piano mover in a bathing suit," the newspaper wrote, "but the Jayhawks' scoring genius has an amazingly delicate touch."

That was the very definition of the man who became the first player to lead the nation in scoring (28.6 points per game) and win the NCAA title in the same year. All these years later, Lovellette remains the only college player to accomplish that. Phog Allen wasn't named the father of basketball coaching for nothing. Allen knew how to use his big man. "Clyde was big for his day," teammate Bill Hougland said. "He didn't have a lot of speed. Phog just told us to get the ball to him, and he'd score."

Allen planned far ahead for the 1952 championship. He sent assistant coach Dick Harp across the state of Kansas to gather the building blocks. Bill Lienhard came from Newton, Bob Kenney from Winfield, and Hougland from Beloit. Lovellette and the other three were seniors in the 1952 lineup and joined by junior Dean Kelley.

Lovellette came from Terre Haute, Indiana. He had already promised Indiana coach Branch McCracken that he would play for the Hoosiers, but that didn't stop Allen from driving to Terre Haute. He saw Lovellette as the final piece in his championship puzzle. Allen talked Clyde into riding back to Lawrence, just to check the place out. Lovellette loved the campus and Allen's plan to win a national championship. He changed his mind. When asked why Lovellette enrolled at KU, Allen told *The Kansas City Star* it was better for the player's asthma. "Up here on the hill, a tall man can stand up straight and breathe the rarified atmosphere," Allen said.

Lovellette also breathed in all the lessons that Allen offered to teach. Allen had studied osteopathy for four years and stressed a shooter's touch, showing the proper pronation and supination of their hands and wrists. Lovellette says he enhanced his "tactile senses" by reading books written by Helen Keller. Allen told his players they could learn the necessity of finger control that was taught by the blind author. Lovellette learned to feel the seams of the basketball and said he could have shot "with my eyes closed." Allen talked about technique and compared shots to the inside curve and outside curve thrown by a baseball pitcher. "If you put the ball inside the little square above the rim, 99.9 percent of the time, it's going to go in," Lovellette said. "But if you're outside that square, you've got to have english on the ball to make it crawl up to where it goes in."

Lovellette scored 33 points in a 74–55 win against Santa Clara in the national semifinals and then had 33 points and 17 rebounds as the Jayhawks handled St. John's 80–63 to reward Allen with his first NCAA championship. Lovellette had scored 30 or more points in six consecutive games and walked away with 13 NCAA tournament records. He was the easy choice as the tournament's Most Outstanding Player.

Allen's dream for 1952 had included an Olympic gold medal, and he joined Lovellette and six other KU players in securing that accomplishment in Helsinki, Finland. It was the last U.S. Olympic team where one college provided half the team. Lovellette, who went on to an 11-year NBA career with four teams, ranks fourth in scoring at KU with 1,979 points and 11th in rebounding with 839. He was elected to the Naismith Basketball Hall of Fame in 1988 and was inducted in the National Collegiate Basketball Hall of Fame in 2012. He lives with his wife, Judy, in a suburb of Indianapolis.

14 Phog's 1952 Title

Talk to any of the members of the 1952 national championship team from Kansas, and they will tell you that head coach Phog Allen and assistant coach Dick Harp formed the perfect tandem for directing the Jayhawks that season. Allen was the motivator and Harp, the first full-time assistant ever at KU, was the strategist. "Dick was the one who told us what to do," guard Bill Hougland said. "Doc was the one who jumped on us if we didn't do it."

That sets the stage for the only true crisis during the 1951–52 season. Kansas opened with 13 consecutive victories, including a 90–88 overtime victory against Kansas State in Kansas City and a 60–59 win at Missouri. But the Jayhawks dropped consecutive games at K-State and Oklahoma State to create some concern for the legendary Allen. He considered changes to his famous pressure defense but quickly abandoned that idea.

Instead, Allen opened his book of motivation. He called a team meeting, the players gathered around, and they paid close attention as Allen read "Casey at the Bat." During the final stanza, tears streamed down Allen's face. Allen then reached for Grantland Rice's lesser-known "Casey's Revenge," and he read of Casey returning to boos from the crowd only to hit the game-winning homer. "He came through hell to scramble back—and prove a champ belongs," Allen read to the Jayhawks.

"You sat there and cried," Clyde Lovellette said. "If Phog cried, everybody cried. Then he would take us out and work us."

The eighth-ranked Jayhawks lost only one more game—in the U.S. Olympic playoffs—after they had traveled to Seattle and defeated St. John's 80–63 for the NCAA championship. Allen had recruited Lovellette, Hougland, Bob Kenney, and Bill Lienhard in 1948 with the intention of winning the Big 7 Conference, the national championship, and Olympic gold in 1952. The Jayhawks didn't strike out like Casey. They went 3-for-3. With Dean Smith, Dean, and Al Kelley, B.H. Born, Charlie Hoag, John Keller, Bill Heitholt, and Larry Davenport filling out the varsity roster, Kansas won the Big 7 with an 11–1 record (Oklahoma State wasn't a conference game yet.)

Everything revolved around Lovellette, Allen's prize center from Terre Haute, Indiana. One of the all-time greats at KU, Lovellette averaged 28.6 points and became the first player to lead the NCAA in scoring and win the national championship in the same year. It's never been done again. He finished the season on fire, scoring more than 30 points in his final six games of the season. That included wins against Texas Christian and St. Louis in the Midwest Region at Municipal Auditorium in Kansas City, Missouri. Lovellette set an NCAA tournament record with 44 points against No. 5 St. Louis. The Billikens' game plan was to cut off KU's outside game and hope Lovellette wasn't at his best. It didn't work, and Kansas won 74–55.

It was 22 degrees outside, but the Jayhawks were headed to the national semifinals, and that called for a party. A conga line snaked along Wyandotte Street and Baltimore Avenue in Kansas City. More than 1,000 people crowded into the lobby of the Muehlebach Hotel to celebrate.

The Jayhawks had a roster full of characters. Smith, the future coaching icon, played sparingly but did help Harp with game plans. Kelley used to worry that Smith's cigarette smoking would get them in trouble in hotels. Lovellette was a prankster. On the plane ride to Seattle for the Final Four, the Jayhawks' flight was in a holding pattern because of bad weather, and fuel was running low. So Lovellette took some flowers from a vase in the plane's lounge and stuck them in Allen's hands. "Phog was leaning back and sleeping, and when I did that, his eyes popped open," Lovellette said. "I said, 'Phog, if we're gonna go down, you're ready. You're ready.' He just chuckled and, of course, we didn't go down. We landed safely."

Before the national semifinal against Santa Clara, Lovellette had been given permission to have dinner with a fraternity friend on a Navy cutter. But heavy fog rolled in, and the boat was late getting back to shore. Lovellette missed his curfew by more than two hours and had to sneak back into the hotel. Fortunately, Allen didn't find out until long after the fact. Lovellette scored 33 points, and the Jayhawks won 74–55. "If he had been in the lobby," Lovellette said, "I shudder to think what would've happened."

There are no great stories from the championship game. Kansas defeated St. John's 80–63, and the players say it was rather ordinary. There were a lot of fouls called as St. John's coach Frank McGuire tried to sag his defense on Lovellette. Lienhard and Kenney each scored 12 points. When the strategy failed, Lovellette took control and finished with 33 points and 17 rebounds. Lovellette hit 12-of-25 shots from the field that night and scored 141 points in four

NCAA games to win Most Outstanding Player honors. Nobody every figured out a way to stop him.

When the team returned to Lawrence, the players boarded a fire truck and came across the bridge from North Lawrence onto Massachusetts Street, where Lienhard said 10,000 people were waiting past midnight. But the best part of all was that Allen—at age 66—finally had his NCAA championship. "It would have been a tragedy if one of his teams didn't win a national championship," Harp said.

15 Late Night in the Phog

Exactly one week after Andrew Wiggins signed his letter of intent with Kansas in 2013, a popular chain of stores that sells KU gear sent out an e-mail offering the first batch of No. 22 T-shirts. "NEW SEASON, NEW FACES" read the ad campaign from Kansas Sampler. "IT'S NEVER TOO EARLY TO GET EXCITED FOR KU BASKETBALL. GET READY FOR LATE NIGHT IN THE PHOG WITH #22 TEES!"

Wiggins wasn't yet listed on an official roster for 2013–14, and this was just before Memorial Day. Late Night in the Phog—KU's version of Midnight Madness—was almost five months away. But it's safe to say that it's never too early for Kansas fans to get pumped up about Late Night. Late Night, after all, is all about anticipation. It's a little bit like New Year's Eve, the start of spring training for baseball, and the first day of summer all rolled into one. Except Late Night is a fresh start for Kansas basketball, something Jayhawks fans yearn for as soon as the previous season ends.

If you think this is a practice and not worth attending, think again. The ultimate Allen Fieldhouse experience is attending a game, but taking part in Late Night is something any Kansas fan should experience at least once. There is dunking and three-pointers, but there's also singing, dancing, costumes, and skits. It's a celebration of everything Crimson and Blue.

The current Kansas coach once appeared as Bill "Vanilla Ice" Self, asking the all-important question, "Yo, Allen Fieldhouse, what's up tonight?" Former coach Roy Williams used to put on his boogie shoes to dance. There was an *American Idol* dance competition in 2006. Ryan Robertson starred in *The Price is Right* sketch in 1997. Scot Pollard scored 14 points, had seven rebounds, and blocked four shots while scrimmaging in Revlon Vixen red polish on all 10 fingernails in 1996.

And even Danny Manning came out of his shell, joining Scooter Barry to sing "My Girl" in 1987. Heck, the Jayhawks went on to win the national championship after that rendition of The Temptations' song. There was no national championship, not even a Final Four, after seniors Jeff Withey, Travis Releford, Kevin Young, and Elijah Johnson danced Oppan Gangnam Style in 2012—but the routine did generate a lot of smiling and screaming.

Late Night is all about having fun, knowing that the first "real" practice—with wind sprints and endless drills—will follow the next morning. Now that NCAA rules do not require the event to start after midnight, it's also at a much more enjoyable time for everyone.

Despite some freshman team vs. varsity team scrimmages that included follies back in the 1950s, history will show that Larry Brown ignited the tradition at KU by introducing "Late Night with Larry" in 1985. A crowd of 6,000 showed up on a Tuesday morning. Many of the students wore T-shirts that read, "Late

Gary Bedore's Top Five

Nobody does a better job covering Kansas basketball than Gary Bedore of the *Lawrence Journal-World*. Bedore has been covering KU hoops full-time since Roy Williams' first season with the Jayhawks back in 1988–89. But he is a KU grad and has attended every Late Night since Larry Brown started the tradition. In the spirit of David Letterman, Bedore offered up his Top Five Moments in Late Night history in an article published October 16, 2009. We checked with Gary after the 2012–13 season, and he said his rankings remain unchanged. So here are Gary's words:

5. Alonzo Jamison shattered the backboard during pre-scrimmage warm-ups in 1988. The dunk gone awry pushed back Williams' first Late Night scrimmage to about 12:40 AM. "Alonzo dunked it, and the goal standard came crashing down," former KU assistant athletic director Doug Vance said. "The crowd went crazy. Glass was everywhere."

4. Eccentric KU senior power forward Scot Pollard proposed marriage to his girlfriend, Mindy Camp, in 1996. She accepted. "Egotistically speaking, I don't think that can be topped. Not many things that go on at Late Night are life-altering

Night With Larry Brown. Starring the 1985–86 Kansas basketball team…all the way to Dallas."

And the Jayhawks did reach the Final Four in Dallas that season.

The next season was special as the student fans welcomed Larry "Bud" Melman of "Late Night With David Letterman" fame to the festivities. The 1987 theme was "Goin' To Kansas City," and that's exactly what the Jayhawks did at the end of the season, winning the national championship at Kemper Arena.

When Brown left, Williams turned the program into "Later with Roy Williams" and eventually switched back to "Late Night." But whatever the name, the event became a tremendous success events," Pollard said. "As far as important, that's as big as it gets."

3. KU charged admission in 1989 to offset the cost of a pair of bands. It's what happened once spectators paid the $5 freight and entered the fieldhouse that really caused a stir. Fans of the bands packed the building and, as at many concerts, decided to light up marijuana joints. "There certainly was an unusual aroma permeating the fieldhouse that night," Vance said.

2. Williams danced...and danced...and danced some more. Williams' dancing stole headlines from 1990 to 2002—his final Late Night. "Coach criticized Mark Randall and my dancing the year before and was always laughing at us, so we thought it'd be fun to get him out there," said Mike Maddox after dragging Williams on the floor to boogie with the Crimson Girls in 1990.

1. The 2008 national title banner was unfurled. KU didn't recognize the Jayhawks' 1988 national title during Williams' first Late Night back in '88. In contrast, the 2008 title was mentioned *a lot* at the '08 Late Night. The crowd unleashed the loudest ovation in Late Night history when the banner dropped in the south rafters at 8:57 PM on October 17. "I almost started crying. I don't think I was the only one," KU coach Bill Self said of the moment.

under Williams. During his tenure, crowds filled the Fieldhouse, and it became a tremendous recruiting tool in addition to a lot of fun.

Television cameras carried live, local coverage as baseball Hall of Famer George Brett and PGA Tour Hall of Famer Tom Watson were among the celebrity coaches for the 1992 game. And in 1998, Pollard stole the show by proposing to his girlfriend, Mindy, before 16,300 of his fans.

Self was there when Brown started the festivities as a graduate assistant on that 1985–86 team. When he came back as head coach in 2003, he changed the name to "Late Night in the Phog," and within an hour after the doors were opened, Allen Fieldhouse was packed to greet the new coach. Officials had to shut the doors. "It was an awesome night," Self said. "The fans were just great. It is a bit humbling to get that kind of reception."

16 Adolph Rupp

The early basketball lineage at Kansas was truly extraordinary. It all started with Dr. James Naismith, the inventor of the game who went on to found the program in Lawrence. His prize pupil was Phog Allen, the man who became the father of basketball coaching. And then Allen, who logged 39 seasons at KU, spawned an entire network of legendary coaches who accomplished greatness in their own right.

At the top of that list was Adolph Rupp, the "Baron of the Bluegrass," who coached 41 seasons at Kentucky and accumulated 876 victories. Rupp delivered the passion of college basketball to Kentucky and through 2013, the Wildcats have won more games than any program in Division I.

Born in Halstead, Kansas, in 1901, Rupp was a player on the 1922 and 1923 teams at Kansas that were later named national champions by the Helms Foundation. Rupp had an unspectacular playing career at KU, but he did enjoy outstanding timing. Rupp not only benefitted from studying in Allen's classroom, but he also could pick the brain of Naismith, who was Allen's assistant at the time. You could call it the ultimate internship.

Rupp reportedly became interested in basketball when he was six years old as Halstead won the first of two consecutive state high school championships. By the time he got to Halstead High

School, he was 6'2". He averaged 19 points his last two seasons, was team captain, and handled unofficial coaching duties.

Rupp made the freshman squad at KU and moved up to the varsity as a sophomore. But he never was a regular for the Jayhawks, and his playing time was reserved for those moments when the game's outcome was no longer in question. That limited playing time left Rupp shy of the qualifications for a letter in basketball. But Allen, who had a special way of looking out for all his players, made sure Rupp got that letter.

Allen wrote this to the Kansas athletic board: "Adolph Rupp has worked for three consecutive years giving the best he had in him for the success of the team. It is an unwritten law among coaches that when a man comes out and does his stint without fail for three successive years that that man should receive a recommendation for a letter."

That took care of that.

Before Rupp arrived in Lexington, the Wildcats had gone through 15 coaches in 26 seasons—quite a contrast from KU. Rupp coached at Kentucky from 1930 to 1972, winning four NCAA championships, an NIT title, and 27 Southeastern Conference championships. Like North Carolina coach Dean Smith, who was part of the 1952 national championship at Kansas, Rupp seemed to absorb a great deal from Allen. He then refined those lessons and became an innovator himself, especially with the use of the fast break and set offenses.

He was superstitious, which earned him the title of "Man in the Brown Suit." He had once worn a blue suit to a game and lost. He was fond of Kentucky bourbon. And the dictionary could have pictured Rupp, his scowl, and his jowls alongside the definition of curmudgeon. None of that bothered him. He embraced his image as a S.O.B.

Rupp seemed to be the anti-Phog. They were competitive but in different ways. Rupp put a lot of pressure on his players. He was arrogant and a real taskmaster. He once said, "Without victory basketball has little meaning." And Kentucky was impacted by the 1951 point shaving scandal, something Allen had warned about as an approaching problem in college sports.

Rupp also was accused of being racist, something he did little to dispel. Ironically, that trait was highlighted by a clash of philosophies in the 1966 NCAA title game when Texas Western's starting five of African Americans defeated Kentucky's all-white starting five. But it took another generation to put those pieces together.

Through the ups and downs, Rupp always showed his respect to Allen. When many past Kansas players got together to honor Allen with a scrapbook for his 25th anniversary of coaching the Jayhawks, Rupp wrote: "I cannot tell you how sincerely I have appreciated knowing you from the first day that I, as a freshman, met you back on Mt. Oread in 1919. From that day on, I have always been an ardent admirer of you and one of your staunchest supporters."

In 1968 Rupp passed Allen on the all-time victory list, jumping to the No. 1 spot. "Bless his bones," Allen said, speaking like the osteopath he was. Rupp stayed at No. 1 until Smith passed him in 1997.

Kentucky's Wildcats traveled to Lawrence on December 10, 1977 and beat the Jayhawks 73–66. That was part of 11 consecutive victories for Kentucky over Kansas, and it was also billed as "Adolph Rupp Night" at KU. Rupp died that night in Lexington, Kentucky, following a battle with cancer of the spine. He was 76. Just months after Rupp's death, Kentucky and head coach Joe B. Hall, a longtime Rupp assistant, honored him by winning the 1978 NCAA tournament.

17 Border War

In 2004 athletic officials at Kansas and Missouri tried to change the name of the Kansas-Missouri series from Border War to Border Showdown. Kansas athletic director Lew Perkins explained the term "war" was inappropriate for athletic events in the aftermath of September 11, 2001. The intent was good, but the change was never fully accepted by players, alumni, or many media outlets for the simple reason that the series was rooted in actual warfare and the two sides really did hate each other.

This was supposed to be one of those "to do" chapters in this book. But we can no longer recommend going to Columbia for a game since the series has been discontinued. Basketball season just isn't the same since Missouri left the Big 12 and headed to the Southeastern Conference in 2012. The greatest college rivalry, at least west of the Mississippi River, has been taken away from fans.

Since 1907 Kansas and Missouri had shared the same athletic conference, traveling from the Missouri Valley Intercollegiate Athletic Association to the Big 6, Big 7, Big 8, and finally the Big 12. But conference realignment—decisions based on greed, television money, and football—have blinded college presidents and chancellors who have no understanding of rivalries and their importance. When the Big Ten passed on Missouri, the MU administration turned to the SEC and killed its ties to the Big 12 with no respect for tradition.

Coach Bill Self has come under attack from the Missouri side for standing against any non-conference scheduling of Missouri. Even with a Big 12/SEC Challenge in men's basketball, Self is not interested. KU plays Florida, and MU takes on West Virginia in the inaugural challenge. During a June 2013 teleconference with

Big 12 writers, Self was asked if anyone had approached Kansas about playing MU in the series. "That would never come up," Self responded. "I don't think Texas is going to play [Texas] A&M either."

Perhaps the current animosity is appropriate. Bad feelings and grudges define the Border War. These emotions date back to pre-Civil War days and have just spilled over to the basketball courts and football fields. Actual acts of violence were waged, one state against the other. And on the morning of August 21, 1863, William Clarke Quantrill, a Confederate guerrilla leader based in Missouri, led his pro-slavery raiders into Lawrence. The Bushwackers killed 183 men and boys, dragging many outside and executing them before their families. Quantrill's Raiders rode out of town as most of Lawrence's buildings burned. "There are a lot of rivalries out there, but few actually stem from real bloodshed," former KU center Scot Pollard told the *Lawrence Journal-World* in 2012. "This rivalry stems from real bloodshed, real war. To lose that rivalry is a huge thing…I don't hate anybody, but I really dislike those Tigers. We really loved beating those Tigers."

These history lessons translated to T-shirts that were popular on both campuses. Missouri students prepared one that illustrated Lawrence burning with the word "Scoreboard" and Missouri athletic logo on the front. The back was emblazoned with Quantrill's slogan: "Raise the Black Flag and Ride Hard Boys. Our Cause is Just and Our Enemies Many." Kansas fans responded with their T-shirt featuring Kansas abolitionist John Brown and the slogan "Kansas: Keeping America Safe From Missouri Since 1854."

Norm Stewart was head coach at Mizzou from 1967 until 1999 and as far as anyone knows he kept his vow to never spend a cent in Kansas even if it meant staying overnight at a Missouri hotel and fueling the bus in Kansas City, Missouri. Other Missouri coaches have followed his lead. Legendary KU coach Phog Allen threatened to quit coaching in 1923 if he couldn't beat the Tigers

The Antlers

After graduation from the William Allen White School of Journalism at Kansas, my first full-time sports writing job was with the newspapers in St. Joseph, Missouri. *Yes, I moved to Missouri.* But St. Joe is close enough that you can see Kansas from there. One of my fellow sportswriters and friends in St. Joe was Jeff Gordon, a Mizzou grad who went on to a distinguished career at the *St. Louis Post-Dispatch*. Gordon is a co-founder of the Antlers, the student section of fans at MU basketball games. I don't know if this means I require intervention, but I do know Gordon has needed help for quite some time. (Just kidding, buddy.)

The Antlers started out in 1976 as a small group with courtside seats. Gordon and another co-founder borrowed an "antler dance" from a Saturday Night Live skit and performed during the playing of *Missouri Waltz*. Members of the media noticed and named the group "the Antlers." As time passed the Antlers became more obnoxious and obscene, especially during games involving Kansas

It became tradition during the week leading up to the KU at MU game that the Antlers would obtain phone numbers of KU players and coaches and then prank call them all week. In 1999 the Antlers booed Kansas guard Ryan Robertson—a graduate of St. Charles West (Missouri) High School—every time he touched the ball. A banner was unfurled that read, "For a good time, call Ryan Robertson" and included his phone number. "They can call it all they want," retorted Robertson, who had 17 points in the 73–61 Kansas victory. "Call it till the wee hours in the morning because I'll be up."

Of course, Kansas students—who don't need a nickname—were well known for despising Missouri coach "Stormin" Norm Stewart. For 32 years, they chanted "Sit down, Norm!" After Stewart retired, KU presented him with a rocking chair. The fans cheered, and Stewart sat down. "This is a very meaningful moment," he said. "I mean that from the bottom of my heart."

twice that year and win the conference championship. Fortunately for KU basketball, the Jayhawks did that, winning at home in the final game of the season to snap Mizzou's 10-game winning streak in Lawrence.

One of the classic moments from Allen Fieldhouse probably wouldn't be allowed today. Steve Stipanovich, Missouri's All-American center from 1980–83, had accidentally shot himself with his own gun but concocted a story about being assaulted by an intruder to his campus room. When the truth was exposed, he was greeted by KU students with "Who Shot Stipo?" signs and a cap-gun salute.

In the finals of the 1951 Big 7 holiday tournament, Kansas center Clyde Lovellette stomped on the stomach of Missouri star Win Wilfong. Lovellette was ejected from the game and reprimanded by Allen. Missouri coach Wilbur Stalcup took the microphone to calm down the Tiger fans and earned the respect of Allen in the process.

Ten years later there was a bench-clearing fistfight between the two teams in Lawrence. At Columbia there was another fight, and fans streamed onto the court after KU big man Wayne Hightower threw a punch following a foul.

Roy Williams lost his first four games against Missouri. "Then we won six in a row to sort of save me," Williams said. "[KU fans] would have lynched me up if it hadn't been for that."

There were overtime games and games when the teams were ranked No. 1 and No. 2 in the nation. Bud Stallworth had his 50-point game against the Tigers and delighted in upstaging Stewart. In 1997 in Columbia, Corey Tate's jumper with five seconds left in double overtime handed KU a 96–94 loss, its only one of the regular season. In 2006 Christian Moody missed two free throws with 0.4 left in regulation, and Missouri won in overtime in Columbia.

As the rivalry came to a close in 2012, the games were never better. Missouri rallied from eight down with less than three minutes left to win 74–71 in Columbia. The Jayhawks returned the favor and more in Allen Fieldhouse, overcoming a 19-point second half deficit to force overtime and ultimately win 87–86. As the curtain came down, longtime observers said they had never heard it any louder in Allen Fieldhouse. Fans from both sides still complain about controversial calls in both contests. In the latter game, junior forward Thomas Robinson had 28 points and 12 rebounds as the Jayhawks wrapped up their eighth consecutive Big 12 regular season championship by tying the largest comeback in a KU home victory. "I'm not the most emotional guy, but that's as good as it gets," Self said. "It's as exciting of a game as I've ever been part of. It's the best home game win I can remember us having. Playing Missouri does mean something to me. But to me, it wasn't about this being the last time we played. To me, it's about our team winning its eighth straight championship."

18 Carolina Connection

Hall of Famer Larry Brown was deeply connected, as well as deeply conflicted, when he arrived at the 2008 NCAA Final Four in San Antonio.

Of course, the Kansas Jayhawks won it all at that Final Four, defeating North Carolina and Memphis to claim the national championship. It was the first for KU since 1988 when Brown was head coach at Kansas. The other Final Four participant in 2008 was UCLA, and Brown had led the Bruins to the Final Four in 1980.

Brown played basketball at North Carolina, and the 2008 Tar Heels were being coached by Roy Williams, who left to return to his alma mater in 2003 after 15 seasons of coaching Kansas. And coaching Memphis was John Calipari, one of Brown's former assistants at Kansas—just like KU coach Bill Self, who was a graduate assistant under Brown when the Jayhawks advanced to the Final Four in 1986.

Brown seemed to be crossing into Six Degrees of Kevin Bacon territory. "When one team wins, then three teams that mean a lot to me will be pretty upset," Brown told *The Philadelphia Inquirer* after accepting invitations from both Self and Calipari to attend that Final Four.

Brown's conflicted situation was, in part, a result of his nomadic life in basketball. He's still the only coach to win an NCAA championship (Kansas) and an NBA championship (Detroit Pistons). The man has gotten around.

But the Carolina Connection was the true force at work. The basketball programs at Kansas and North Carolina are intrinsically linked to one another. And if the story was ever turned into a movie, Bacon might be perfect in the role of a young Dean Smith. Without Smith there might not be a Kansas-Carolina Connection. KU and UNC do rank in a different hierarchy among college basketball teams. Along with Kentucky, they are the only programs to win more than 2,000 games.

And the two basketball programs were introduced to one another on March 23, 1957 when the Tar Heels toppled Wilt Chamberlain and the Jayhawks 54–53 in a triple-overtime national championship game played in Kansas City, Missouri. It remains one of the classic NCAA title games of all time.

But Jayhawks and Tar Heels will forever be linked together because of Smith. The coach with 879 victories was born in Emporia, Kansas, graduated from Topeka High School, and attended the University of Kansas. Smith was a role player on the 1952 team that won the NCAA championship. He didn't play much, but there are pictures and video of Smith in the Kansas locker room with coach Phog Allen. In his book, *A Coach's Life*, there is a picture of his KU teammates swarming Smith after a win at Kansas State. The caption says, "I sank a free throw late in the game to help us beat rival Kansas State on the road. Al Kelley and I celebrate a happy moment for Kansas basketball."

Born in Emporia, Kansas, and having played under Phog Allen, Dean Smith (left) and Larry Brown, a UNC alum who coached the Jayhawks to a national title, are two of the many connections between the schools of Kansas and North Carolina. (Getty Images)

Smith's teammates remember that he was already showing signs of his coaching ability. He would help Allen and assistant coach Dick Harp scout opponents. In his book Smith remembers an exhibition game in the 1952 season, and Allen told the players he wanted to see the four-man weave against the zone. Smith walked over to Harp and said, "Dick, we can't weave against the zone."

"Shut up, Smith, and do what Doc said!" Harp replied.

It wasn't always that way. Smith made some valuable contributions. He said he wasn't conscious of it at the time, but he had met two of the most interesting basketball authorities in the game in Allen and Harp. "It was impossible to play for those men and not learn something," Smith says in his book.

Smith was just four years out of Kansas when the Jayhawks and Tar Heels met in the 1957 title game. At the time he was an assistant coach at the Air Force Academy. In 1958 he moved to Chapel Hill as an assistant and began a stay at North Carolina that would last until his retirement in 1997. In 1961, Smith replaced UNC coach Frank McGuire and took over a program that was on NCAA probation. It took a while for Smith to bring success back to the program, but when that happened in the late 1960s, Kansas fans found themselves envying the national stature of the North Carolina program being run by a Kansas product.

The Jayhawks didn't win another national championship until 1988—under Brown with North Carolina native Danny Manning leading the way. Harp, who replaced Allen when he was forced into retirement, became known as the Kansas coach who lost the national title with Chamberlain. Harp resigned in 1964 and later accepted a long-standing invitation to join Smith's staff at North Carolina from 1986 to 1989. Harp and Smith are two of only six men to have both played and coached in the Final Four, and both had the experience as a player under Allen.

After winning his first national championship in 1982, KU athletic director Monte Johnson tried to bring Smith home to Kansas in 1983 after the firing of Ted Owens. Smith declined, and Brown was hired. Of course, Johnson consulted Smith on the hiring of Brown. But Smith was much more involved in 1988, endorsing his unknown assistant after Brown left KU and returned to the NBA. Once Williams, that previously unknown coach, established himself as a prominent coach and endeared himself to KU, Jayhawks fans found themselves in the annual position of worrying about losing Ol' Roy back to North Carolina when Smith retired. That created a new tension between the schools—and again Smith was at the center of it all.

When Smith finally walked away in 1997, it was just before the start of the season, and the Tar Heels did not pursue outside candidates. Longtime assistant Bill Guthridge took over until 2000, and that's when the call came to Williams. With Kansas fans fearing the worst, Williams waited a week and then announced "I'm staying," as more than 15,000 fans cheered at KU's Memorial Stadium where they watched on the scoreboard Jumbotron. "If we have another press conference like this, it will be either when I'm retiring or dying," Williams said.

But given a second chance to return to his alma mater three years later, Williams couldn't turn down UNC again. Matt Doherty, who had been Williams' assistant at Kansas from 1992–99, fell out of popularity at his own alma mater. Doherty resigned but later said he felt he was pushed out of his job in order to make way for Williams. Former KU assistant coaches Joe Holladay and Steve Robinson went to Chapel Hill with Williams. Former Jayhawk C.B. McGrath is a staff member as was Jerod Haase—until he was hired as head coach at University of Alabama at Birmingham.

19 Dean Smith

Few Jayhawks have returned to Allen Fieldhouse, only to be greeted by a chorus of boos. In fact Dean Smith may be the only member of that club. The legendary North Carolina coach was booed for wearing the wrong color sport coat.

Dean vs. Roy

It was mentor vs. student. Kansas coach Roy Williams made his Final Four debut on March 30, 1991 against his alma mater, North Carolina, and Tar Heels coach Dean Smith—the man who recommended Williams for the Kansas job. Williams hated every moment of it with the exception of winning the game 79–73.

The game may be remembered most for Smith's ejection. The Hall of Fame coach, who studied under Phog Allen at KU and was known for keeping his composure on the court, received two technical fouls from referee Pete Pavia with 35 seconds remaining in the national semifinal. North Carolina was trailing 76–71.

Smith said he was asking Pavia how much time he had to make a substitution for Rick Fox, who had fouled out. Pavia said Smith was outside the coaches' box. Smith called the ejection "ridiculous" and "an embarrassment." It was only the third of his coaching career at UNC. Williams was clearly upset and later blamed the official's action for overshadowing his team's victory.

On his way off the floor, Smith shook hands with Williams, the KU players, assistant coaches, and support staff. "That's something I would have normally done after the game," Smith said. "But my game was over with then. I wasn't going to come back out."

Smith, though, would defeat Williams when they faced each other for a second and final time in the NCAA tournament. North Carolina beat Kansas 78–68 in the 1993 Final Four en route to winning the national title.

There are two important things to remember here. First, Kansas fans simply aren't very tolerant about colors outside of Crimson and Blue (make that Kansas blue). And this was in February 2007 when the wounds from Roy Williams' departure were not completely healed.

Smith showed up at the 55-year reunion of KU's 1952 national championship team wearing a Carolina Blue blazer. Athletic department officials had the former players stand at their seats behind the bench during the first media timeout. *The Kansas City Star* reported, "there was mostly applause, but a quick burst of boos could be heard from the student section" when Smith's name was announced.

Smith said he gave no thought to the color of his sport coat that day. But when asked how many people in Lawrence that weekend had mentioned the name of Roy Williams, Smith said, "The whole town has."

The booing came with a touch of embarrassment for KU, given Smith's importance in Kansas—and college basketball history. "I hope Kansas fans understand that KU produced arguably as good of a coach as our profession has ever known," Jayhawks coach Bill Self said. "We should be so proud of that."

And Kansas fans are glad to be associated with Smith, who received his basketball education at KU and then compiled a record of 879–254 in 36 seasons as head coach at North Carolina. But there were times when Smith became a polarizing figure in Jayhawks history, and that certainly was the case when his protégé went back to North Carolina.

In 15 seasons at KU, Williams became immensely popular while winning 418 games. But as soon as Williams began enjoying success, nervous Jayhawks fans started worrying about his eventual departure back to his alma mater. Williams had been an apprentice under Smith, serving 10 years as an assistant before getting the KU job when Larry Brown left in 1988.

Williams showed an unusual level of reverence toward Smith, and that bothered some Kansas fans, who wanted nothing but total devotion from Williams. He never referred to Smith as "Dean." Instead Williams called him "Coach" or "Coach Smith." When they appeared at clinics together, Williams always made sure that special attention was given to the details of Smith's trip, all the way down to holding doors open for Smith.

That created tension and jealousy for Kansas fans living with the fear that Smith would retire and Williams would be North Carolina's first choice in the replacement pool. Williams told North Carolina no thanks when Smith's successor, Bill Guthridge, stepped down in 2000. But despite directing Kansas to the Final

Four in 2002 and 2003, Williams could not reject Smith or the Tar Heels when the job opened again in 2003. Lost in the anger aimed at Williams and Smith was the fact that North Carolina assistant Dick Harp, the former KU coach, and Smith had done so much to influence the hiring of Williams in 1988.

Smith was offered the Kansas job after Ted Owens was fired in 1983 and again when Larry Brown left in 1988. Both times Smith declined. The late Bob Frederick, the KU athletic director who eventually hired Williams, said Smith laughed and said he couldn't leave the school that had recently opened a basketball arena bearing his name.

Kansas truly was in Smith's blood. He was born in Emporia, Kansas, in 1931 and later moved to Topeka, where he attended high school. He didn't play much for the basketball Jayhawks but at the side of Allen and Harp, he learned a great deal about coaching. In addition to that 1952 national championship team, Smith played for a squad that lost in the 1953 national title game.

Smith was an assistant coach at Air Force in 1957 when Kansas and North Carolina staged their first historic contest, that triple-overtime contest when the Tar Heels prevailed over Wilt Chamberlain's Jayhawks in the national championship game. Air Force coach Bob Spear had invited Smith to stay in a two-bedroom suite with two other coaches at Kansas City's Continental Hotel. One of the other coaches was North Carolina's Frank McGuire. "I still had deep emotional ties to the Jayhawks, and here I was sleeping in Frank's living room," Smith wrote in his biography *A Coach's Life*. "I was crushed [after the loss]. It was a profound disappointment for me and anyone else who cared about the KU program, and I took it extremely hard. After the game I was so low I didn't feel like going out, so I went back to the hotel suite."

Smith found the entire North Carolina team in the suite. McGuire asked all the coaches to say a word or two to the Tar Heels. "I certainly wasn't cheering for you," Smith told the Carolina players.

The young coach wasn't sure how McGuire would react but sensed that he liked it. Over breakfast the next morning, McGuire asked Smith to join his staff as an assistant coach. Three years later Smith replaced McGuire as North Carolina's head coach.

20 Ol' Roy Doesn't Give a...

Kansas played Syracuse for the national championship on April 7, 2003, but there was a strong aura of North Carolina Tar Heel in the New Orleans Superdome that night. Kansas fans actually had two results on their minds as the game began: the final score and the battle for Roy.

Two days after the Jayhawks defeated Arizona 78–75 to advance to the Final Four, Kansas had a familiar distraction. Coach Roy Williams was in the running for the North Carolina coaching job again. Matt Doherty, the former Tar Heel player and former Kansas assistant coach under Williams, had resigned under pressure. Kansas fans thought the North Carolina issue had been put to rest three years earlier when Williams turned down the Tar Heels. They should have known better. And the timing couldn't have been worse.

As the Jayhawks prepared to play Marquette in the Final Four, Williams got a phone call from North Carolina athletic director Dick Baddour. Williams didn't address the situation with the media in New Orleans, but it was a well-known fact that the KU coach wasn't seeing eye-to-eye with Al Bohl, who had replaced Bob Frederick as Kansas athletic director.

Williams had directed the Jayhawks to the Final Four for the second consecutive season, a true tribute to him and a roster that included Nick Collison, Kirk Hinrich, Keith Langford, Wayne Simien, and Aaron Miles. The journey wasn't quite as smooth as the previous season when the Jayhawks finished 33–4 overall and went undefeated in the Big 12. Drew Gooden had departed for the 2002 NBA Draft, but the rest of the cast seemed determined to win the championship that eluded them the season before.

After a shaky 3–3 start, including losses to North Carolina and Florida in the Preseason NIT in New York, the Jayhawks rattled off 10 straight wins, dropped consecutive games to Colorado and Arizona, and then ended the regular season by winning 11 of the last 12 to win the Big 12 with a 14–2 record. They did that even though Simien, averaging 14.8 points, dislocated his right shoulder on January 4 and never returned to full strength before reinjuring it February 26 and shutting down for the remainder of the season. "If you told me before the year we wouldn't have Wayne, I'd have said it'd be difficult [winning the Big 12]," Williams said. "To go 30–2 in this league the last two years is something we're really proud of."

There was a loss to Missouri in the Big 12 tournament, and then the Jayhawks got past Utah State, Arizona State, Duke, and Arizona to reach the Final Four. Hinrich scored 28 points and made six three-pointers as the Jayhawks avenged their loss to Arizona earlier in the season at Allen Fieldhouse. "It's the best feeling in the world," Hinrich said.

It kept getting better in New Orleans—at least in a 94–61 win against Marquette in the semifinal. Even with the distractions surrounding Williams and North Carolina, the Jayhawks played a near perfect game offensively, grabbing a 59–30 halftime lead and lifting Williams into the championship game for the first time since 1991. KU made 53.5 percent of its field goal attempts on the way to a rare Final Four rout.

That set the stage for the final dramatic scene. Would Williams win his first national title and then leave for North Carolina? Would he lose, stay at KU, and keep trying? No one knew exactly how it would play out. Syracuse fans may remember Gerry McNamara and Carmelo Anthony combining for 9-of-15 shooting from three-point range or KU struggling against coach Jim Boeheim's 2-3 zone defense. Maybe they remember Kansas coming back from an 18-point deficit or the Jayhawks missing 18 free throws. But they definitely remember Hakim Warrick blocking Michael Lee's three-point attempt with about three seconds remaining to seal Syracuse's 81–78 victory.

Kansas fans remember Collison and Hinrich walking off the floor for the final time without the championship trophy and rings they had coveted for four years. KU had finished 30–8 overall, the national runner-up once again.

And Kansas fans definitely remember the interview Williams conducted with Bonnie Bernstein of CBS immediately after the game. Bernstein very professionally stated that a lot of people watching the game wanted to know Williams' level of interest in the North Carolina job. "Bonnie, I could give a flip about what those people want," Williams said. "As a journalist you have to ask that question, I understand that. But as a human being…all those people that want that answer right now, they're not very sensitive."

Bernstein then asked Williams if he would take the job if North Carolina offered it. Williams said he had not thought about it for one second. "In tough times people should be more sensitive," Williams said. "I could give a shit about North Carolina right now. I've got 13 kids in that locker room that I love."

Within 48 hours, T-shirts were selling in Lawrence that read "I Don't Give a SH*T About North Carolina Either!" But one week after the championship game, even though Bohl had been fired as AD at Kansas, Williams accepted an offer to coach at North Carolina.

KEN DAVIS

21 Wilt and the 1957 National Championship Game

Frank Deford, perhaps the preeminent sportswriter of our time, called the 1957 national championship game the "greatest game ever played in college basketball" and "the beginning of the process which made college basketball big time." Given another chance today, Deford might alter his rankings a bit. Maybe not.

Regardless, when North Carolina prevailed 54–53 in triple overtime at Municipal Auditorium in Kansas City, Missouri, it was a bitter pill for the Jayhawks to swallow and has remained that way ever since. This was supposed to be the coronation of Wilt Chamberlain, the team's star big man. In his first varsity season, winning the NCAA title would have been emblematic of everything Chamberlain had accomplished to that point in his basketball career. And it was supposed to be a win for Kansas, playing in the NCAA title game for the third time in six seasons.

It would have been a lifetime achievement for KU coach Dick Harp, the man who replaced Phog Allen under difficult circumstances. And in many ways, it would have been another trophy for Allen, who recruited Chamberlain to KU but never had the opportunity to coach Wilt the Stilt. Chamberlain, the seven-foot center from Philadelphia, led the Jayhawks in scoring that season with 29.6 points per game. Forward Gene Elstun averaged 11.3 points, the only other Kansas player to average in double figures. Maurice King, Ron Loneski, and John Parker were the other top scorers on a team that won its first 12 games before losing at Iowa State on January 14.

The Jayhawks finished first in the Big 7 Conference and lost only one other game—at Oklahoma State—before heading into the NCAA tournament on a four-game winning streak. After beating

72

SMU and Oklahoma City in the Midwest Region in Dallas, the Jayhawks headed back to Kansas City for the Final Four. A crowd of 10,500 jammed into Municipal Auditorium to see the Jayhawks play their best game of the season in a national semifinal against two-time defending champions San Francisco—minus star center Bill Russell, who had moved on to play professional basketball. KU went on a 16–0 run in the second half, Chamberlain scored 32 points, and Elstun added 16.

That set up the national championship game between No. 2 KU and No. 1 North Carolina. The Tar Heels needed triple-overtime to win their semifinal against Michigan State. With Chamberlain dominating and facing a tired Carolina team, KU became the favorite in Kansas City. North Carolina coach Frank McGuire, who had coached St. John's in the 1952 championship game won by Allen and the Jayhawks, made it clear he intended to rattle Chamberlain from the very start. McGuire sent his playmaking guard, Tommy Kearns, to jump against Wilt the Stilt at tip-off. Kearns was just shy of six feet. Chamberlain won the jump, but the Tar Heels led 29–22 at halftime.

North Carolina sagged everyone around Chamberlain, and that worked better than Harp's box-and-one strategy against Lennie Rosenbluth, Carolina's top scorer. Chamberlain led a comeback for the Jayhawks in the second half, but when they grabbed a 36–35 lead, Harp decided to sit on the ball. KU's Bob Billings said the game might have been exciting for the fans, but it was boring for the players. "We wanted to run," Billings said in the book *Max and the Jayhawks*. "There was a lot of standing, holding the ball, and it was a great disappointment."

Kansas led 44–41 with 1:45 left, but Elstun missed a free throw after Chamberlain had passed to him from the high post. Kearns hit from the line to send the game into overtime tied at 46. The tension built and so did the cigarette smoke in the auditorium as the first two overtimes passed.

In the third overtime, Elstun hit two free throws to put Kansas ahead 53–52. But with six seconds remaining, Carolina's Joe Quigg pump-faked, drove against Chamberlain, and was fouled by King. Quigg hit both free throws. KU tried to throw the ball into Chamberlain, who had 23 points and 14 rebounds, but Quigg batted the pass away, Kearns grabbed the deflection, and the Tar Heels had won 54–53.

Despite advancing to the national championship game in his first season as coach, Harp was condemned by many Kansas fans for not winning it all. He seemed to second that notion. "There's no virtue in second place," Harp said. "There just isn't."

Chamberlain felt he had let his teammates down, and that burden stayed with him for years. He was tagged with a loser label that followed him well into his professional career. "It may have changed Wilt's whole direction," Billings said. "If we had won that title, it might have changed Wilt's life."

22 Dick Harp

In many ways Dick Harp has become the forgotten coach in Kansas basketball history. Perhaps more than anything else, that is a product of bad timing. "There's an old saying; never be the guy who follows a legend," said Ted Owens, the man who took over for the man who followed KU's coaching legend—Phog Allen.

Harp was the unfortunate one asked to fill Allen's shoes in 1956. It seemed natural because Harp had been considered Allen's understudy. He served as Allen's assistant for eight seasons, returning to Lawrence at Phog's request after two seasons as head coach at William Jewell College in Liberty, Missouri. When the Jayhawks won the national championship in 1952, Harp had been at Allen's side and he was there again the next season when KU returned to the title game and lost. "He was happy to do what he was doing and let Doc take all the credit," said Bill Hougland, KU star from 1950–52. "Dick scouted [opposing teams]. He'd go to games, come back, and have it all written up. Dick was really good at that. Doc was the motivator. Dick was the one who really got us playing the way we had to play to win."

Harp had played basketball under Allen at KU as well. He lettered from 1938–40 and was one of the starting guards and a co-captain on the legendary 1940 team that lost to Indiana in the NCAA title game. Harp had been born in Kansas City, Kansas, so his resume was all Jayhawk. "I had always wanted to play at Kansas and I think I maybe even said something in high school about wanting to coach," Harp said in John Hendel's book *Kansas Jayhawks History-making Basketball.*

Allen had done so much for Kansas basketball—not to mention the perception of the sport nationally and internationally. He convinced the inventor of the game, Dr. James Naismith, that the sport could be coached and he won 590 games in 39 seasons as the leader of the Jayhawks. That made it a hard act to follow. On top of all that, keep in mind that Allen didn't want to retire. The state of Kansas said it was mandatory because Allen was 70, and that was the law. Allen Fieldhouse had just been christened in 1955, and Allen was aching to coach his most noteworthy recruit of all-time, a tall lad from Philadelphia by the name of Wilt Chamberlain, who was preparing for his first season with the varsity. "Wilton could make a successful coach out of anyone," Phog wrote in a letter to friends on June 7, 1956. "Lucky is the man who inherits Wilton for three fairy-tale years."

Harp was that "lucky man." Chancellor Franklin Murphy told the KU athletic board to elevate Harp. Former player Jerry Waugh, who had become coach at Lawrence High School, was hired as Harp's top assistant. "I never put it in terms of following Doc because that's not possible," Harp said. "I never gave that a thought." But Harp couldn't control what others thought. And Allen certainly hadn't helped matters by stating that KU could win the 1957 national championship with "Wilt, two Phi Beta Kappas, and two aggressive coeds."

Harp had a 121–82 record in eight seasons as Kansas coach, leading the Jayhawks to two conference titles and two NCAA tournament appearances. It doesn't require a history degree to know that Harp and Kansas didn't win a national title with Chamberlain. Kansas went 24–3, won the Midwest Regional in 1957, and reached the championship game, but North Carolina prevailed 54–53 in triple overtime. KU dropped to 18–5 the next season and didn't make the NCAA tournament despite Chamberlain's 30.1 scoring average.

Chamberlain left, and Harp didn't reach the tournament field again until 1960 when forward Wayne Hightower and center Bill Bridges combined to produce more than 33 points per game. The Jayhawks were eliminated by Cincinnati and Oscar Robertson. KU was banned from the tournament in 1961 and 1962 after the NCAA charged that "KU boosters provided Chamberlain with a 1956 Oldsmobile convertible" while he was in school.

A deeply spiritual and Christian man, Harp became disillusioned with college basketball. After losing seasons in 1962 and 1963, KU finished 13–12 in 1964. Harp resigned and spent the next the 13 years as director of the Fellowship of Christian Athletes before joining Dean Smith's staff at North Carolina—yet another connection between the schools. "After he became [Kansas] coach, he was never happy," Waugh said. "This is a guy who lived his lifetime dream—and couldn't enjoy it."

Harp, who died in 2000, remains one of only six men to have both played and coached in the Final Four. "No one ever loved KU more than Dick Harp," said Harry Gibson, who played for Harp from 1962 to 1964. "He was proud of the tradition, proud to be a Jayhawk. I think he felt that all young basketball players should want to come to KU just because it was KU."

23 Bill vs. Roy

Kansas basketball endured an emotional breakup in 2003. When Roy Williams left for North Carolina one week after the Jayhawks lost the national championship game in New Orleans, Kansas fans felt betrayed and orphaned. One week later, those same fans were asked to shake Bill Self's hand, welcome him to Lawrence, and hand the keys over to Ol' Roy's office, program, and players.

KU basketball had never experienced anything like it. The former coach was being called a traitor. The new Kansas coach was being asked to cope with a popular ex-coach who had moved in with another nationally prominent program and was chasing the same championship trophy. "The thing I heard most was how pissed they were at Roy," Self said of his first season, "which basically told me they would rather have him as their coach than me."

Williams made it clear he absolutely, positively didn't want to play Kansas unless the two happened to meet in the NCAA tournament. But given the success of both programs, it was bound to happen. In fact it happened three times from 2008 to 2013. And once everybody emerged alive and well after the first time, the entire situation has calmed down—just a bit.

Through 2012–13, the scoreboard reads decisively in favor of the undefeated Self—Bill 3, Roy 0. (Kansas fans do seem to be counting.) The first meeting took place in San Antonio on April 5, 2008. The Jayhawks dominated a national semifinal game, winning

Roy Williams (left) shakes hands with Bill Self prior to a 2013 NCAA tournament game in Kansas City, Missouri, which Kansas won 70–58 to advance to the Sweet 16. (Getty Images)

84–66. Two nights later Self led KU to its first national title since 1988 with an overtime victory against Memphis.

In 2012 the Jayhawks won 80–67 in the Midwest Region championship in St. Louis, Missouri, sending Self to his second Final Four. And in 2013 the setting was the Sprint Center in Kansas City, Missouri, a familiar venue for both coaches. KU, the Midwest's No. 1 seed, advanced to the Sweet 16 after a 70–58 victory against Williams and the Tar Heels.

Before the most recent meeting, Self said enough time has passed that the focus should be on the two teams trying to make their own history in March. "Nobody can ever take away that he did a fabulous job [at Kansas]," Self said. "On the flip side, I don't really see after 10 years it's near as big a deal as maybe the story line would be."

But that story line was magnified enormously at the 2008 Final Four. True to their personalities, Self laughed off the questions, and Williams became increasingly annoyed as the game approached. The Jayhawks jumped out to a 40–12 lead with five minutes left in the first half. It was absolutely astonishing. KU executed perfectly on both ends of the floor. Self called it the best 15 minutes ever played by one of his teams. The Jayhawks swarmed around North Carolina big man Tyler Hansbrough, the National Player of the Year. When he handled the ball, he was greeted with a minimum of double coverage. Cole Aldrich came off the Kansas bench to play his best game of the season.

No one expected a Roy Williams team to roll over and stop playing. The Tar Heels closed within four points, but Brandon Rush, who led KU with 25 points, made clutch baskets down the stretch to hold off North Carolina. Williams started to hear the haunting Rock Chalk Jayhawk chant with 1:36 remaining. It must have seemed odd for him to hear it from the opposing bench. "They hit us right between the eyes," Williams said. "We probably rushed things a little bit. And they just kept hammering."

Two nights later when KU beat Memphis, Williams was handed a Jayhawks sticker as he headed to his seat. He wore it throughout the game and cheered for Kansas, a display that didn't go over well with some in Chapel Hill. Williams didn't think that was fair. But time has removed most of the tension, and both coaches seem at ease. "It's over with now," Williams said. "And time, as they say, will heal a lot of things. I don't think [facing KU] will ever feel good for me, regardless of the outcome…It was 15 years of my life that I felt like that I gave my heart and my body and my soul. And the people were wonderful to me."

24 Ted Owens

If Bill Self continues on his current pace of 30 wins a season at Kansas, he will pass Ted Owens on the school's all-time coaching victories list in the second half of the 2014–15 college basketball season. Until then, Owens will hold on to the third spot on the KU charts with 348 victories, trailing only Phog Allen (590) and Roy Williams (418).

Owens, an Oklahoma farm boy and a guard on the University of Oklahoma teams from 1949–51, arrived in Lawrence as an assistant coach on Dick Harp's staff in 1960. There was no assertion that he might succeed Harp, but that's exactly what happened in 1964 after Harp resigned. He had produced excellent results with the freshman team, and Owens was selected as head coach over Dean Smith and Ralph Miller, two of Allen's prize pupils. "My family had such great respect for teachers and coaches," Owens said in a 2008 interview. "To be offered the job wasn't overwhelming, but it was a dream come true."

The dream was his for 19 years, a stretch of time that saw dramatic changes in the world of college basketball and the NCAA tournament. Owens took over at a time when KU basketball needed an injection of life. Harp's last three teams had combined for a 32–43 record, and the Jayhawks had tied for seventh place in the Big 8 in 1962. Owens ordered a paint job for the locker room, including a tribute to past great players at KU.

Owens had a likeable personality and an ever-present smile. To those around the program, he became known as "Smiling Ted." "He was always, always shaking hands, always smiling," said Roger Morningstar, who played for Owens from 1974–75. "He tried to be mean, but he really had a hard time with it."

By winning the Big 8 holiday tournament his first three seasons, Owens got off to a good start with the KU fanbase. And he won seven of his first eight against Kansas State, which had assumed the position of conference power. Owens had a .657 winning percentage (348–182) at Kansas, won six Big 8 Conference titles, and advanced to the NCAA tournament seven times. He doesn't get enough credit for taking the Jayhawks to the Final Four in 1971 and 1974. His 1966 team might have won the NCAA tournament, but the Jayhawks were stopped short when a potential winning basket by Jo Jo White was waved off by an official who said White had stepped out of bounds.

White was one of five All-Americans coached by Owens. The others were Dave Robisch, Bud Stallworth, Walter Wesley, and Darnell Valentine. Owens was named Big 8 Coach of the Year five times and was named National Coach of the Year by *Basketball Times* in 1978 when Valentine, John Douglas, Ken Koenigs, Donnie Von Moore, and Paul Mokeski went 24–5 but received a tough draw in the NCAA West Regional and lost to UCLA in the first round. KU reached the NIT final in 1968 before losing to Dayton.

Owens made his final NCAA trip in 1981. After a 13–16 record in 1983, athletic director Monte Johnson fired Owens, even though he had put together a team with great potential that had Carl Henry, Kelly Knight, Ron Kellogg, Calvin Thompson, and Greg Dreiling. "We had a couple of down years at the end that you shouldn't have at Kansas," Owens said. "The thing that was disappointing was that I wanted a chance to get the program going again. I felt the responsibility of it being down. I wanted to turn it around, but they made the decision."

Owens lives in Oklahoma and enjoys his regular visits back to KU for reunions and anniversaries for his teams. His son, Teddy Owens, who was born in Lawrence, is an assistant coach who recently made the move from the staff at Oklahoma to Nebraska.

25 Jo Jo White

After Wilt Chamberlain left Lawrence in 1958, Kansas basketball fell on some lean times. There were three losing seasons between 1959 and 1963 and a 13–12 record in 1964 before Ted Owens replaced Dick Harp as coach. What KU needed was a fresh face, a new star on the court, a game changer who would restore the winning tradition. Enter Joseph Henry White—better known as Jo Jo.

Jo Jo White was a 6'3" guard from St. Louis who played at Vashon High School under legendary coach Jodie Bailey. White didn't know a thing about the University of Kansas, and nearly 250 schools were recruiting him. White was considering Cincinnati because Oscar Robertson was his hero. But Bailey suggested that White visit KU, and that was the first break the Jayhawks caught with the star guard. "First and foremost, I was in awe of the university," White said. "It was way beyond what I imagined a college campus would even be about. Then I had the opportunity of seeing this great [football] player play by the name of Gale Sayers. I was spellbound by how he moved on the field and all the plays he made. Then I got a chance to meet him. It started there."

The next break can only be described as hustle by recruiter Sam Miranda, the newest assistant coach on Owens' staff. Miranda, who had played for Branch McCracken at Indiana and spent 13 years at Kansas, gave the Jayhawks an edge with recruits especially from the area between St. Louis and Chicago. Miranda was one of the few who knew White was graduating from high school a semester early and would have the unusual opportunity to join the KU varsity midway through the 1965–66 season. "Rather than wait until the fall season, Coach Owens wanted me to come to school then, so as a freshman, I could play half a year," White said. "The team they had assembled had a chance to go all the way. And Ted felt I played a vital part in upgrading the backcourt. Just to have the opportunity was great."

Owens already had a good team with Walt Wesley, Al Lopes, Delvin Lewis, Riney Lochmann, and Ron Franz. But White would add to it with a game that was mature beyond his years. He had a beautiful shooting stroke, could handle the ball, and was tremendously quick. "His greatest strength was that he had no weaknesses," Owens said. "He was a great defender and an excellent passer in addition to being a great shooter."

It was a tricky move for a coach, bringing in a high school star in the middle of the season. But White's teammates were outstanding. Lochmann told Owens the players wanted White to start, even though that meant Lochmann would losing his starting role. White debuted February 12 and scored the first time he touched the ball. After dominating Oklahoma State 59–38, KU basketball had its swagger back. The Jayhawks won their last six games, finished first in the Big 8 with a 13–1 record, and reached the NCAA tournament for the first time since 1960.

After White joined the team, Kansas' average margin of victory was 26.4 points that season. Owens and the staff thought a national championship trophy might be waiting for the Jayhawks at the end of the season. But in one of the most controversial NCAA games in KU history, Texas Western defeated the Jayhawks 81–80 in overtime. In that Midwest Regional final (what would now be called the Elite Eight), referee Rudy Marich ruled that White stepped out of bounds before hitting what would have been the winning shot in regulation—a 28-footer at the buzzer. White maintains that he never put his heel down or beyond the sideline. "[I] executed what I was out there to do for the play we had to run," White said. "But when Kansas won it all in 2008, it was like poetic justice."

White was KU's Most Valuable Player three straight seasons and an All-American in 1968 and 1969. His 1,286 points rank 29th in KU history. His teams won two conference championships and three Big 8 holiday tournaments and made two NCAA appearances. In 1968 White's Jayhawks lost to Dayton in the NIT finals. White was an Olympic gold medalist with the U.S. team in 1968 before the Boston Celtics selected him with the ninth overall pick in the 1969 draft. He played 10 of his 12 NBA seasons in Boston, won two NBA championships, was the NBA Finals MVP in 1976, played in seven All-Star games, and had his No. 10 retired by the Celtics.

He returned to KU as an assistant coach from 1982–83. And he is a regular visitor to Allen Fieldhouse for reunions and anniversaries at KU. "It's the loyalty. It's the alumni. Those are the things that keep it incredible all these years," White said. "You can always go back to Kansas as an athlete and you feel welcomed and you feel appreciated for your accomplishments at that university."

26 Self vs. Calipari

Andrew Wiggins, the Canadian skywalker who has been compared to almost every legend who has played in the NBA, signed with the Kansas Jayhawks on May 14, 2013. Kentucky coach John Calipari held a press conference the next day. Calipari called his May 15 session a "summer press conference" to address the state of the Kentucky program.

That's cool. Not every college coach gives the media a 40-minute opportunity to catch up with offseason news. But outside the Bluegrass State, the timing appeared a bit suspicious and politically motivated. Wiggins, Bill Self, and the KU program had dominated the news cycle for a full 24 hours, and social media had simply exploded. Was Calipari invoking the equal-time rule and trying to pull attention back to the Wildcats? Draw your own conclusion.

But it seems pretty clear Kansas vs. Kentucky is back on the roster of college basketball's most compelling rivalries. Or is it Self vs. Calipari that is suddenly commanding our attention? Either way, it feels like fun. This is not Phog Allen vs. Adolph Rupp. That's so old school.

The subplots are delicious. While it is not pupil vs. mentor like the Allen-Rupp rivalry, Self and Calipari were both assistants under Larry Brown at Kansas. The Wildcats and Jayhawks rank No. 1 and No. 2, respectively, in all-time Division I victories (Kentucky has 2,111 and Kansas 2,101 entering the 2013–14 season). And the coaches have squared off in the national championship game twice in the last six years. Self beat Calipari's Memphis team in overtime in 2008. And Calipari, with his roster full of NBA talent, prevailed over Self and KU in 2012—the first time these blueblood programs had met in the championship game. It was also the second time

Williams vs. Pitino

When Allen Fieldhouse celebrated its 50th anniversary in 2005, voters on KUSports.com ranked a Kansas victory against Kentucky No. 2 among the most memorable moments in its history. During the regular season game on December 9, 1989, Kansas was just off NCAA probation, and Rick Pitino was in his first season with a Kentucky program that had only eight scholarship players after a major NCAA investigation devastated his program.

The final score: Kansas 150, Kentucky 90. Kansas led 80–61 at halftime. The final total represented the most ever scored by Kansas and the most ever against Kentucky. It was a tough night for Doug Beene, official scorekeeper at KU since the 1963–64 season. The NCAA scorebook only has space for recording 136 team points. "I had to manufacture the rest of it in the book," Beene revealed in the book *Beware of the Phog.*

The game also demonstrated some friction between two great coaches trying to rebuild their programs following NCAA investigations. "I was standing next to Coach Pitino when Coach Williams yelled down to him, 'Rick, what do you want me to do? We've got the third team in,'" Mark Randall told the *Lawrence Journal-World.* "Coach Pitino shouted an expletive at Coach Williams. I think Pitino was trying to prove a point with his team. They were trying to establish themselves."

Williams, in his second season as KU coach, said he had no intention of running up the score. Kentucky's pressure defense played into the hands of Williams' running game, and KU shot 61 percent and forced 27 turnovers. Kansas fans, who had seen Kentucky win 16 of the previous 18 meetings, didn't seem to mind. "It was like Custer's last stand," Pitino said.

the schools met that year after Kentucky defeated the Jayhawks in a November contest at Madison Square Garden.

USA TODAY covered the off-the-court battle between the schools—Calipari's interestingly timed press conference—this way: "Missing out on the nation's No. 1 recruit didn't dampen University of Kentucky basketball coach John Calipari's excitement about the 2013–14 season. He called a press conference

Wednesday, a day after Andrew Wiggins signed with Kansas, to rave about the guys he did get—a recruiting class still considered one of the best of all-time—and how good the Wildcats could be.

Calipari said the Wildcats are chasing perfection, greatness, and "things that have never been done in the history of our game." When asked about not getting Wiggins, Calipari said, "I'm as confident before and after his decision and I wish him well. I mean, he's a great kid, and he's going to be a terrific basketball player. It didn't change me any. I was confident in this team, and the group we had before and after."

Maybe Wiggins' decision didn't change Calipari. After all, Kentucky's 2013–14 roster features eight former McDonald's All-Americans and 10 players who were top-50 recruits nationally. But when Wiggins chose Kansas over Kentucky, North Carolina, and Florida State (the school Wiggins' parents attended), it changed the landscape and the outlook.

Kansas was a surprise call by the 6'8" wing player, who wasted no time impressing Jayhawks fans with some amazing moves and dunks during summer camp games. The choice didn't just end KU's period of gloom and doom that was still in session after losing to Michigan in the 2013 NCAA tournament, it gave Self a bolt of career enthusiasm.

Top recruits are taking a closer look at Kansas now. Jahlil Okafor, a 6'10" post player and one of the top prospects in the class of 2014, blogged for *USA TODAY* shortly after Wiggins' decision. He wrote: "A lot of people say that Kansas doesn't want a freshman to just come in for a year and have a huge impact then leave. I've never believed that, but I know Andrew will prove that it's not true so that's why it's big. I'll definitely be watching close to see how they handle a player of his talent level. I know Coach Self will do a good job with it."

27 Bud Stallworth

Isaac "Bud" Stallworth took his first step on the KU campus as a 17 year old from Hartselle, Alabama. He had no idea who coach Ted Owens was, and his goal in life had nothing to do with playing basketball for the Jayhawks. Stallworth was attending Midwestern Music Camp in Lawrence. He could have made his parents happy just by achieving first-chair trumpet in the band. "I was the next Louis Armstrong," Stallworth likes to tell anyone who might ask. He usually follows that up with a big laugh. "I was playing intramurals with the other campers when somebody told me I was wasting my time. He told me I should go [to Robinson Gym] and play with some guys during the noon hour."

Stallworth would bolt from camp at lunch, head over to Robinson for some serious competition, and then make sure he wasn't late for rehearsal. "If you were late, they called your parents," Stallworth said. "That was a no-no in my world. So I would always be back over there ahead of time. And luckily, I never got hit in the mouth. All bets would've been off. I wouldn't be here today."

It turned out he was holding his own against Vernon Vanoy, Al Lopes, Jo Jo White, and some other KU players, who were coming off two consecutive NCAA tournament appearances, including the infamous 1966 game against Texas Western. Those players wasted no time notifying their coach about the camper who could make sweet music with his shooting touch. When he got back to his dormitory, the camp counselor told him Owens had been calling to ask about him. "Now I'm thinking somebody knows I like to play basketball, and they're going to play this little joke on me," Stallworth said. "I figured I'd go along with it and see what the punch line is."

When Owens told him he was KU's coach, and those Kansas players thought Stallworth could play for the Jayhawks, Stallworth reacted by saying, "Are you serious?" Stallworth politely asked Owens to wait until his return to Alabama before calling his parents. His father was a principal, and his mother was a teacher. "My dad used to tell me to leave the ball alone and don't be stupid," Stallworth said. "You had to be an A student, be in the band, and then you could play basketball. He also said, 'In order to be the best, you've got to play against the best.'"

Stallworth, a 6'5" guard, would spend the next few years playing against the best, going to the Final Four in 1971, being named Big 8 Conference Player of the Year in 1972, and then playing in the NBA until 1977. He was a first team All-American on the court in 1972 and an Academic All-American in 1971, demonstrating that strong emphasis on education that was instilled by his parents. Playing at a time when freshmen were not eligible, Stallworth scored 1,495 points in three seasons at KU, and that ranks 20th on the all-time career scoring list. That was without a three-point line. "Everybody knows that I liked to take long shots, which was not one of Coach Owens' favorite things," Stallworth said. "But the way that I could shoot from the perimeter really made things easier for Dave Robisch and Roger Brown, who were our inside guys."

Robisch, Brown, Stallworth, Pierre Russell, and Aubrey Nash led KU to a 27–3 record in 1971. The Jayhawks won the Big 8 with a 14–0 record and reached the Final Four before losing to national power UCLA 68–60. "I thought I was going to the Final Four every year," Stallworth said. "That's one of the reasons I chose Kansas."

But Stallworth's senior season was a huge disappointment for the team. He averaged 25.3 points—fifth highest in KU history—but the Jayhawks finished 11–15 overall and 7–7 in the conference. Stallworth scored 659 points in 1971–72 (12th at KU) and made

277 field goals (eighth). He also attempted 620 field goals that season, third all-time at KU behind Clyde Lovellette (742 in 1952) and Danny Manning (653 in 1988). Wilt Chamberlain is fourth with 588 in 1957.

Stallworth is remembered by a generation of Kansas fans for the moment that came in his final game at Allen Fieldhouse. On February 26, 1972, with the 1952 national champions gathered for a reunion, Stallworth scored 50 points as the Jayhawks defeated rival Missouri 93–80.

Only Chamberlain—with 52 points against Northwestern as a sophomore in 1956—ever scored more for Kansas in a single game. Stallworth averaged 27.8 points in conference play that season. He had 19 field goals and 12 free throws against the Tigers and—thanks to assistant coach (and future athletic director) Bob Frederick, who urged Owens to get him back on the floor in the final moments—he set the Big 8 single-game scoring record.

But Stallworth, who loved competing against Missouri, enjoyed beating MU coach Norm Stewart the most. Before the game, Stewart had told reporters that MU star John Brown should be Big 8 Player of the Year over Stallworth. Bud's roommate showed him the article, and Bud took it personal. "It was Missouri, man," he said. "It doesn't get any better than that. Norm Stewart and I had a running feud for a couple of years. He really had his guys hating the University of Kansas. When you played Missouri, it was like you stole something from their mommas. Every time I played against them, I had one of my better games. It motivated me. My thing was if [Stewart] was going to be like that, I was going to show him. We let Norm know we had one more bullet left in our gun."

28 Take a Photo with Big Jay and Baby Jay

How many college mascots were "hatched" during a halftime ceremony? Well, that's how Baby Jay entered the world on October 9, 1971, at halftime of KU's homecoming football victory against Kansas State. Just like that, the world was no longer such a lonely place for a Jayhawk.

If you are a true Kansas fan, that means there's a pretty good chance the family photo album includes a picture of you or someone in your family posing for a picture with Big Jay, Baby Jay—and possibly even C Jay. (C Jay is Centennial Jay. The university's third mascot, honoring the original Jayhawk drawn up in 1912, was introduced during a first-half timeout of the Kansas–Missouri basketball game on February 25, 2012, and was retired after the centennial celebration.)

Unlike most birds the Jayhawk does not fly away when being photographed. In fact, Big Jay and Baby Jay love to strike a pose. If you attend a game, a pep rally, a parade, or any other KU function, you should have your camera ready. Do it—or regret it later. Big Jay and Baby Jay are two of the most photogenic mascots in college athletics. They might be wearing basketball uniforms, football uniforms, lab coats, tuxedos, or graduation gowns, but these birds are usually smiling and approachable. Take a photo or shoot a video but make sure the kids get into the shot. In fact a couple of the official duties in Baby Jay's job description are "entertaining children" and "giving hugs to youngsters."

Student Amy Sue Hurst saw a bumper sticker depicting a Jayhawk and hatchlings back in 1970, and that inspired her to create a new mascot. After talking to a friend, who portrayed Big

Jay, and getting approval from the KU Alumni Association, Hurst created Baby Jay at her Ohio home the summer after her freshman year. Then Baby Jay was transported to Lawrence by the family station wagon. The original Baby Jay costume, now on display at the Kansas Union, cost $53. Now it is replaced every two years at the cost of $5,000.

The evolution of the Jayhawk can be traced to that drawing back in 1912. Henry Maloy, a cartoonist for the student newspaper, gave that blue bird with the yellow beak a pair of shoes—for kicking opponents, of course. Three different drawings emerged in the 1920s, one perched on a KU monogram (1920), one resembling a duck-like creature (1923), and one rather grim-faced bird with dangerous talons (1929). Gene "Yogi" Williams opened the bird's beak in 1941, giving the Jayhawk a more threatening appearance.

But it is Harold D. Sandy's 1946 design of a smiling Jayhawk that has withstood the test of time. The only change since then came in 2005 when the KU lettering was changed to a Trajan font.

The costume now known as Big Jay appeared in the 1960s. Tryouts for Big Jay and Baby Jay are held every year, and mascots are selected "based on their appropriateness and entertainment value." To try out for Big Jay, you must be 6'1" to 6'5". For Baby Jay the requirement is 4'11" to 5'1". Mascots receive a $300 scholarship per semester and an additional $50 semester for maintaining a GPA of 3.0 or higher. The mascots make about 250 appearances a year besides football and basketball games.

"It is awesome to be part of the mascots because you're literally the face of the university," mascot coach Kamille Ratzlaff told the *Lawrence Journal-World* in 2012. "You can just change someone's day by walking into a room, and all they want is a high-five."

29 Waving the Wheat

When Nellie from *South Pacific* sings that song about her "wonderful guy," she proudly proclaims she's "as corny as Kansas in August." Well, that's nice. And there is a lot of corn in eastern Kansas at that time of year. But wheat is the really big deal all across Kansas. It's big business, too. Kansas is the top wheat-producing state in the nation with almost 20 percent of the total supply in the United States coming from within the state borders. Anyone who has ever driven from Kansas City to Denver can tell you about wheat fields. Those golden fields of grain stretch as far as the eye can see, and when a gentle prairie breeze passes through, the wheat gently sways in a dance that makes any Kansan proud.

So, with all the great tradition associated with Kansas athletics, it only makes sense that the waving of the wheat was adopted as a significant ritual at basketball and football games. All you need is a group of fans standing in a crowd, arms raised to the heavens, sharing in a waving, side-to-side, back-and-forth motion that resembles that breezy Kansas wheat field.

At Memorial Stadium, fans wave the wheat after every scoring drive in football. Inside Allen Fieldhouse, the tradition is carried out when an opponent fouls out and is headed to the bench—and at the conclusion of every Jayhawks victory.

Unlike most traditions at Kansas, the ritual's origin isn't known. There is a photo from the late 1930s showing Jayhawks fans at the Lawrence train depot, waving their arms in a warm welcome home to a KU team. And in the 1937 *Jayhawker* yearbook, there is a photo of a waving arm used to illustrate an essay on the renewed school spirit associated with the 1936 football season.

Suffice it to say, Kansas fans have engaged in this unusual practice for a long time. In 1971, the KU band department got in on the act and "waving the wheat" was taken to another level. Trombone player Frank Thompson asked senior band member Jim Barnes to write an arrangement of the Wheaties jingle from the popular cereal commercial starring NBA Hall of Famer Willis Reed. In the commercial, Reed missed a dunk because "he had not eaten his Wheaties that day."

Barnes, who went on to become a music professor at KU, remains on campus more than 40 years later. But he executed that 1971 request to perfection, adding lyrics to the popular jingle. And when coach Ted Owens took the Jayhawks to the Final Four in Houston in that same year, the cereal makers at General Mills sent 5,000 flat Wheaties boxes to help KU fans support the Jayhawks.

Kansas lost to UCLA at that Final Four, but the pep band's involvement with waving the wheat was secured. Eventually, fans stopped singing the words, but the band continued playing the song. The school says there are no official words, but for those who have passed through Allen Fieldhouse over the years, this is the accepted refrain:

So long, you didn't have your Wheaties.
So long, we hate to see you go.
Too bad, you didn't have your Wheaties,
So sad, you didn't win the game.

The tradition continued unquestioned for years, at least until political correctness marched into the college arena. In January 2004 a Kansas State player fouled out in Lawrence, and *Lawrence Journal-World* sports columnist Chuck Woodling noticed a woman who stood and began waving her arms above her head. But the band did not join in with the Wheaties jingle. "The woman looked around, saw she was in the minority, and sheepishly sat down,"

Woodling wrote. "Slowly word has trickled down that the KU band no longer performs its longtime Wheaties rite. The Big 12 Conference considers it unsportsmanlike, and Kansas has complied by shutting the band down."

Tom Stidham, then director of the basketball band, had been told by KU administrators that NCAA rules stated the band could only play before and after the game, at halftime, and during time-outs—not during other dead-ball situations. That's when Mary Burchill, a season-ticket holder since 1968, pulled together the words and asked KU fans to sing—even if the band had been silenced. "The traditions are what make the game fun," Burchill told the *Journal-World* on February 6, 2004. "If they have the words, I have confidence students will do it. All it takes is a few to start to get it going."

Jayhawks do not let go of their traditions easily. Before the 2003–04 season ended, KU officials gave in. And by the Big 12 tournament in Dallas, the KU Alumni Association had reached an agreement with General Mills. "We looked at it again and again and again and decided it didn't violate the spirit of the NCAA rule book," KU associate athletic director Jim Marchiony said of the reversal. "Anything that adds to the game and reflects on the tradition of KU basketball is very exciting."

About 2,500 special-issue Wheaties cereal boxes, brandishing a giant Jayhawk on the front and lyrics to the jingle on the back, were put on sale before KU's game against rival Missouri. Most of the boxes had cereal, but others were stuffed with commemorative "Wave the Wheat" T-shirts that became pop-culture collectors' items.

30 Paul Pierce

Coach Roy Williams found the early building blocks to success on the West Coast. Williams developed a California pipeline, starting with point guard Adonis Jordan, who left Reseda, California, for Kansas—even as KU dealt with NCAA probation left over from Larry Brown's final season. Scot Pollard, Jerod Haase, Jacque Vaughn, and Paul Pierce followed Jordan to Lawrence, and they were there as Williams constructed a dynasty in the Big 8 and later the Big 12.

Pierce, a McDonald's All-American who grew up a Los Angeles Lakers fan at nearby Inglewood High School, turned out to be the best of them all. Pierce became a 1998 first-round pick of the Boston Celtics, a 10-time NBA All-Star, and the 2008 NBA Finals' Most Valuable Player. But on December 2, 1995, Pierce was just a freshman playing his first home game at Allen Fieldhouse. And the opponent just happened to be that legendary school from Los Angeles—the UCLA Bruins. UCLA entered the Phog with an 8–0 record against the Jayhawks with the last four victories coming in the NCAA tournament.

It looked like more of the same in the first half. After 17 minutes UCLA led the No. 2 Jayhawks 41–22. It was an embarrassing first half. But Williams switched to a zone defense after the break, and that changed the complexion of the game. UCLA missed four consecutive shots and became rattled. Vaughn and Pierce, who both chose Kansas over UCLA, pulled their games together in the second half. Vaughn finished with 22 points; Pierce had 14 points and eight rebounds. Down 15 at the half, KU rallied to win 85–70. The Jayhawks finally had a victory over the Bruins, and Pierce's career was off to an impressive start. "I don't have to go back to L.A. and hear everybody's mouth," Pierce said. "This was a must-win game."

In his book with Tim Crothers, *Hard Work: A Life On and Off the Court*, Williams described Pierce as the final piece to a recruiting puzzle. "Recruiting is like putting together a puzzle, and I mean that literally," Williams said. "When we recruited Paul Pierce at Kansas, we had four starters coming back, but we had no small forward. I asked my assistant Steve Robinson to make a little puzzle. He cut pieces out of a cardboard box; there were four corner pieces that represented our four starters, and he left the centerpiece missing. We sent Paul the four corner pieces and then two days later, we sent the centerpiece in the shape of a star with Paul's picture on it and a message that read, 'You are the missing piece to the puzzle.' That's what Paul turned out to be when we got him. Recruiting is about convincing kids that they are the missing piece that we need to be complete."

Power forward Raef LaFrentz was from Iowa—not California—but he joined with Pierce to give the Jayhawks a potent front-line scoring punch for three consecutive seasons. One memorable moment came on March 9, 1997 in Kansas City, Missouri, at the inaugural Big 12 tournament. Pierce scored 30 points and was named the tournament's Most Valuable Player after the Jayhawks crushed Missouri 87–60 in the championship game. "It was just one of those days," Pierce said. "I was definitely feeling it, and my teammates recognized that."

Pierce left for the NBA after his junior season, but in his three years at KU, the Jayhawks went 98–11, won three conference titles, and lost only four league games. Despite all that success, Pierce never played in a Final Four. Syracuse defeated KU in the West Regional final his freshman year. His sophomore season ended with one of the most crushing defeats in KU history, an 85–82 loss to Arizona in the Sweet 16. And his final game as a Jayhawk came in Oklahoma City, where Rhode Island upset Kansas 80–75 in a second-round game.

After averaging 20.4 points as a junior, he exited with 1,768 points—eighth all time at Kansas behind Danny Manning, Nick Collison, LaFrentz, Clyde Lovellette, Sherron Collins, Darnell Valentine, and Keith Langford. In 1998 Pierce was a consensus first team All-American, a John Wooden Award finalist, and a first team All-Big 12 selection. He ranks among KU's all-time leaders in free throws made, free throw attempts, rebounding, and steals.

Nicknamed "the Truth" by Shaquille O'Neal in 2001, Pierce was the 10th pick overall in 1998 and was named to the NBA All-Rookie first team in 1999. Pierce is quite simply the best NBA talent KU has produced since Wilt Chamberlain and he became an icon in Boston, a pro sports town that warmly embraces its championship teams. Pierce endured difficult and lean seasons with the Celtics early in his career and almost died while trying to separate fighters at a Boston dance club in 2000. He was stabbed 11 times and was rushed to a nearby hospital where he needed lung surgery to repair damage. But Pierce remained steady and loyal to the Celtics until the fabled franchise added Kevin Garnett and Ray Allen to form a new Big Three that won the 2008 NBA Finals. Pierce averaged 21.8 points, 6.3 assists, and 4.5 rebounds to earn Finals MVP honors as Boston beat his hometown Lakers for the crown. "I know we didn't have a lot of great years, but you guys stuck with me, and now we bring home a championship to you," Pierce said. "They don't hang up any other banners but championship ones, and now I'm a part of it."

After 15 seasons with the Celtics, Pierce, and Garnett were traded to the Brooklyn Nets on July 12, 2013. Allen had left for Miami one year earlier. Boston fans mourned a sad ending to the Big Three era. Pierce scored 24,021 points—second only to John Havlicek's 26,395 in Celtics history. *The Boston Globe* headline read, "Celtics made painful decision to start over."

31 Jacque Vaughn

Halfway through my first interview with Kansas guard Jacque Vaughn, it struck me that I had never met another athlete quite like him. Almost 18 years later, I still feel the same way. The feeling wasn't solely based on his extraordinary ability to play point guard, though it was a thing of beauty to watch him essentially coach his team on the floor. It wasn't about his grade point average, even though he was a gifted student. The 1997 Academic All-American of the Year led his team to a 34–2 record during that same year. He also was "America's point guard laureate," who found writing poetry to be a form of introspection. "I take a lot of pride in [being an example]," Vaughn said. "Kids can realize it's okay to be a student and an athlete. They can realize being a student doesn't constitute you as a nerd."

Vaughn wasn't a nerd; he just had the total package. He was a *Sports Illustrated* cover boy. He had a 3.72 GPA as a business administration major at KU. He was a two-time Academic All-American, but he was a two-time All-Conference selection and the Big 8 Player of the Year in 1996. He received the Arthur Ashe Jr. Scholar-Athlete Award and left KU as the all-time Kansas and Big 8 assist leader with 804. (Aaron Miles would break that record with 954.) Vaughn had 10 assists in a single game 18 times in his KU career. He started 100 straight games. But numbers never defined Vaughn. "You'll never fully appreciate Jacque by looking at his statistics," teammate Scot Pollard told *The New York Times* during 1997.

And you couldn't truly appreciate his poems because he didn't share them publicly. "It's pretty personal," Vaughn said. "It's something where I can sit down, and if I'm feeling frustrated, I can write about frustration. If I'm tired, I can write about being tired. It's a way of me ridding my emotions. And often, I get a lift from reading other poets' works. It works for me both ways."

Named head coach of the NBA Orlando Magic in July 2012, Vaughn had great speed during his playing days. If you didn't see him play, check out his videos or photographs. Vaughn even looked fast in freeze frame. Hall of Fame coach Jim Calhoun talked about Vaughn's speed as his UConn team prepared to play the Jayhawks in 1995 at Kemper Arena in Kansas City, Missouri. "Our speed problem is his ability to go by pressure defenses," Calhoun said. "I don't know if he knows teams are pressing sometimes because he's already at halfcourt by the time a team sets up its presses and traps."

When Vaughn was a senior at John Muir High School in Pasadena, California, he attracted attention from many of the top coaches in college basketball. Indiana coach Bob Knight made a visit to the Vaughn home and truly made himself at home. When Knight propped his feet on the family coffee table, the Vaughns were not impressed. Jacque and his family were much more comfortable with Roy Williams, and the coach returned the favor with immediate trust in Vaughn's freshman season.

Williams introduced his former point guard on December 21, 2002, when Vaughn's No. 11 jersey was raised to the rafters on the south side of Allen Fieldhouse. As he talked, Williams pointed to places on the court where Vaughn created memories for the ages. "Right over there, freshman year against Indiana with one second left in overtime hit a three. Over there, spin move against UCLA," Williams said. "If there's ever been a better leader, I've never seen it. If there's ever been a better student-leader, I've never seen it. Jacque, I love you, son."

Vaughn broke down as he spoke to the crowd. He said he never imagined his jersey hanging from the rafters. He said it was tough to describe what it meant to him.

An All-American in the classroom and on the court, Jacque Vaughn started 100 straight games at Kansas before having his No. 11 jersey retired.

"When all is said and done," Vaughn said, "I hope you remember me as someone who played hard, played smart, played unselfishly, who played because he loved his coach, loved his teammates, loved his institution, and loved Kansas basketball."

32 Darnell Valentine

From 1977 to 1981, when he wore jersey No. 14 in Allen Fieldhouse, every day was Valentine's Day. But Darnell Valentine was a fan favorite at Kansas before he played his first game. As a schoolboy playing at Wichita Heights High School in Wichita, Kansas, he became a legendary figure in Kansas high school sports and was heavily recruited from the Class of 1977.

KU needed to land this recruit with the magical name and an immense amount of talent. The Jayhawks needed his help. They had been to the Final Four under Ted Owens in 1971 and 1974. They won the Big 8 again in 1975 but lost to Notre Dame in the first round of the NCAA tournament. Then times got a little tough.

Juniors Norm Cook and Herb Nobles, sophomores Clint Johnson and Ken Koenigs, and freshman center Paul Mokeski all averaged more than 10 points in 1975–76, but KU finished 13–13 overall and tied for fourth in the Big 8. The addition of transfer John Douglas didn't help much the next season, and the Jayhawks finished fourth in the conference again.

But Valentine's arrival in 1977–78 generated excitement for the program again. The freshman guard with the tree trunk thighs led the team in scoring with a 13.5 average. Valentine was a playmaker with outstanding court vision. A great decision maker, he knew when to pass and when to shoot. The Jayhawks were simply better with the ball in his hands. His on-ball skills were extraordinary, too, affording him the ability to impact the game at either end of the court. "Darnell was a tremendous defender," Owens said. "Darnell just disrupted the other team's offense. When you have a point guard who can dominate the opposing point guard, then you just disrupt everything they do. He would just steal a ball and go down and lay it in."

His defense would frustrate Big 8 opponents so much that they would resort to retaliation and intentionally knock him to the floor. In one game against Oklahoma, Valentine got decked, and Owens thought a flagrant foul should have been called. "I'm really upset and I went charging down the court," Owens said. "As I went by [Sooners coach] Dave Bliss, I shoved him on the shoulder, which was stupid and I got reprimanded by the league. It was ridiculous. You don't do things like that. But I felt the other coaches were trying to get back at Darnell."

Surrounded by Douglas at the other guard and three talented big men—Koenigs, Mokeski, and senior Donnie Von Moore—the Jayhawks rolled to a 13–1 championship record in the Big 8 and had only four losses going into the NCAA tournament. "We had seniors on the team, but the final piece was Darnell," Koenigs said. "His coming in as a freshman added another dimension. I think that put us over the top. He was ready to play as soon as he hit the door. The thing I remember about that year was how nice it was to be successful. We had really struggled my sophomore and junior years."

Kansas carried an eight-game winning streak into the Big 8 tournament. But after beating Kansas State three times in the regular season (during the Big 8 holiday tournament—a popular Kansas City event, which took place from 1946 to 1978—and home and away contests), the Wildcats got revenge with an 87–76 win against the Jayhawks in Kansas City. It was a costly loss for KU. Instead of a possible path through Wichita and Lawrence to the Final Four in St. Louis, the Jayhawks were shipped to Eugene, Oregon, and met John Wooden's UCLA Bruins in the NCAA tournament again.

Mokeski had 18 points and 12 rebounds, Johnson scored 15 points, and Douglas 14. Valentine had 11 points and six assists but fouled out as did Koenigs and Johnson. KU was called for 30 fouls to UCLA's 14. The Bruins outscored KU 27–8 from the free throw line and won the game 83–76. With Kansas leading, Owens gambled with nine minutes remaining and left Valentine in the game with four fouls. Valentine was called for a charge on the next play. "I looked like the dumbest coach around for leaving him in," Owens said.

Valentine averaged more than 16 points the next two seasons, but KU didn't return to the NCAA tournament until his senior season. After considering leaving early for the NBA, he came back for one more shot at the Final Four. Kansas tied for second in the Big 8 in 1981, but Valentine and Tony Guy really came on strong in the postseason. After beating K-State to win the Big 8 tournament, the Jayhawks opened NCAA play in Valentine's hometown of Wichita.

KU defeated Mississippi 69–66 in the first round of the Midwest Regional, and Guy scored a career-high 36 to spark an 88–71 upset of Arizona State in the second round. As a reward KU moved on to New Orleans against in-state rival Wichita State. KU had refused to play the Shockers for 25 years, and WSU had put together a talented team led by Cliff Levingston and Antoine Carr. Headlined by Valentine vs. his hometown school, the story lines were rich. The Shockers pulled a huge upset—at least in the eyes of Kansas fans. The Jayhawks fell 66–65, and Valentine's career ended on a 24–8 team that wanted more. "It was painful," Valentine told the *Lawrence Journal-World.* "It's a game I think we were capable of winning and moving farther in the tournament."

Valentine departed with 1,821 points, 609 assists, and 336 steals. He still ranks sixth in scoring, fifth in assists, and is the all-time KU leader in steals. Mario Chalmers is second with 283. "I am surprised I'm still there," Valentine said of the steals mark. "What that means is I had great teammates. They allowed me to take a lot of chances and get a lot of steals."

Valentine was a three-time Academic All-American and received All-American honors on the court after his senior season. He won the team MVP award four times and is the only KU player to be named first team All-Conference four times. Before becoming a first-round pick of the Portland Trail Blazers in the 1981 Draft, Valentine did much more than pile up stats at KU. In four years of Valentine Days for the Jayhawks, he set an example to follow. "I instilled an incredible work ethic," Valentine told the *Journal-World.* "I worked extremely hard to get to the point to where I could achieve things at Kansas. I was at every practice. And I was consistent."

33 Beware of the Phog

In 1988 a pair of fifth-year architectural students hung a sign that captured the spirit of an entire arena, reflected the character of the school's most famous coach, and inspired the school's players for years and years to come. Their work of art was 35 feet long and six feet high. The message was painted on a canvas of 10 stolen dormitory shower curtains (poor McCollum Hall) held together by those straight pins used to make foam core models in architecture classes.

NCAA Games in the Phog

Coach Ted Owens and the players on the 1977–78 Kansas team still wonder what might have happened if the NCAA had awarded the Jayhawks games in Wichita and Lawrence on the way to the Final Four in St. Louis. Instead KU lost to Kansas State in the semifinals of the Big 8 Conference championship, and the Jayhawks were sent to Eugene, Oregon, where they lost to UCLA 83–76. Meanwhile, Digger Phelps' Notre Dame team defeated DePaul in Allen Fieldhouse to advance to the Final Four against Duke.

Allen Fieldhouse was the site for 37 NCAA postseason games from 1956–79, including two that featured KU. In 1967 No. 3 Kansas and Jo Jo White fell to Elvin Hayes and No. 7 Houston 66–53. The next day Kansas beat No. 2 Louisville 70–68 in a consolation game.

Cincinnati's Oscar Robertson scored 56 points in a 97–62 NCAA victory against Arkansas on March 15, 1958. That's still the Allen Fieldhouse record for most points scored by an individual player. In the NCAA's final act in Lawrence, Larry Bird and Indiana State began the trek to the national championship game against Michigan State and Magic Johnson with an 86–69 win against Virginia Tech at Allen Fieldhouse.

It read, Pay Heed, All Who Enter: BEWARE OF "THE PHOG." Simply stated, and yet classic at the same time, the phrase has become part of the standard Kansas vocabulary.

The students' names were Todd Gilmore and Mike Gentemann, but legend has it they were affectionately known as "Gumby" and "the Mauu." Gilmore or "Gumby" is credited with those nine magical words. Gentemann or "the Mauu" provided the distinctive lettering that set the banner apart from all others. The two students had combined for one other banner for a game against Kentucky in 1985 that read, "On the Sixth Day, God Created Manning."

"Beware of the Phog" debuted on February 20, 1988, when Duke visited Allen Fieldhouse for a late season non-conference game worth remembering. The Blue Devils won 74–70 in

106

overtime. The Jayhawks would lose 11 games that season but only two more the rest of the way—to Oklahoma in Norman on the road and to Kansas State in the Big 8 tournament in Kansas City, Missouri. The Jayhawks went on to avenge all three losses in the NCAA tournament, beating K-State, Duke, and Oklahoma in succession to win the national championship.

The 1988 season would turn out to be a very special, of course, with "Danny and the Miracles" winning the national championship under coach Larry Brown. And introducing such a banner was nothing unusual at this point in Kansas basketball history. It really was a renaissance age for student fans who started traditions such as camping out before games, yelling "Whoosh" on made free throws, and tossing a student in the air during timeouts.

Gilmore was one of the first campers and he believed the Fieldhouse needed its own branding. He says "Pay Heed" just came to him "out of nowhere." But "Beware of the Phog" played off an ad for a John Carpenter movie called *The Fog*. Of course, the spelling was changed to honor the coach who built the Fieldhouse.

For the book, *Beware of the Phog*, Gentemann told authors Doug Vance and Jeff Bollig, that all the materials for the banner—other than the shower curtains—were "scrounged from studio supplies. It wouldn't have been like us to go out and purchase anything special." Another friend of "Gumby" and "the Mauu" was a person they referred to as "Kippen." And "Kippen" was sent on a scavenger hunt for materials. "Let's just say that the residents of McCollum Hall woke up the next day to find their showers had no curtains," Gentemann said. "I don't know that they were clean, but they were sturdy, dry, and the eyelets made them custom made for hanging."

Gilmore described his own history of the sign. "We put it in our design studio for the night to dry and we went home," Gilmore wrote. "It took a *long* time for the paint to dry, so there was no time to have it sewn together before the game. We were kind of worried how it would hold up, but luckily it didn't come apart. That would have been a disaster. The day before the game we started to camp out in front of the fieldhouse, so we could get our usual seats for the game. We brought the banner with us and showed it to Assistant AD Floyd Temple, and he gave us permission to hang it up. While we were making the banner we had strung a 100-foot rope through the top of the shower curtains. We knew the only way we could hang it would be to tie it in between the catwalks at the top of the fieldhouse. That ended up being difficult. For obvious reasons they wouldn't let us climb up on the catwalks. We got around this problem by tying a shoe to the end of the rope and throwing it over the catwalk and then tying it down by the last row of seats. On the second toss, the shoe came loose and landed right on top of the catwalk. So Ferd [another friend named Brad Oliver] had to go through the game without one shoe. After we had it tied down, we realized that the middle was too heavy and sagged so badly you couldn't read it. We were at a loss what to do when Floyd pointed out a rope hanging down in just the right place, which even had a clip on the end of it. It held the middle up perfectly. It was at exactly that point that we knew we had something special."

The original banner greeted visitors until the 1998–99 season when the shower curtain material started to fail. A replica took its place in 2000. The original banner now is on display in the Booth Family Hall of Athletics.

Hanging on the north wall of the Fieldhouse, visiting teams are still warned of the hazards of entering the Phog. If that doesn't get their attention, the five national championship banners directly underneath usually do the trick.

34 Make a Pilgrimage to the Naismith Hall of Fame

The Naismith Memorial Basketball Hall of Fame sits on the banks of the Connecticut River, just off Interstate 91 in Springfield, Massachusetts, the city where James Naismith invented the game. Springfield is a short drive from Connecticut, where I have lived and worked since 1985. Coverage of the annual enshrinement ceremonies has become part of my reporting routine.

Every Hall of Fame class is historic for one reason or another, but the 2007 ceremony had special meaning because of my life-long connection with Kansas basketball. Coach Roy Williams had already left KU and returned to North Carolina, his alma mater, by the time he was elected in 2007. Anyone who knew Williams understood he wanted to share his election with the both the Tar Heels and Jayhawks despite lingering resentment from Kansas fans over his move in 2003.

The man did spend his first 15 seasons as a head coach at KU, building his reputation as one of the top college coaches. So before delivering his acceptance speech Williams told reporters, "If I had to pick a hat [to wear in the Hall], I'd have one special made that would be half-Tar Heel, half-Jayhawk."

After that press conference, Williams and I were talking and strolling through the Hall of Fame lobby when a tall gentleman approached him with hand extended. I had never met Clyde Lovellette until that moment, but there was no mistaking the face of the former star from Kansas. With that handshake two great eras of Kansas basketball came together at the center of the Hall of Fame building. Lovellette congratulated Williams and told him he was proud. For that instant, Lovellette seemed to be speaking for Jayhawks everywhere.

I cannot guarantee you a Jayhawks memory as special as that one, but any true Kansas basketball fan should schedule a pilgrimage to Springfield and tour the Naismith Basketball Hall of Fame at least once in a lifetime. The Hall is close to Boston and not far from New York. Any basketball fan visiting New England should get to Springfield. The fact that Naismith's name is on the building is enough reason for Jayhawks to visit. He may not have invented the game in Kansas, but he brought basketball to KU in 1898 and lived in Lawrence until his death in 1939.

Here's the fact every Jayhawk fan needs to know: Kansas has more inductees in the Naismith Hall of Fame than any other Division I school. *Seventeen.* That's right, 17 former Jayhawks—16 men and women's great Lynette Woodard—have been immortalized there. In addition, longtime KU radio voice Max Falkenstien was awarded the Curt Gowdy Award that honors members of the electronic media. Falkenstien was honored in 2004, the same year Woodard was enshrined.

Naismith, of course, is one of the 17. The only losing coach (55–60) in Kansas history was elected in 1959. Naismith once told his pupil, F.C. "Phog" Allen, "You don't coach basketball, Forrest; you play it." Luckily, Allen paid no attention to that advice. Phog was elected in 1959 after winning 590 games in 39 seasons as coach of the Jayhawks.

Adolph Rupp, the legendary Kentucky coach known as the "Baron of Basketball," Dean Smith of North Carolina, and Ralph Miller of Oregon State, were all pupils of Allen and have earned spots in Springfield's shrine. Larry Brown, who sat in the head coach's chair at Kansas before Williams and was the sixth head coach in KU history, was elected in 2002. And John McLendon, the first African American coach elected to the Hall in 1978, was actually mentored by Dr. Naismith.

Lovellette, the two-time All-American center who led Kansas to the 1952 national championship is there. So is the legendary Wilt

Chamberlain. One of the all-time greats, Chamberlain, who went on to an incredible NBA career, died in 1999—21 years after he was elected into the Hall.

Paul Endacott, 1923 National Player of the Year and a member of the 1922 and 1923 teams that were recognized by the Helms Foundation as national champions, was elected in 1972. John Bunn lettered in basketball three years at KU before going on to a 42-year coaching career. Arthur "Dutch" Lonborg was an All-American at KU in 1919 and went on to a long career in coaching and athletic administration, including athletic director at Kansas. And Bill "Skinny" Johnson, an All-American in 1933 when the Jayhawks won a third straight Big 6 title, was elected in 1977.

Kansas baseball fans who remember old Quigley Field, the baseball park next to Allen Fieldhouse, will be delighted to know that E.C. Quigley went into the Hall back in 1961. He is best known as a referee and official. He presided over about 1,500 basketball games in 40 years as well as 5,400 major league baseball games and six World Series.

The most recent inductee from KU is Al Kelley, who entered the Hall in 2010 as part of the 1960 U.S. Olympic basketball team that won a gold medal in Rome. Kelley was on the same Olympic team as Jerry Lucas, Oscar Robertson, and Jerry West.

The Hall of Fame celebrated its 50th anniversary in 2009. A new facility, with its spectacular silver, shiny globe structure opened in September 2002 with a new Honors Ring that overlooks Center Court, a full-size regulation basketball court. The Hall of Fame is home to almost 300 inductees and more than 40,000 square feet of basketball history.

Lovellette may not be there to shake your hand at the entrance, but you can feel the strong Kansas presence whenever you decide to visit.

35 Paul Endacott

Phog Allen once called him "the greatest player I have ever coached." No, he wasn't talking about Clyde Lovellette or Wilt Chamberlain. Allen never got a chance to coach Wilt the Stilt.

The player Allen heaped that high praise on was Paul Endacott, a true Jayhawk born in Lawrence. He was the 1923 National Player of the Year, a member of two Helms Foundation national championship teams, and an inductee into the Naismith Basketball Hall of Fame. Not a bad basketball resume, huh? Well, off the court, Endacott also served as president of Phillips Petroleum later in his life. He even kept a hula hoop in his office at Phillips, but more on that later.

Endacott was the first truly great Kansas basketball player. He arrived at KU shortly after Allen returned for his second stint as coach of the Jayhawks in 1919. Endacott made his debut in the 1920–21 season, and Kansas basketball entered into a special era.

Those two national championships came in 1922 and 1923, when there was no tournament to determine a title winner. Instead, the Helms Athletic Foundation based in Los Angeles put together a panel of experts to select championship teams and name All-America teams in a number of college sports, including football and basketball.

The Jayhawks finished 16–2 in 1922. The next season, the Helms Foundation honored Kansas again when the Jayhawks posted a 16–0 in the Missouri Valley Conference and went 17–1 overall. In addition to Endacott, that 1923 team included John Wulf, Tus Ackerman, Charlie T. Black, and a seldom-used player named Adolph Rupp, the future coaching legend at Kentucky. The Jayhawks shared the Missouri Valley title with Missouri in

1922 when both teams finished 15–1. The rivalry with the Tigers was evolving, and Allen wanted to end a period of domination by Missouri coach Walter Meanwell.

Allen put his players through a rigorous training program and intense practices, demonstrating how serious he was about the Jayhawks winning the title outright. "He was a very unusual, odd person," Endacott said of Allen. "He was full of fire, very aggressive. He had all the kinds of ideas, and they worked out. He liked to get into controversies. He liked the publicity."

The Jayhawks traveled to Missouri on January 16, 1923, for one of the biggest games early in Allen's coaching career. After a difficult trip to Columbia, Missouri, Endacott and Ackerman led the Jayhawks to a 21–19 victory. This was at a time when the rules allowed a player to tip the ball himself in a jump ball situation. Allen liked to tell the story that Endacott tipped the ball to himself 16 times, several of those at the end of the victory. "He leapt for it, he dived, he lunged, he plunged, with no thought of himself," Allen wrote. "The ball was the thing…A greater exhibition of man's doggedness has not been witnessed before or since."

In his book on Allen, *The Kansas City Star* sportswriter Blair Kerkhoff reports that "newspaper accounts of the game do not detail a series of jump ball at the end" of the game. After years of answering questions about the game, Endacott typed up a recollection in 1991, saying that Allen "greatly exaggerated" the incident. "He insisted that this was not the case and that he had a record to prove it, although he never showed it to me," Endacott wrote.

Endacott, who passed away in 1997, was inducted into the Basketball Hall of Fame on April 20, 1972. His biography refers to him as a "tenacious defender" and points out he was named to the Associated Press All-Time All-American second team and Allen's National All-Time College team. After graduation with his engineering degree, Endacott played Amateur Athletic Union basketball for five seasons with the Phillips 66 Oilers.

Now, about that hula hoop. Phillips entered the plastics business in 1951 and three years later introduced Marlex polyethylene, a product that became immensely popular for its use in a large ring of plastic tubing known as the hula hoop. Endacott was said to be so delighted, he kept a hoop in his office for "impromptu demonstrations."

36 The Fight Song

"I'm a Jayhawk" has been the Kansas fight song longer than most people can remember. Any child growing up in the state of Kansas with the hope of becoming a KU student one day learns "I'm a Jayhawk" at a very early age. But for many Kansas graduates, the lyrics to the song today are a little different from the ones every Jayhawk knew and sang for years.

George "Dumpy" Bowles was a student in the class of 1912 when he wrote, "I'm a Jayhawk." The song became extremely popular with Kansas students in 1920. According to KU, Bowles had longed to make "a great contribution to KU spirit," but he wasn't athletic enough to succeed with the Jayhawks on the athletic field. Bowles, though, was a talented musician and produced several outstanding musical shows.

"I'm a Jayhawk" was a song in one of those shows. A burst in school spirit in 1920 led renewed interest in the song. It was rolled out as part of fund-raising drives that helped build the KU football stadium and student union as World War I memorials. The lyrics remained unchanged until 1958 when alterations were necessary because of changes to the membership of the Big 8 Conference. Yes, realignment is nothing new —just more prevalent these days.

114

The song's popularity grew, and it became the school fight song. Although there are many anthems, or "Songs of Old KU," associated with Kansas athletic teams, "I'm a Jayhawk" is the primary song associated with the KU marching band, pep bands, and the basketball band.

"I'm a Jayhawk" has been included on several collections of college fight songs, including the 2009 release of songs in MP3 format titled Fight On: The Greatest College Fight Songs. The KU song, among many others, was included along with Michigan's "Hail to The Victors," the Michigan State University fight song, the "Notre Dame Victory March," Oklahoma's "Boomer Sooner," "The Eyes of Texas," and "On, Wisconsin."

One of the most unusual performances of "I'm a Jayhawk" came in 2010 when the KU men's glee club appeared on the popular game show *The Price is Right* and was introduced by none other than Bob Barker. These are the well-known lyrics associated with the version written by George Bowles:

"I'm A Jayhawk"

Talk about the Sooners, the Cowboys, and the Buffs,
Talk about the Tiger and his tail,
Talk about the Wildcats and those Cornhuskin' boys,
But I'm the bird to make 'em weep and wail.
Chorus:
'Cause I'm a Jay, Jay, Jay, Jay Jayhawk
Up at Lawrence on the Kaw
'Cause I'm a Jay, Jay, Jay, Jay Jayhawk
With a sis-boom, hip hoorah.
Got a bill that's big enough to twist the Tiger's tail,
Husk some corn and listen to the Cornhusker's wail,
'Cause I'm a Jay, Jay, Jay, Jay Jayhawk,
Riding on a Kansas gale.

The lyrics went untouched when the Big 8 expanded to the Big 12. But in June 2010, when longtime rivals Nebraska and Colorado departed for the Big Ten and Pac-12, respectively, some KU alumni asked the Alumni Association about adapting the lyrics for the first time in 50 years.

A contest was held and a panel of judges selected the new lyrics submitted by Matt Schoenfeld over five other submissions. Schoenfeld talks about the Sooners, Cowboys, and other rivals. His lyrics alter the first verse and one line of the chorus. It was out with the Cornhuskers, and in with the Longhorns.

"I'm A Jayhawk" (October 2010)
by Matt Schoenfeld

Talk about the Sooners, Cowboys, and the Bears,
Aggies and the Tiger and his tail.
Talk about the Wildcats and the Cyclone boys,
But I'm the bird to make 'em weep and wail.
Chorus:
'Cause I'm a Jay, Jay, Jay, Jay, Jayhawk,
Up at Lawrence on the Kaw—
'Cause I'm a Jay, Jay, Jay, Jay, Jayhawk,
With a sis-boom, hip hoorah,
Got a bill that's big enough
To twist a Tiger's tail,
Rope some 'Horns and listen
To the Red Raiders wail—
'Cause I'm a Jay, Jay, Jay, Jay, Jayhawk,
Riding on a Kansas gale.

Schoenfeld attended Baylor but had followed KU basketball teams since the time Ted Owens served as coach. "I remember sitting with my two roommates from Kansas City and tuning the radio until we could pick up the crackly voices of Bob and Max down in Waco," he said in the release, referring to longtime KU broadcasters Bob Davis and Max Falkenstien. "I saw a *Sports Illustrated* story on the contest and I sat down that night with my kids to work on lyrics."

Note that the rival Missouri Tigers, who left for the Southeastern Conference at the start of the 2012–13 school year, are still in the lyrics. The KU athletics web page on "Traditions" states that, "Future conference changes will not automatically dictate further changes to the lyrics."

37 Crimson and Blue

Warning: Some information in this chapter could be disturbing to Kansas basketball fans still smarting from Michigan's 87–85 overtime victory against the Jayhawks in the Sweet 16 round of the 2013 NCAA tournament.

There is no doubt that the school colors at the University of Kansas are crimson and blue. Those are the colors KU has used for many years, dating back to the early 1890s. After all, the school's alma mater, sung before every athletic event, is titled "Crimson and the Blue."

But they are not the originally adopted colors by the university board of regents in the 1860s. (And here comes the disturbing part you were warned about above.) The regents originally decided on the University of Michigan's colors—maize and blue. In fact, Kansas was represented by maize and blue at early oratorical meets and that combination may have been used when the Kansas crew competed in rowing events in the middle 1880s.

Seeing Red

When the Jayhawks took the floor at Reunion Arena in Dallas wearing crimson uniforms for their 1986 national semifinal game against Duke, it was a jolt to die-hard Kansas basketball fans accustomed to seeing KU in white at home and blue on the road.

Duke won 71–67, and KU fans called a foul on coach Larry Brown, who was superstitious enough to pack the crimson outfits away and vow never to use them again. Brown had done his research and learned that Phog Allen's 1952 team won the national championship in bright red uniforms and red sneakers. The fact is KU had a lot of success in road red from the Allen era through Ted Owens' tenure. But the Jayhawks also suffered some difficult losses in crimson, including the 1953 and 1957 NCAA championship games—and that excruciating 1966 loss to Texas Western when Jo Jo White was called for stepping out of bounds.

The crimson uniforms were put away until the 2003–04 season when Bill Self bravely brought them out of storage for a 72–52 win against UC–Santa Barbara on December 20, 2003. The Jayhawks are 9–1 in regular season games wearing red in the Self era, the only loss coming January 22, 2005, when Villanova routed the second-ranked Jayhawks 83–62 while more than a foot of snow shut down the Philadelphia airport and cancelled KU's flight home—just an all-around bad road trip.

But did you know the 1988 national champions are the only KU team ever to put on yellow uniforms? KU's outfitter offered the yellow alternative, and Brown chose them for an early December road game against Western Carolina. The Jayhawks won 68–63 despite giving up 17 unanswered points late in the game. But Jayhawk fans called the basketball office phone and buried Brown in letters until he promised never again to wear anything close to Missouri's Old Gold color. "They'll never be seen again," Brown said. "I like them, but they're history."

The fact that Brown liked them should not matter. This is the same man who coached the ABA Carolina Cougars wearing bib overalls in the mid-1970s. Speaking of questionable wardrobes, what were the folks at Adidas thinking when they introduced those postseason "camo" uniforms for Kansas, Cincinnati, Notre Dame, Baylor, UCLA, and Louisville in 2013?

But football arrived at KU in 1890, and a genuine clamor arose in support of Harvard's Crimson as a way to honor Colonel John J. McCook, a Harvard man who had provided money for an athletic field at KU. That field ran east and west in the general proximity of the north bowl of Memorial Stadium on the Lawrence campus today. Because of the intensity of the rivalry between Harvard and Yale, the Yale graduates among the faculty at Kansas insisted that their academic lineage be included. They wanted the Yale blue (a dark blue rather than Michigan's navy bluish color) to be represented as well. Support for the Michigan colors dropped. In fact, no one put up a battle to retain the original maize and blue colors. Crimson and Blue prevailed. And in May 1896, those were the colors officially adopted for the university.

The 2002 Final Four Team

Enjoy the journey.

During 15 seasons at Kansas, that became coach Roy Williams' motto. His critics turned it against him and said that was his way of deflecting attention away from all the heartbreaking losses that left him short of a national championship at Kansas. Those less cynical accepted it as the man's philosophy, and the motto applied to the 2001–02 Jayhawks better than any other group during Williams' tenure.

Reaching the NCAA tournament was never a problem. The only time in the Williams era that didn't happen was 1989, when the Jayhawks served their NCAA sanctions in his first season at KU. But heading into 2001–02, the Jayhawks had fallen short of the Big 12 championship each of the past three seasons. And Kansas hadn't been to a Final Four since 1993. Four times under Williams, the Jayhawks were a No. 1 seed but fell short of the national semifinals.

The Jayhawks had two of the top frontcourt players in the country in Drew Gooden and Nick Collison, KU's leading scorers, in 2001–02. Point guard Aaron Miles directed the offense, and Kirk Hinrich and Jeff Boschee completed the scoring attack. Wayne Simien and Keith Langford joined Miles in one of the nation's top freshman classes. That was the group that rewrote the Kansas record book. They averaged 90.9 points a game—second to the 1989–90 squad (92.1)—but set the record with 3,365 points in one season. They also set the record for most assists in conference games and averaged more than 22 assists per game in Big 12 games.

The season started off on a bad note, a 93–91 loss to Ball State in the Maui Invitational on November 19. But the only regular-season loss after that came against UCLA in Los Angeles on January 12. The most enjoyable part of the journey was a 16–0 record in the Big 12 Conference. The Jayhawks were the first team in Big 12 history to go undefeated in league play. "Honestly, I wouldn't have believed we could have done it if you'd have asked me in the beginning of the season," Collison said.

KU held off Colorado with a late run and beat the Buffaloes 97–85 on January 5, 2002. One day later No. 1 Duke lost at Florida State, and the Jayhawks moved into the top spot for the first time since 1997. Coming off the UCLA loss, the Jayhawks went to Gallagher-Iba Arena in Stillwater and defeated Oklahoma State 79–61. They won at Iowa State, and Drew Gooden scored 26 points in front of 20 NBA scouts as KU blasted Missouri 105–73 in Allen Fieldhouse. There was a 110–103 overtime victory against Texas, the first game in school history to produce 100 or more points on each side. Seniors Jeff Carey, Chris Zerbe, Lewis Harrison, Brett Ballard, and Boschee started and gave KU a 7–0 lead on the way to a 103–68 Senior Night rout of Kansas State.

The conference curtain came down in Columbia, Missouri, on March 3. Collison hit a 17-footer with 1:36 left to give KU the lead, and the Jayhawks held on for a 95–92 victory, a sweep of the Tigers, and a sweep of the conference schedule. The Jayhawks enjoyed running off the floor that night at the Hearns Center as a quiet Missouri crowd headed to the parking lots. "Unbelievable," Boschee said. "To be able to do something like this, to run through the conference like we did, I never thought we'd be able to do that."

The Jayhawks rolled to the title game of the Big 12 tournament before they laid an egg. KU managed just 19 points in the first half against Oklahoma, and the guards were outscored 41–11 as the Sooners won the tournament championship 64–55. If that wasn't reason for concern, Kansas fans went into full panic mode in the first round of the NCAA tournament.

When Holy Cross jumped on the Jayhawks early and Hinrich suffered a second-degree sprain of his left ankle just before halftime, it looked as if the Jayhawks would be the first No. 1 seed to fall to a No. 16. But KU rallied and fought, beating Holy Cross 70–59. "We knew we couldn't play any worse," Collison said, "So we just felt like we needed to go out and play to win and not play to lose."

Hinrich healed remarkably fast. Just 48 hours after the injury, he scored 15 points and dished out eight assists in an 86–63 win against Stanford. Casey Jacobsen of the Cardinal said Hinrich had played with one leg "and with more heart than anyone else out there." Victories against Illinois (then coached by Bill Self) and Oregon lifted the Jayhawks into the Final Four, but the journey ended short of the national championship once again. Gooden said playing Maryland in the national semifinals was like looking in a mirror. The Terps had scorers on the perimeter and inside, liked to run, and could get up and down the court.

Maryland was back after losing to Duke in the Final Four just one season earlier, and Gary Williams' team had won 17 of its last 18 games. KU opened well and closed well, but in the middle portion of the game, Juan Dixon and the Terps dominated on the way to a 97–88 victory. The No. 2 team in the nation had been eliminated with a 33–4 record.

The Kansas locker room was silent. Williams wept in the postgame interview session again. But the tears were for his players—not for himself. "I thought we were going to be pretty good this year," Williams said. "But I didn't think we were going to be as good as we were. This was really a good basketball team. This was a basketball team that, boy, gave me a lot of fun."

39 Fred Pralle

If the NCAA tournament had started in 1938 rather than 1939, Fred Pralle might have led Kansas to another national championship. Alas, he didn't have that opportunity, but he certainly ended his KU career with a stunning array of honors.

Other Kansas players had been named All-Americans before Pralle's senior year. But he became the Jayhawks' first consensus selection, starting a tradition that later included Clyde Lovellette, Wilt Chamberlain, Danny Manning, Raef LaFrentz, Paul Pierce, and Thomas Robinson—among others.

Pralle helped his team win championships and that led to multiple individual awards. KU won three Big 6 conference titles from 1936–38. He was named All-Big 6 three times. And he led the Jayhawks in scoring his last two seasons, averaging 10.7 points in 1938. His conference scoring average was 12.1 that season. During that senior season, the 6'3" Pralle was team captain and led KU to an 18–2 record and a 9–1 mark in the Big 6. "I can tell you that Pralle was the one-man team," Bob Allen said in the book *Kansas Jayhawks History-making Basketball.* "They won the [Big 6] championship with a bunch of no-names and Pralle, who was an absolute great. In my personal opinion, he was the greatest guard that KU ever had."

The Jayhawks won their final nine games, including a season-ending victory on March 3, 1938, against Missouri in Lawrence. Pralle went out in style, scoring 22 points in a 56–36 win against the Tigers. According to the book, *A Century of Jayhawk Triumphs,* Dr. James Naismith was in attendance at that game played in Hoch Auditorium. The crowd gave him a huge ovation when the game ended.

Pralle finished with 539 career points. That number, though, does not truly demonstrate the kind of workhorse he was. Pralle started every game except one in his three seasons and played every minute of KU's conference games, barring the final seconds against Oklahoma and Missouri when he fouled out.

He was a member of the 1936 Kansas team that was one win away from representing the United States in the Olympics. And he went on to a tremendous AAU career with the Phillips 66ers. Pralle's jersey was retired on January 15, 2003.

Coach Phog Allen wrote that Pralle "had one of the greatest shooting eyes from long distance and the best coordination of any man I have seen, not excluding Hank Luisetti." Luisetti, who played at Stanford, was one of the dominant players of that time, and is credited with developing the running one-handed shot.

40 Harvesting the Iowa Crop: Collison, Hinrich, and LaFrentz

One of the finest media relation campaigns in Kansas basketball history welcomed the start of the 2002–03 season. With the Jayhawks coming off a Final Four appearance and led by Nick Collison and Kirk Hinrich, the KU athletic department featured the returning seniors in a series of promotional shots that blended them into historic KU photos. Perhaps the best of the bunch inserted Collison and Hinrich into the famous 1923 sepia photo featuring Phog Allen with his team. Adolph Rupp is in the top row, Hall of Famer Paul Endacott sits in front holding the ball marked 1923, and Allen sits in the middle seat flanked by Collison and Hinrich in their 2002 blue uniforms. "Old School" was the promotional theme. And, boy, were they ever.

Nick and Kirk. Kirk and Nick. KU fans couldn't have one without the other. They were All-American boys from Iowa.

Coach Roy Williams never hesitated to recruit Iowa after landing power forward Raef LaFrentz from Monona, Iowa, in the class of 1994. In retrospect, those were three of the most important commitments of the Williams era. All three played in the NBA, but all three stayed four years at Kansas. That speaks to their upbringing and character, the type of players Williams truly enjoyed recruiting.

In fact, Williams says it was a good thing Collison, Hinrich, and Drew Gooden came along when they did. Not long before he discovered them, he came home and told his wife, Wanda, that he didn't know whether he could cope with the dark side of the recruiting world any longer. Williams was frustrated by the growing number of players who viewed college as a "bus stop" on the way to the NBA. "Their recruitment was such a joy, and it showed me there are situations out there that are still really good," Williams

*Seated next to Jeff Graves (right) during a 2003 NCAA tournament victory
against Arizona State, Nick Collison (left) and Kirk Hinrich (middle) are two
of the stars Roy Williams recruited from the state of Iowa.*

said. "You've just got to look for them a little harder. When Nick
and Kirk decided to come back for their senior year, I had two
NBA people call me and ask, 'Roy, what is it that they're afraid of?
What's wrong with them?' And I said, 'You know, it is okay just to
enjoy college and it's okay to get an education.'"

It's easy to understand their Midwestern values. All three Iowa
guys had fathers who were high school basketball coaches. When
Williams was inducted into the Naismith Basketball Hall of Fame,
he pointed out that Collison and Hinrich came to Springfield,
Massachusetts, too, and brought their dads. "Boy, do I love that
part," Williams said. Kansas fans connected with all three families
as they traveled with the team and rarely missed home games. It
wasn't uncommon to catch the Hinrich family hanging out at the
Lawrence Steak 'n Shake, grabbing burgers and fries. It was part
Norman Rockwell painting and part *Happy Days* episode.

Ron and Ellen LaFrentz named their son after a character George Peppard played in the movie *Home from the Hill*. They moved to Lawrence during Raef's time at KU, renting a condo from former Jayhawks guard Rex Walters. "You know what the one thing people don't know about me is? I'm just a dork," LaFrentz said to *Sports Illustrated*. "I like to just hang out with my friends and be myself." When LaFrentz chose KU over Iowa, the decision was broadcast live on radio. LaFrentz got hate mail and nasty phone calls. "It was just a bunch of crap," he told *Sports Illustrated*. Ron, who played at Northern Iowa, said it was never even close; Raef always wanted to go to Kansas.

Collison, from Iowa Falls, was a power forward like LaFrentz. Collison, who cried on Senior Night when talking about his grandparents, is KU's second all-time leading scorer (2,097), third all-time leading rebounder (1,143), and fourth all-time leading shot blocker (243). LaFrentz is third in scoring (2,066), second in rebounding (1,186), and 11th in blocked shots (138). Hinrich, a guard from Sioux City, who was comfortable handling any of the perimeter duties, is 10th in scoring (1,753), fourth in assists (668), sixth in steals (206), and third in three-pointers made (236).

Collison played 142 games; Hinrich played 141. They led KU to back-to-back Final Fours in 2002 and 2003 but fell short of a national championship both times. The 2002 KU team remains the only undefeated (16–0) team in the history of the Big 12. LaFrentz and Collison join Danny Manning as the only KU players to score 2,000 points. LaFrentz won four Big 12 championships but, unlike the other two, never reached the Final Four.

They were just three "Old School" guys who got to hang out, be themselves, and deliver plenty of good times to Kansas basketball. A thank you note to Iowa might be proper, but there's still the issue of all that hate mail.

41 Merry Christmas, Jacque

Freshman point guard Jacque Vaughn gave Kansas fans an early Christmas present on December 22, 1993. Years and years later, his game-winning three-point shot against Indiana is the gift that keeps on giving. Coach Bob Knight brought his Hoosiers, complete with Damon Bailey and Alan Henderson, to Allen Fieldhouse that day. It was quite the stage, with two fabled programs, both ranked among the top 12 teams in the nation, and future Hall of Fame coaches going against one another in one of college basketball's shrines.

The game more than lived up to the hype and Vaughn, playing in just his 11th game in a Kansas uniform, made it one for the ages with his three-pointer from the right wing with 0.2 seconds remaining in overtime to give the Jayhawks an 86–83 victory. "Sometimes special people are put in special situations like that," said Kansas coach Roy Williams. "Sometimes youngsters are given an opportunity to make big plays, and Jacque made that. He'll remember that for the rest of his life."

Bailey, who scored 30 of his 36 points after halftime, hit a three-pointer to tie the game with 18.3 seconds left. Vaughn brought the ball down and patiently tried to set up the offense and a shot for Steve Woodberry, who had scored seven of his 13 points in overtime. But the screen that was supposed to set Woodberry free for an open 12-foot shot never developed. "I didn't think I could get it to Steve, so the best thing I could do was shoot the ball," Vaughn said. "I got a good release, a good arc, and it went in."

Vaughn calmly shot faked and then hit the jumper over Indiana's Todd Leary to trigger an explosion of emotion from the Allen Fieldhouse fans and Vaughn's teammates, who swarmed him with a team hug. It wasn't the first time Vaughn had broken Knight's heart. As the Indiana coach went out recruiting a guard to replace Bailey, he found Vaughn in Los Angeles. But Williams found him, too, and KU's coach won the recruiting battle.

And on that December night in Allen Fieldhouse, Kansas fans began their love affair with Jacque Vaughn. "I just remember going Christmas shopping during the three or four days we had off after that game, and all anybody wanted to talk about was that game and Jacque's shot," former Jayhawk Greg Gurley told the *Lawrence Journal-World* in 2010.

After a decorated college career in which he earned 1996 Big 8 Player of the Year, Vaughn played 12 years in the NBA. He became the head coach of the Orlando Magic in 2012.

42 A Fine Line

Ted Owens steadfastly believes that Kansas should have won the national championship in 1966. "I'm not sure there was a more powerful team in the history of Kansas basketball," Owens said.

That would have changed history drastically. Kansas fans wouldn't have been forced to wait from 1952 until 1988 to celebrate another national championship. And Texas Western wouldn't have gone on to become the first NCAA champion with five African Americans in the starting lineup. There would have been no *Glory Road* book or movie, chronicling the story of coach Don Haskins and his Miners.

On the way to making history with a statement over the racism of Kentucky and coach Adolph Rupp, Texas Western defeated Kansas in double overtime for the Midwest Region championship.

It's not a stretch to say that game, played in Lubbock, Texas, remains the most controversial loss in Jayhawks history.

The Miners led 38–35 at halftime, and regulation ended in a 69–69 tie. With the score tied at 71 and seven seconds remaining in overtime, Kansas called a timeout. Jo Jo White, a sophomore with only eight games of experience but loaded with a ton of confidence, looked at the coaches during that huddle and said, "Let me have the ball."

The coaches designed a play for White, one that would spring him open off a series of screens. He dribbled to create space and took a shot about 28 feet from the basket as the clock was about to expire. The ball swished through the net. But as the Kansas players started to celebrate, they saw referee Rudy Marich pointing to the sideline. Marich waved off the shot, saying White's heel had been on the line.

Texas Western won 81–80 in double overtime and went on to make history. Owens felt the nation's two best teams had met in that game. The way the game played out certainly backed up his belief. But to this day, no one on the Kansas side, especially White, thinks he stepped on the line. "It still bothers me in terms of the opportunity at the national level and the team's opportunity to win the whole thing," White said in 2008. "We certainly had the pieces in all the right places. But again, it got down to someone else's opinion. It was a tough pill to swallow. But at the same time, I did and executed what I was out there to do."

That loss ended a 10-game winning streak for Kansas. The Jayhawks finished the season 23–4 after winning the Big 8 title at 13–1 and were ranked No. 4 by both the Associated Press and United Press International polls.

Opinions on the call depend, in large part, on your perspective, of course. For pure cinematic sensationalism, the producers of the 2006 film *Glory Road* didn't worry about the sequence of events and showed White well over the line, missing the final shot of the game.

Eddie Mullens, the longtime sports information director at Texas Western (which later became the University of Texas at El Paso or UTEP), wrote the game was "wilder than a lone deuce in a college poker game" and that he admired Marich's "integrity" for making the call. "I was seated at the scorer's table as White trotted back to his bench where he was met by coach Ted Owens." Mullen wrote. "It appeared from where I sat that Owens asked White if he was indeed out of bounds. White nodded his head, and Owens immediately turned back to his huddle. All business. All class. Don't get me wrong. Utah and Kentucky were great opponents, but truthfully if Rudy Marich hadn't made that call, Kansas would have been in College Park that weekend. And the 1966 trophy, which now resides in El Paso, could easily be sitting alongside all of the other hardware in Lawrence, Kansas."

43 Dickie V Gives Collison A Standing O

The Jayhawks needed someone to come up big against Texas on January 27, 2003, and Nick Collison really rose to the occasion. And that is an understatement. What Collison did against the Longhorns that night in Allen Fieldhouse was legendary. It was so remarkable that it brought announcer Dick Vitale to his feet. Not at the end of the game—but during it.

When Collison fouled out with 1:18 to play, Vitale took off his headphones and stood to applaud the senior from Iowa Falls, Iowa. Collison walked off the floor with 24 points and 23 rebounds to lead the Jayhawks to a 90–87 victory against third-ranked Texas. Collison's performance that night ranks among the top

Unstoppable Opponents

Although Collison put on a performance for the ages, sometimes it has been a star player from the opposition who has wowed the Jayhawks. Jackson State's Lindsey Hunter was a classic scorer and he certainly proved it against KU on December 27, 1992, in the Rainbow Classic in Honolulu, Hawaii. Hunter's 48 points rank as the most scored by one player against Kansas. Hunter had his shot falling, but his Jackson State team fell 93–85. Kansas State's Mike Wroblewski's performance may have been even more impressive. He scored 46 points to lead the Wildcats to a 91–72 victory in Allen Fieldhouse on February 7, 1962. That's still the most scored by an opponent in a Kansas loss.

Here are the other top guns who have scored 40 or more points against Kansas:

45—Randy Rutherford, Oklahoma State, March 5, 1995, Lawrence
44—Glenn Robinson, Purdue, March 24, 1994, Knoxville, Tennessee
43—Anthony Peeler, Missouri, March 8, 1992, Lawrence
43—Oscar Robertson, Cincinnati, March 12, 1960, Manhattan, Kansas
42—Craig Brackins, Iowa State, January 24, 2009, Ames, Iowa
41—Rayford Young, Texas Tech, February 13, 1999, Lubbock, Texas
40—Thomas Gardner, Missouri, January 16, 2006, Columbia, Missouri

individual performances in the history of Allen Fieldhouse. Those 23 rebounds tied for the 13th-best single-game record in school history. They were the most for a Jayhawk since Dave Robisch grabbed 26 against Iowa State in 1970.

Vitale will never forget what Collison did. And Vitale's audience will never forget what he did in response. "There have been very few occasions where I got up as a broadcaster and gave a player a standing ovation," Vitale wrote on his website after the game. "David Robinson of Navy was one…and Collison on Monday night when he fouled out with a minute-plus left. Kansas was on the verge of its third straight loss, something that hasn't happened since 1994. Collison helped will the Jayhawks to the winner's circle."

After winning 10 consecutive games, the Jayhawks lost back-to-back games at Colorado and then at home against No. 1-ranked Arizona. The Jayhawks let a 20-point lead slip away against Arizona, a true rarity at home. Collison sensed the Jayhawks needed a spark. "I just made up my mind that I was going to be very aggressive," Collison said. "We really needed a win. We really needed a lot of rebounds against a big, physical Texas team. I think it might be my best game."

Collison wouldn't get an argument on that point. "I don't know if I've ever seen a person be so relentless on the backboard as Nick Collison was," KU coach Roy Williams said. "If those [24] NBA scouts sitting over there tonight say there's anybody in the world with a bigger heart, then they're just blind."

What prompted Vitale's salute through a standing ovation? "I was just so passionate," Vitale told the *Lawrence Journal-World* in 2010. "I got caught up in the moment and did what I thought the kid deserved—a standing ovation."

Texas coach Rick Barnes visited the Kansas locker room after the game just to shake Collison's hand.

In addition to Barnes' visit and the standing ovation from Vitale, Collison's effort sparked another rare response. The Kansas fans stormed the floor, something that longtime observers said had not happened in the Williams era. "I didn't put a lot of thought into it," Williams said. "I just wanted to get into the locker room and dance a bit."

44 Visit Booth Hall

Allen Fieldhouse has earned special status as one of college basketball's shrines. In this age of modern arenas with luxury suites and fancy amenities, there aren't many old fashioned gyms in use anymore. Enter the Phog, and that first goose bump is the sense of history, the feeling that you just entered one of the world's great museums.

And since 2006, there actually is a 26,000-square-foot museum adjacent to Allen Fieldhouse that gives fans a chance to experience the history and tradition of Kansas basketball and the rest of KU athletics. The Booth Family Hall of Athletics, which was expanded in 2009, should be on the bucket list of every Kansas fan—and basketball fans everywhere.

It's open year-round Monday through Saturday, so there's no need for a basketball game on the schedule to see all the displays and artifacts. Just enter the doors where the statue of Phog Allen stands guard, facing out toward Naismith Drive. Thanks to this tremendous facility, the legacy of Wilt Chamberlain, James Naismith, Danny Manning, and Allen will never be lost. If you want to see trophies, photos, and stories related to those KU icons, in addition to women's stars such as Lynette Woodard and coach Marian Washington, the "Basketball Legacy" exhibit will satisfy all those needs.

One of the best displays in the collection is the original center court floor of Allen Fieldhouse. This section of hardwood—with its red center circle and bold blue letter "K"—anchors everything in the building and can't be missed. The Story of Sport display will walk you through the history of KU athletics, beginning in 1879, and includes two Olympian cases as well as the fascinating display

Every Kansas fan should visit the Booth Family Hall of Athletics, which has a statue of Phog Allen gracing its entrance. (Getty Images)

dedicated to Chamberlain. Recent athletes and achievements from all 18 teams are highlighted in Game and Gear section. Kansas traditions, including the marching band, cheerleading, and rivalries can be found along the KANSAS Experience Wall. There you find a media display that includes artifacts from Max Falkenstien's legendary 60-year radio and television career.

The Hall of Champions includes a collection of conference and national championship trophies and the Hall of Fame wall. The two hallways leading into Allen Fieldhouse should not be missed. The original Beware of the Phog banner has been preserved on one wall, and retired basketball jerseys are there, too. If you are doing a little research there are touch-screen kiosks that allow searches for any athlete, team, coach, or administrator in KU history. The hall also includes new ticket offices, a KU gear store, a lounge, and meeting rooms for alumni, donor, and recruiting events.

Kansas fans are always skeptical about additions or refurbishments to Allen Fieldhouse, but the initial $8 million project was completed with a façade of natural stone to match the building's original exterior and with matching windows. The Hall is named for the late Gilbert and Betty Booth, staunch Kansas supporters who lived on 1931 Naismith Drive just down the street from the fieldhouse. More than $5 million came from donations from the Booth children and grandchildren. "We are doing this in memory of our parents," David Booth said at groundbreaking ceremonies in 2005. "This year marks 20 years ago my dad passed away and 10 years ago my mom. This is a good way to reconnect back and a way that would have been really special to them. It's about as good as it gets."

In 2009, the Hall was expanded, and exhibits were added as part of a $7.9 million renovation to Allen Fieldhouse. Credit Candace Dunback, director of traditions for the K Club and the Booth Family Hall of Athletics, for her tireless work with artifact donations and keeping the exhibits fresh. Booth has to be considered one of the most positive developments during the tenure of athletic director Lew Perkins. "It's going to give an opportunity for many people to share in the memories, the excitement, and the history of KU athletics," Perkins said at the groundbreaking.

45 Watch *There's No Place Like Home*

Kansans generally are quite sensitive about references to Dorothy, Toto, and anything else related to *The Wizard of Oz*. There's nothing more annoying than visiting another part of our great country and hearing someone remind you that you're "not in Kansas anymore." We, though, have discovered a classic exception to that rule.

When ESPN's *30 for 30* series decided to chronicle a KU fan "on his quest to bring Naismith's original rules of basketball to

Dr. James Naismith's Original Rules of Basketball

1. The ball may be thrown in any direction with one or both hands.
2. The ball may be batted in any direction with one or both hands (never with the fist).
3. A player cannot run with the ball. The player must throw it from the spot on which he catches it, allowance to be made for a man who catches the ball when running at a good speed if he tries to stop.
4. The ball must be held in or between the hands; the arms or body must not be used for holding it.
5. No shouldering, holding, pushing, tripping, or striking in any way the person of an opponent shall be allowed; the first infringement of this rule by any player shall count as a foul, the second shall disqualify him until the next goal is made, or, if there was evident intent to injure the person, for the whole of the game, no substitute allowed.
6. A foul is striking at the ball with the fist, violation of Rules 3,4, and such as described in Rule 5.
7. If either side makes three consecutive fouls, it shall count a goal for the opponents (consecutive means without the opponents in the mean time making a foul).
8. A goal shall be made when the ball is thrown or batted from the grounds into the basket and stays there, providing those

Kansas," the directors could not have picked a better title. *There's No Place Like Home* perfectly captures the mission depicted by this documentary. I'm not sure any film has ever done a better job of wrapping itself around the feelings of pride, history, and tradition that exist with the Kansas basketball program and the relationship between Jayhawks fans, boosters, coaches, and players.

This story begins in November 2010 when Kansas City native Josh Swade saw a story in *The New York Times* about a truly unique artifact coming to Sotheby's auction house in New York. Among the three historic objects that were up for sale were the 13 original rules of basketball, which were typewritten on two pages by Dr. James Naismith in 1891.

---

      defending the goal do not touch or disturb the goal. If the ball rests on the edges, and the opponent moves the basket, it shall count as a goal.

9. When the ball goes out of bounds, it shall be thrown into the field of play and played by the person first touching it. In case of a dispute, the umpire shall throw it straight into the field. The thrower-in is allowed five seconds; if he holds it longer, it shall go to the opponent. If any side persists in delaying the game, the umpire shall call a foul on that side.

10. The umpire shall be judge of the men and shall note the fouls and notify the referee when three consecutive fouls have been made. He shall have power to disqualify men according to Rule 5.

11. The referee shall be judge of the ball and shall decide when the ball is in play, in bounds, to which side it belongs, and shall keep the time. He shall decide when a goal has been made, and keep account of the goals with any other duties that are usually performed by a referee.

12. The time shall be two 15-minute halves, with five minutes rest in between.

13. The side making the most goals in that time shall be declared the winners. In case of a draw, the game may, by agreement of the captains, be continued until another goal is made.

Swade, a devoted KU fan, made it his purpose in life to bring the rules to Kansas. Even though the rules were written in Springfield, Massachusetts, Swade believed they belonged in Lawrence, where Naismith spent most of his life and started the KU basketball program. Swade knew people were willing to pay millions of dollars for a set of rules unlike any other in the sports world. "I didn't know how much it was worth," Swade said as part of the documentary's narration. "But I knew there's only one place they belonged."

Sotheby's auction estimate was above $2 million. "Quite frankly, I thought they'd sell for more than that," Swade said in an interview with *The Kansas City Star*. "So I knew we needed a lot of money. So from that point, it just becomes about trying to get in front of people and really giving them the reasons why this would be so monumentally important."

Swade had no resources. He had a photographer friend who shot the video. The documentary tells the story of Swade's frantic effort to pull the plan together before the December 10, 2010 auction. He approached the school's most affluent boosters. He talked to Larry Brown, Roy Williams, and Bill Self.

No need for a spoiler alert here. Most Kansas fans know the ending to the story. Kansas alumnus David Booth purchased the rules for $4.3 million. At the time it was the highest price ever paid for sports memorabilia. Even with that knowledge, the documentary's detail regarding Swade's power of persuasion and Booth's decisions during the bidding process creates tense dramatic emotion that literally leaves Kansas fans sweating out the final decisive bid over the interested party representing Duke.

The Booth family should be thanked every day for preventing the rules from rotting away in Durham, North Carolina. "They're incredibly important and they should be at the University of Kansas," Booth told the *Lawrence Journal-World*. "Naismith was there 40 years. He invented basketball, and Phog Allen was one of the key figures in making it so popular. Nobody else was to going to [buy the rules to bring them to KU]."

The exact price, according to Sotheby's was $4,338,500. That same day the auction of a copy of the Emancipation Proclamation signed by president Abraham Lincoln—and once owned by Robert F. Kennedy—drew $3.7 million.

In April 2013 KU announced the rules will have a permanent home on Naismith Drive in Lawrence. The university announced plans to build an $18 million facility that connects to Allen Fieldhouse and will house the document. The three-story facility will be known as the DeBruce Center in honor of donors Paul and Katherine DeBruce. There will be dining and meeting space available for students, faculty, and visitors. "The DeBruce Center will serve not only as a 'must-see' destination landmark for sports fans and history buffs but also as an important, integral part of campus benefitting students, faculty, and visitors alike," Kansas athletic director Sheahon Zenger said.

Zenger is right. The new home for the rules will be a "must-see" destination. To understand the effort given by Swade—and the financial sacrifice made by Booth—the documentary is also "must-see" viewing. Just click your heels together three times and repeat, "There's no place like home."

46 Camp Out for Tickets

Freshmen make mistakes befitting their youth. It's a fact of basketball life. But this certainty isn't just reserved for the players on the court. Consider the case of this rookie camper at the University of Kansas.

Maggie Hirschi, a 2012 senior from St. Louis, Missouri, learned a difficult lesson during her freshman year, according to *The University Daily Kansan*. Hirschi overslept her camping shift. She woke up at 5:55 AM for her 6 AM shift at Allen Fieldhouse before a game against Texas. But that was cutting it too close. Hirschi bolted into action, rushed from her Oliver Hall dorm room, but was told she was too late upon arrival. She lost her group's No. 3 camping spot.

Take heart, Maggie, you aren't alone. It has happened before. It will happen again. The fine art of waiting in line for the best seats at Allen Fieldhouse requires practice, experience, and dedication.

Give the campers credit. They are the ones who bring Allen Fieldhouse alive on gameday. They bring the signs, the props, the cheers, the costumes, and the enthusiasm. They are the ones who generate the earsplitting noise that raises the decibel level from November to March.

Campers showed up from time to time during the 1970s when Ted Owens was coach. But the arrival of Danny Manning and coach Larry Brown in the mid-1980s generated bigger crowds, more excitement, and an increased interest in camping for the best seats. The KU athletic department makes it clear that students don't have to be part of a camping group to get seats. But students who desire a better seat location can form a camping group and then must follow the rules of camping.

There are basic rules. Camping begins at Allen Fieldhouse at 6 AM the morning following the previous home game. Each group may have a maximum of 30 members. A list of groups in order is posted on a door, and new groups sign up at the bottom as they arrive. Camping takes place from 6 AM until 10 PM on weekdays and 8 AM to 10 PM on weekends. That schedule has solved many of the problems and concerns that came with allowing all-night camping outside the Fieldhouse. A mandatory roll call requires that each group has a representative present at those times. There are random roll calls throughout the day. And at the final roll call, each group receives its final standing for entry.

Bigger games obviously trigger bigger crowds—and an earlier arrival of campers. The north concourse of Allen Fieldhouse becomes its own tent city—without the tents that existed when campers were kept outside the building. Clusters of students can be found hanging out in sleeping bags, on air mattresses or lawn chairs. Pillows and blankets are regular accessories. Some students sleep, while others study—or at least try to. Books, laptops, iPhones, iPods, and any other portable entertainment sources are typical. "There were times when it gave the appearance of a crowded homeless shelter," a longtime athletic department employee said in *Beware of the Phog.* "You came in the morning for work and saw all of those kids asleep on the floor and you felt guilty if you made noise."

Brown, Roy Williams, and Bill Self have all supplied food to the campers. Brown started bringing coffee with Joe's Donuts in the morning. He would deliver Pyramid Pizzas at night. And the late Floyd Temple, director of facilities in addition to being baseball coach, was well known for bringing added comfort, cover, warmth, and storage space over the years. In recent years, players from the men's and women's teams have delivered pizza at night. In 2012 forward Kevin Young pushed teammate Thomas Robinson around in a laundry hamper as they made the delivery of pies.

When Missouri visited Allen Fieldhouse for the final time as a member of the Big 12 Conference late in February 2012, the camping was intense. "Mizzou ones just are always fun because you see the dedication students have to come to these games," Hirschi told *The UDK.*

47 The Comeback Hawks of 2012

Senior guard Tyshawn Taylor still had tears welling in his eyes after Kentucky defeated Kansas 67–59 in the 2012 national championship game in New Orleans. "I'm proud of my team for how we competed and how we've been competing all year," Taylor said as he choked back more tears. "As a senior this is a bad feeling because I don't get the chance to make it up to these guys. And so it's a pretty bad feeling, man. I love how we fought. In a couple days, I might look back and say this a great year. But right now it's just a bad feeling."

Kansas made its 14th Final Four appearance in 2012, and Jayhawks fans would smile and agree that KU's ticket to New Orleans may have been the most unlikely of all. One year earlier, Kansas had been a No. 1 seed and lost the Southwest Regional final in painful fashion to VCU. Starting over without four starters from that team, the Jayhawks had no Final Four expectations heading into 2011–12. That's what made it such a pleasant journey. In his time at Kansas, coach Bill Self never had a more resilient team than this one. "I'm really proud of our guys," Self said after the Jayhawks defeated Roy Williams and North Carolina to reach the Final Four. "They've come together well. We haven't been a team that very many times has had five guys hitting on all cylinders. We've kind of had to piece it together. One thing these guys have done—they've been pretty tough."

Perhaps that toughness spread from the inspiration provided by forward Thomas Robinson. After the death of his mother and two grandparents the year before, Robinson returned to get his chance as a starter. He responded with a school-record 27 double-double performances, including 18 points and 17 rebounds against

Kentucky in the title game. He was a consensus first team All-American and a finalist for National Player of the Year.

Taylor cut down on his turnovers and became a more efficient, more mature point guard in his final season. Center Jeff Withey emerged as a shot-blocking force and was a dominant defender in the NCAA tournament. Travis Releford started and embraced his defensive role while adding the occasional offensive outburst. And guard Elijah Johnson found his own offensive groove as the Jayhawks marched to the Final Four. Self turned in perhaps his best coaching effort at Kansas and was rewarded with the Naismith Coach of the Year Award.

What really set this team apart was its never-say-die attitude. Call them the Comeback Kids, the Cardiac Kids, or the Comeback Jayhawks, this Kansas team never faced a deficit it didn't think it could overcome. "Somehow these guys find ways to win games," Self said. "This is kind of who we are."

In KU's final meeting with Missouri as a conference opponent, the Jayhawks erased a 19-point deficit in the second half to beat the Tigers 87–86 in overtime at Allen Fieldhouse. That matched the largest deficit ever overcome by KU at the Fieldhouse. (It tied the 1995 UCLA game.) In the NCAA tournament, Kansas trailed Purdue the first 37 minutes and rallied for a 63–60 victory. Against North Carolina State the Jayhawks led by eight with 3 minutes, 48 seconds left but then went without a field goal until Johnson scored on an inbounds pass with 14.8 seconds left to preserve a 60–57 win to reach the Elite Eight. In the national semifinal against Ohio State, they trailed by 13 in the first half and led for a grand total of four minutes and 20 seconds. But when the buzzer sounded it was Jayhawks 64–62. "It's just been our thing all year, coming back," Robinson said. "I don't like doing it, but for some reason my team is pretty good when we're down."

Robinson was right. But the Jayhawks weren't good enough to overcome falling behind Kentucky by 18 late in the first half. The

Wildcats had a cast of future NBA draft picks on the floor. Kansas had one more rally in the bank. With 3:52 remaining, KU was down nine. In 2008 against Memphis, the Jayhawks rallied from nine down with 2:12 remaining and won the national championship in overtime. "I reminded them of that," Self said. "But we just didn't have the mojo tonight."

Kentucky held the trophy as confetti fell from the roof. While the Jayhawks answered questions about a surprisingly successful season that nearly fulfilled everyone's dream, there were tears. But underneath the tears, there was another layer of satisfied smiles. "I'm just glad I got a chance to be part of this team," Robinson said.

48 T-Rob

When Kansas fans enter Allen Fieldhouse for a game, there is an unwritten rule to check any emotional baggage at the doors. Basketball is important. So are winning streaks. But walking into the Phog is an invitation to 40 minutes of diversion and a break from daily concerns. It's an escape. It doesn't always work that way. Sometimes the real world intersects with Naismith Drive at Allen Fieldhouse Drive.

That was the case when more than 16,000 fans filed into Allen Fieldhouse on the afternoon of January 22, 2011. Many of those already had heavy hearts. Just more than 12 hours earlier, the 37-year-old mother of KU sophomore forward Thomas Robinson had died of an apparent heart attack in Washington, D.C. After Robinson's younger sister delivered the news to him by telephone, word spread quickly across the Internet and by word of mouth.

Blue-Collar Bill

Rebounders speak of "blue-collar pride." Coaches insist any player should be able to rebound the basketball, and former New Jersey Nets enforcer Buck Williams once said his motto was, "The ball belongs to me." Put that all together and you've got Kansas rebounding legend Bill Bridges.

Bridges, from Hobbs, New Mexico, was a 6'5" center who started for coach Dick Harp from 1959–61. He grabbed 1,081 rebounds in three seasons, a total that ranks fourth on KU's all-time list behind Danny Manning, Raef LaFrentz, and Nick Collison—all of whom played four seasons. Bridges averaged 13.9 rebounds, which is why KU's annual rebounding award bears his name.

He waited 43 years to have his KU jersey No. 32 retired in 2004. When Bridges returned for his jersey ceremony, he expressed his dissatisfaction that players from his era had been ignored by KU. "I was very disconnected to KU when I left," said Bridges, who also had 1,028 points to rank 50th on the all-time KU list. "There was a time here that wasn't remembered."

Bridges teamed with 6'8" forward Wayne Hightower in 1960–61. Hightower led KU in scoring both of those seasons and sits at No. 40 on the all-time scoring list with 1,128 points. Hightower followed Wilt Chamberlain to Overbook High in Philadelphia and then on to Kansas. He logged time with eight different NBA and ABA teams before retiring in 1972.

Bridges played 13 seasons in the NBA and eventually reconnected with KU. "I feel I belong here. It's always been a privilege to be a Jayhawk," he said.

Just before midnight, teammates and coaches started gathering at Robinson's Jayhawker Towers apartment. "Thomas couldn't stop crying," junior guard Tyshawn Taylor said the next day. "Coach [Bill] Self was there. He cried. It was just real emotional."

Robinson had already climbed into the hearts of KU fans with his hard work, tenacity, and energizing play off the bench. He was growing and excelling, making progress every game in front of Jayhawk Nation, who affectionately called him T-Rob.

But this had become a story of unbearable sadness. Lisa Robinson's death followed the death of her mother in late December and the death of her father just one week before her own passing. In that short period of time, Thomas Robinson lost his grandmother, grandfather, and then his mother. And suddenly he was shouldering much more responsibility for his younger sister.

With all that going on, No. 2 Kansas was supposed to take the floor against No. 10 Texas on national television with a 69-game home winning streak on the line. Somehow, Thomas Robinson played. Self called it remarkable. Robinson scored two points and grabbed five rebounds but picked up four fouls in eight minutes. Through it all, it seemed the fans at Allen were trying to wrap Robinson in a blanket of hugs. "It's unbelievable," Self said. "Stop and think about it. He's got a nine-year-old sister left in his family, and she's half the country away and how his life has changed so much overnight. It's a pretty sad thing. People deal with it all the time, and he'll deal with it like a man, but still your heart certainly hurts for [him] and his family."

The 69-game winning streak—the longest in school history—was broken. Texas won 74–63. The Jayhawks funneled their emotion into a good first half and led 35–23 at halftime. But Texas outscored the Jayhawks 51–28 in the second half as KU made just eight of 30 shots. Out of respect to Robinson, no one on the Kansas side placed blame on the distractions. But it was obvious that KU ran out of gas in the second half. The Jayhawks looked drained. "I couldn't care less about the streak," Self said. "I couldn't all along."

Texas was put in a bad situation as well. The game was important in the Big 12 standings, but the Longhorns knew the Kansas players had their minds elsewhere. "I can't even imagine the burden and the weight that was on [Robinson's] shoulders today," Texas coach Rick Barnes said. "When you have a team and a player loses his mom, it affects everybody, and I'm sure it's weighed really

Thomas Robinson, whose Kansas teammates helped him cope with losing loved ones, flexes after scoring two of his 28 points during the Jayhawks' overtime victory against Missouri in the teams' final game as Big 12 opponents.

heavily on Bill. I'm sure he's had a really tough time. You only have one mom."

Like other Kansas teams, this one stressed family. The mother of twins Marcus and Markieff Morris lived in Lawrence, as did the mother of Taylor. They all chipped in and went to Robinson's apartment at midnight that night. The entire team traveled to Washington, D.C., the next week for the funeral. Robinson handled everything with class and maturity. The KU community's outpouring of support allowed him to get through the darkest moments.

Instead of rushing to the NBA prematurely, Robinson returned for his junior season and became KU's shining star in 2011–12. After starting just three games his first two seasons, he started all 39. He raised his scoring average from 7.6 to 17.7 and his rebounding average from 6.4 to 11.9. Robinson was a consensus first team All-American and was second to Kentucky's Anthony Davis in Player of the Year balloting. In an exciting and unexpected season, he led the Jayhawks to the national championship game before losing to a cast of NBA-ready Wildcats.

That's when he decided the time was right to turn pro and take care of his sister. Even then, it was a tough for T-Rob to say good-bye. "I have been up all night trying to come up with a thank you note or something to show my appreciation, but I couldn't get anything out because I think it is beyond words what this program meant to me and how much support I felt coming from my situation," he said. "It's going to be hard leaving, and I am going to miss my teammates, the coaching staff, the fans, and just the town—period, but this puts me in a situation to take care of my family, my little sister."

49 Hoch Auditorium

Before the Jayhawks moved into Allen Fieldhouse in 1955, Kansas played its home games in Hoch Auditorium, a building that was built for anything except basketball. But by 1928 the popularity of the team meant the Jayhawks had outgrown Robinson Gymnasium, which had served KU for 20 years and was actually quite special when it opened in 1907–08 with 3,000 seats for spectators.

Original Home-Court Disadvantage

One week after the Kansas basketball team played its first game—and lost to the Kansas City YMCA—the Jayhawks posted their first victory. On February 10, 1899, Kansas defeated the Topeka YMCA 31–6 in a rare home game. Games in Lawrence were few and far between because the Jayhawks didn't have a proper practice court or gymnasium for games.

Snow Hall's basement served as the first site, but it was woefully inadequate. The court was 36 feet wide and 84 feet long. There were support posts running down the middle of the floor, and it was impossible to arc a shot since the ceiling was 11 feet above the floor and just one foot above the rim.

James Naismith moved his team to a roller skating rink on Kentucky Street until that building was destroyed by fire. The next stop was the Massachusetts Street YMCA until it, too, burned down in 1902. Robinson Gymnasium, designed by Naismith to resemble the YMCA in Springfield, Massachusetts, was finally opened in 1907.

Hoch, which cost $350,000 to build, was a tremendous upgrade, but it was better known as the "Opera House" because it was much better suited for concerts and theater than playing basketball. It was referred to as a 3,500-seat multi-purpose arena. The traditional Gothic architecture set it apart.

But there were basketball idiosyncrasies everywhere in the building. The wooden floor at Hoch sat directly on top of concrete. This was not a cushioned surface, and it took a toll on the Kansas players. They soon started calling their new home the "Shin Splint Palace." Coach Phog Allen, who had earned his only college degree from the Central College of Osteopathy in Kansas City, Missouri, was always concerned about injuries to his players, so he kept the majority of practices at Robinson Gym.

The cramped floor was squeezed into Hoch's tight confines and created other hazards. In one corner the convergence of one baseline and one sideline directly abutted a wall. "I loved playing there, even though it was confined," said Al Kelley, a KU guard from 1952–54 who went on to be a member of the 1960 U.S. Olympic team that won gold in Rome. "You bet it was dangerous. But you sure felt important there because of the closeness of the fans and the noise they raised. Like any home court, it inspired you to do your best. I think everyone who played there has a soft spot in their heart for Hoch."

Soft spot? That may have been the case for the home team. Visitors were not so crazy about the place. Coach Henry Iba, hired by Oklahoma A&M (now Oklahoma State) in 1934, referred to Hoch as "The House of Horrors." The building may have set a record for most nicknames, and most were not favorable. "Horrible Hoch" was another.

In addition to the tight area surrounding the court, the building featured curved walls and decorative latticework directly behind the backboards. It has been said that the curvature of the walls made the backboards appear to be moving. Thus, opponents tended to miss free throws.

Kansas defeated Washington (Missouri) University 29–26 in overtime in its first game in Hoch Auditorium on January 6, 1928. That season, KU split home games between Hoch and Robinson. But the first full season in Hoch, 1928–29, turned out to be a nightmare for the Jayhawks. It was one of the most forgettable campaigns in Kansas history. Allen suffered through his first losing season as a coach, and KU finished 3–15 with a 2–8 record in the newly formed Big 6 Conference that included Kansas State, Missouri, Iowa State, Nebraska, and Oklahoma.

In the last game at Hoch, Kansas lost to Nebraska 66–55 on February 19, 1955. With Allen building his Hall of Fame coaching career and winning the NCAA championship in 1952, the Jayhawks completed their run in Hoch with a 204–38 record. Not bad for an "Opera House" subbing as a basketball gym.

After basketball games moved down the hill to Allen Fieldhouse, Hoch was better known for its lecture rooms, musical performances, political speeches, and other gatherings. The annual Rock Chalk Revue, a variety show performed by students now held at the Lied Center, was a popular Hoch feature for many years.

Acts like Kansas, REM, Bob Marley and the Wailers, and Chuck Mangione were among the many who performed concerts at Hoch. The Marley concert, just 17 months before the reggae star died, is considered one of the most memorable concerts ever in Lawrence. Hoch was struck by lightning on June 15, 1991, and a fire destroyed the interior. The building was rebuilt and now is known as Budig Hall with three giant lecture halls retaining the name Hoch Auditoria.

50 Kansas City: KU's Second Home

There really is no place like home—especially if home is Allen Fieldhouse. But the Jayhawks don't mind an occasional trip to Kansas City, Missouri, where they can act like they are on the road and still have the support of a passionate home crowd.

Kansas City's Sprint Center sometimes even hosts the Big 12 tournament and the opening rounds of the NCAA tournament in the same season. That was the case during the 2012–13 season when the Jayhawks went 8–0 in the Sprint Center. First, they beat Washington State and Saint Louis in the College Basketball Experience Hall of Fame Classic in November. "It was great to have a road trip, or kind of a road trip, you know," Kansas center Jeff Withey said of playing in Kansas City. "We were right down the street." The Sprint Center is adjoined to the College Basketball Experience, which includes the National Collegiate Basketball Hall of Fame.

The Jayhawks also defeated Oregon State in a regular season game in Kansas City. KU claimed the Big 12 tournament title by beating Texas Tech, Iowa State, and Kansas State before downing Western Kentucky and North Carolina in the NCAA tournament there.

Kansas has a 207–78 record all time in games played in Kansas City. With almost 300 games played there, it's obvious this isn't a recent trend for KU basketball. In fact, KU's first game ever—a 15–6 loss to the Kansas City YMCA on February 3, 1899—was played in Kansas City before a modest crowd of about 150 people.

After those eight wins in 2012–13, the Jayhawks were 22–4 in the Sprint Center with Big 12 titles in 2008, 2010, 2011, and 2013. Kansas was 80–24 in Kemper Arena, the Kansas City arena that was home to the NBA Kings, NHL Scouts, and college basketball tournaments. It is, of course, where KU fans and the Jayhawks celebrated the 1988 national championship. That was a truly special moment for Kansas City sports history since it was the 50th Final Four, and the event featured special exhibits and parties honoring the history of college basketball and the NCAA tournament. After winning the national title, the parties spread from the Country Club Plaza all the way back to Lawrence.

At the start of the 1987–88 season, all signs truly pointed to a Kansas City conclusion. The 1987 edition of Late Night at Allen Fieldhouse went with a "Goin' To Kansas City" theme. The preseason issue of *Basketball Times* magazine featured a picture of Danny Manning leaning against the road sign on the entrance ramp to I-70 in Lawrence with an arrow pointing east to Kansas City.

With 11 losses during the regular season, there were concerns the Jayhawks would find the road to Kansas City closed. Instead, KU got contributions from unlikely sources, and Manning was the superhero everyone wanted him to be. In the championship game, Manning had 31 points and 18 rebounds as KU upset Oklahoma

83–79 with a little help from the hometown faithful. "This feels great to be able to close out my career like this in Kansas City in front of people that have cheered for me and supported me for four years," Manning said. "It's a great feeling, and something we deserved."

That victory by Manning, Larry Brown, and the Miracles helped wipe away the memory of three previous championship losses in Kansas City. The Jayhawks fell to Indiana in 1940 and 1953 and then lost to North Carolina in a classic triple-overtime game involving Wilt Chamberlain. All three of those games were at Municipal Auditorium.

In this era of domed multi-sport arenas, Kansas City's rich Final Four and NCAA tournament heritage has become somewhat forgotten. Through 2013 Kansas City has hosted more NCAA games (128) and more championship games (10) than any other city. The last Final Four was that memorable one in 1988 at Kemper Arena. But Municipal Auditorium still ranks second in tournament games (83) and first in championship games (9). "This city has had a love affair with college basketball," Duke coach Mike Krzyzewski said of Kansas City.

The city issued an official proclamation declaring October 13, 2011 as "Municipal Auditorium Recognition Day for being a centerpiece of Kansas City for 75 years." The 75th anniversary celebrations of both Municipal Auditorium and the NAIA championship, along with the College Basketball Hall of Fame inductions and the CBE Classic, made Kansas City a prime spot on the college hoops calendar that season. And with KC just 40 miles down I-70 from the Lawrence campus, the Jayhawks never mind joining the party.

51 Jeff Withey

There isn't a college basketball coach in the country who wouldn't want to find an athletic seven-footer under his Christmas tree. Bill Self of Kansas enjoyed that experience on Christmas Eve 2008 when Jeff Withey's transfer from Arizona to KU became official.

But Withey didn't arrive in Lawrence with great expectations, and Self certainly couldn't have predicted what the future held for this Southern California, volleyball-playing, laid-back dude. Even after Withey became eligible in 2009–10—playing in 15 games, averaging 3.0 minutes, and blocking six shots—no one would have been bold enough to predict he would depart as KU's all-time leader in blocked shots with 311. But he did, and 2012–13 became a Withey "Block Party" at Allen Fieldhouse, complete with his own scoreboard video and website.

He rejected 146 shots in 37 games to be named Big 12 Defensive Player of the Year for the second consecutive season. Withey also became the Big 12 career blocked shots leader. In a 70–57 victory against San Jose State at Allen Fieldhouse on November 26, 2012, he became just the second KU player to officially record a triple-double with 16 points, 12 rebounds, and 12 blocks. "I've been wanting that for a while now, and it's only me and Cole [Aldrich] that have it, so it's pretty special to me," Withey said. "They kept on driving in, and I just kept on blocking it. It's what I do."

Opponents found it almost impossible to get Withey off his feet with pump fakes or shot fakes of any kind. And Withey was more than a swatter. Rarely did his blocks go flying out of bounds. Statistical services showed Kansas gaining possession of the ball on more than 70 percent of Withey's blocks—a key stat as the Jayhawks often used the blocked shots as a starting point for their fast break. "Most of the time—I'm guilty of it, too—we get caught standing around watching Jeff like a fan or something, and that's when we need to snap back to it," point guard Elijah Johnson said. "Jeff saved us a lot of times."

The school record for blocked shots fell during an 83–62 romp against Kansas State at Allen Fieldhouse on February 11, 2013. Withey rejected a shot by Thomas Gipson with 16:28 left in the first half and moved past Greg Ostertag, who recorded 258 blocks from 1992–95. Note that blocked shots were not recorded as an official stat during the days of Wilt Chamberlain, so his name does not appear among the top 20 in Kansas history. And Chamberlain likely had some triple-doubles of his own.

The Big 12 record came when Withey blocked two shots against Texas to pass former Longhorns center Chris Mihm with 265. "It definitely means something to me," Withey said. "I put a lot of hard work into getting it. Hopefully I can put some distance on it and make sure it doesn't get touched for 20 years or so."

Playing behind Aldrich and then the Morris twins, Withey's first two seasons were far from sensational. He entered his junior season with just 25 blocks. Even in February 2012, Self didn't feel Withey was giving his maximum effort. After a 74–71 loss to Missouri in Columbia, Self could barely recall Withey being on the floor. He missed his only shot, had four rebounds, and two fouls in 23 minutes.

Self expected Withey to be angry and motivated when he arrived at practice before the next game against Baylor. Instead, Withey was too laid-back for the head coach. Self pointed to the stairs in Allen Fieldhouse and told Withey to start running. Withey wasn't happy. But that played directly into Self's hand because Withey's effort drastically improved. "That was my way of trying to get back at him by playing even harder," Withey said. "I think [Self] definitely knows how to get under my skin."

When the Jayhawks traveled to Waco, Texas, and defeated a talented Baylor team 68–54, Withey was the big story. He scored a career-high 25 points on 8-of-10 shooting from the field. He had five rebounds, one assist, two steals, and three blocks. Self didn't have any trouble finding his center on the floor that night. "I just got tired of watching him not go after the ball and not being aggressive," Self said. "And the other players did, too, to be honest with you. They jumped him."

Self's high-low offense was perfect for Withey, who teamed with Thomas Robinson to spark a run to the 2012 national championship game before losing to Kentucky. Withey also benefitted from the coaching of Danny Manning, who helped him with his footwork.

Withey's experience as a volleyball player aided his jumping skills, and there were times he appeared to be on a pogo stick. He had 20 blocked shots in the four NCAA games that KU won on the way to the 2012 Final Four. Withey had 10 blocks against North Carolina State. His energy and success made an enormous difference in KU's tournament success.

And in the final home game of his Kansas career, Withey made a lot more noise than he did when he first arrived in Lawrence. On Senior Night against Texas Tech, Withey had 22 points, nine rebounds, four blocks—and hit the only three-point shot he attempted in a KU uniform. "The fieldhouse has been good to us, and the fans have been good to us," Withey said. "This is going to be a night that we will remember for a long time."

52 Ben McLemore

On the night of the 2013 NBA Draft, former Kansas guard Ben McLemore looked resplendent in his suit, crisp white shirt, and red-and-blue bow tie. Any KU fan with a discerning eye would have noticed the tie's color scheme. But there was another tribute to his college team hidden inside his suit coat. The unusual accessory was visible only when he took his right hand to pull the jacket back and pose for a photographer. A replica of his No. 23 KU blue jersey had been sewn inside.

After 37 games and one remarkable season in a Kansas jersey, McLemore walked across the stage of the Barclays Center in Brooklyn, New York, as the No. 7 selection in the draft, wearing the cap of the Sacramento Kings. It was the beginning of his professional career and a key moment in his personal version of a rags-to-riches story.

Kansas wasn't too far into its 31–6 season in 2012–13 before an entire nation recognized McLemore's athleticism and talent would limit his stay in Lawrence to one season. College basketball fans also heard coach Bill Self talk about his star's reluctant nature and lack of killer instinct. But it was a story by Eric Prisbel of USA TODAY that revealed the depths of poverty McLemore experienced growing up in St. Louis. McLemore told about nights when as many as 10 relatives would sleep inside the family's less-than 600-square foot home. "It's hard to play basketball when nothing is inside of you," McLemore told the newspaper. "It's a hard feeling—just starve."

That should no longer be a problem after McLemore received a multi-million dollar contract from the Kings. McLemore slipped a bit from original predictions that he could have been the first or second pick in the draft. Perhaps teams were scared off by his laid-back reputation or the fact his scoring average dropped from 17.4 points in Big 12 Conference play to 11.0 in KU's three NCAA tournament games. "The consensus was that he could go anywhere from No. 1 to 7," coach Bill Self said. "I would've been surprised if he fell lower than seventh, but I wasn't shocked by any means. With this draft, was there ever any idea where anybody was going? I didn't see [it] as a negative in any way, shape, or form."

McLemore was a redshirt freshman who practiced with the Jayhawks in 2011–12 but was ineligible for games due to academic reasons. Former KU coach Larry Brown, who attended numerous practices that season, regularly reminded Self that McLemore was the best talent on a team that advanced to the national championship game and lost to Kentucky.

McLemore finally got a chance to prove that and, in the process, accomplished something most people thought was impossible. He broke Danny Manning's freshman scoring record. McLemore scored 589 points, shattering the mark Manning established with 496 in 1985. McLemore's average of 15.9 was higher than Manning's 14.6 as well. He also set Kansas freshman records for field goal attempts (400), free throws (120), free throw percentage (87.0), minutes played (1,191), and games started (37).

His career-high came March 2 against West Virginia when he hit 12-of-15 shots and scored 36 points. He had 30 against Kansas State and 33 against Iowa State, including a banked-in three with 1.3 seconds left in regulation to send the Jayhawks to an overtime victory. That shot—and many of his athletic dunks—will remain part of KU lore.

When he announced his intention to enter the draft on April 9, McLemore wiped away tears as he left the press conference. But he knew he made the right decision, and Kansas fans couldn't ask for anything more than he had done in one season. "All my teammates and coaches said, 'If it's your time, it's your time.' It was my time," he said. "As a kid growing up, [playing in the NBA was] what I wanted to do. Now I've got the opportunity to do that and provide for my family. I'll remember this place the rest of my life."

53 A Trio of Unforgettable Point Guards

When Kansas won its third NCAA championship in 2008, *Sports Illustrated* published a commemorative issue with Mario Chalmers on the cover and the headline "Jayhawks Return To Glory." Among the features inside was an all-time KU team titled "The Team of Your Dreams." Rightfully so, the team was dominated by big men. In Jayhawks history, any dream team must include center Wilt Chamberlain—along with forwards Danny Manning and Clyde Lovellette. Guards Jo Jo White and Paul Endacott rounded out the starting five. That's a squad that represents the history of the program quite nicely.

White certainly would be comfortable bringing the ball up the floor for that team, and Phog Allen, the coach on this dream team, would have trusted the do-everything player. But Kansas basketball has a proud tradition at the point guard spot that wasn't really reflected by that dream team. The bench players on this roster did include Jacque Vaughn and Darnell Valentine, so ball handling and leadership is very well represented. *SI* could have put either of those players on the starting five, and there would have been no argument. At the very least, one should be designated the sixth man.

The list of great KU point guards has grown dramatically since Valentine departed in 1981. The discussion must include floor quarterbacks such as Kevin Pritchard, Russell Robinson, Sherron Collins, Tyshawn Taylor, and Kirk Hinrich.

But three other players tend to get bit overlooked and, based on their accomplishments, Final Four appearances, and career statistics, that doesn't seem fair. Here's our unforgettable trio:

Aaron Miles (6'1", Portland, Oregon, 2002–2005): Miles has a strong presence in the KU record book. He is the all-time leader in assists with 954, breaking Vaughn's mark of 804. And Miles ranks third in steals with 264, trailing only Valentine and Chalmers. Miles played in 138 games and burst on the scene as a freshman in 2001–02, when he started 36 of 37 games. He shattered Vaughn's freshman record of 181 assists with 252. Miles played in two Final Fours; had a double-double (12 points, 10 assists) against Maryland in the 2002 national semifinal; and had 18 points, five rebounds, and four assists against Marquette in a 2003 national semifinal. He finished his career with three of the top five season assist totals in KU history.

Adonis Jordan (5'11", Reseda, California, 1989–1993): Jordan was Roy Williams' first Kansas recruit. He ranks seventh all-time in assists at KU with 568 and ninth in steals with 181. As a freshman, Jordan came off the bench, backing up Kevin Pritchard, and the Jayhawks were a surprising 30–5 in Williams' second season. Jordan started the next season, averaged 12.5 points and had 154 assists as the Jayhawks reached the Final Four before losing to Duke in the national championship game. Two years later he combined with Rex Walters in the backcourt as the Jayhawks advanced to the 1993 Final Four. Jordan ranks 25th in career scoring with 1,373 points and he has one of the best names in college basketball history. "A Greek god," he said. "I can live with that."

Cedric Hunter (6'0", Omaha, Nebraska, 1984–1987): He ranks third all-time in assists—behind Miles and Vaughn—with 684 and 17th in steals with 157. He holds the single-season assist record of 278—set in 1986 when the Jayhawks reached the Final Four under coach Larry Brown. One year later Hunter had 209 assists, the 10th highest season total. Hunter averaged 9.1 points as a starter on KU's 1986 Final Four team that included Danny Manning, Ron Kellogg, Calvin Thompson, and Greg Dreiling. He had 16 assists against Oklahoma on March 8, 1986, the second-highest single-game total ever at KU.

54 Tyshawn Taylor

For point guard Tyshawn Taylor, the standard assist-to-turnover ratio wasn't enough. Taylor needed a big play-to-knucklehead moment ratio. That stat would have reflected the wide spectrum of his play during a career that thrilled KU fans one moment and left them in agony the next. He was a study in the art of contradiction.

Never was that more evident than his senior season when Taylor and the Jayhawks advanced to the 2012 national championship game before losing to Kentucky in New Orleans. During a 64–62 national semifinal win against Ohio State, Taylor capsulated his career in two seconds. KU took a 64–61 lead with 8.3 seconds remaining, but Ohio State had the ball. When Taylor intercepted a pass intended for William Buford of the Buckeyes, it appeared he could simply dribble out the clock for a KU victory. But Taylor saw teammate Elijah Johnson streaking to the basket for a potential dunk or layup. Faced with a decision, Taylor did the wrong thing and fired a bullet pass that Johnson had no chance of catching. The ball skidded behind Johnson and came to rest on the Kansas bench, coming closer to coach Bill Self than Johnson. "Tyshawn can make plays you can't coach, which was the steal against Buford," Self said. "And he can make a play that looks like he's never been coached, which was the pass two seconds after that." Luckily for KU, it didn't cost the Jayhawks, who still won the game.

Taylor led the Jayhawks in assists during his junior (164) and senior (186) seasons. On December 10, 2011, Taylor had 13 assists in a game against Ohio State in Lawrence, tying for the fifth highest single-game total in KU history. Taylor also holds the KU single-game record for turnovers with 11 against Duke just days earlier in the Maui Invitational.

Oh, the contradiction of it all.

That's the way his senior season started. Taylor was an early-season candidate for the Bob Cousy Award that goes to the top point guard in the nation. He was so inconsistent that he fell off the midseason list and then reappeared when the finalists were named. "I had a nickname earlier in the season—'Tyshawn Turnover Taylor.' I had that nickname, but I haven't heard that in a while—not because I haven't been turning the ball over, but we've been winning, and nobody cares," Taylor said at the 2012 Final Four. "There's a lot more positivity now. We're in the national championship game. If you're a true fan, how can you not respect that?"

Taylor truly was one of the most active Twitter posters in college basketball. When he started his senior season with 58 turnovers in 14 games (4.1 average), fans lashed out at him with tweets, posts, and comments. If people thought he would fold under pressure, they found just the opposite. "It's cool," he said. "Coming from [my background in Hoboken, New Jersey], it's all fun and games. I live with it, I enjoy it, I embrace it. And criticism is just motivation. I have fun with it. I don't take it too hard. I don't go crying in my room when people say I suck. I laugh at it. I show it to my teammates. Then it's over with it. I won't think about it the next day. It's water down my back."

After that horrible start to his senior season, Taylor turned things around and had his best stretch of games, beginning in early January—just in time for the Big 12 season. That continued all the way to the Final Four.

Taylor left KU with a 127–21 record. His 127 starts rank seventh all time at KU. He was only the third player in KU history with the combination of 1,400 points, 500 assists, and 150 steals. The others are Darnell Valentine and Kirk Hinrich. "Ty has had a great career," Self said in 2012. "He's one of the better guards that has ever played here. He's been a little bit up and down, inconsistent. We've had a good relationship, but it's better this year.

There's no question. It's been a little combative from time to time. He was probably as criticized going into this season as any player we've had since I've been here. He brought a lot of that on himself. He gets in his own way a little bit. He's emotional. But that's also what makes him good."

55 Attend Senior Day

Unless you've been in Allen Fieldhouse on Senior Day, it's virtually impossible to understand the emotion that fills the building. It matters not if it is Senior Day or Senior Night; there is always laughter and always tears. Most schools settle for one ceremony before the game. There are handshakes and hugs, parents escort their players to the court, a framed jersey is presented to the player. The head coach hugs Mom, Dad, all the brothers and sisters— sometimes wives and kids.

That's not enough at Kansas.

When KU says good-bye to seniors, there are pre and postgame ceremonies. The more seniors, the merrier, and student-mangers, cheerleaders, and band members are included. It has become tradition that KU fans—so attached to their heroes—throw roses, carnations, or other flowers on the court to show their appreciation. The crowd arrives early, too. Nobody wants to miss out. After the game the seniors give their speeches. Broadcaster Max Falkenstien used to emcee the event, but coach Bill Self introduces the players these days. Some speeches are too long, some speeches are better than others, but they always come from the heart.

The Jayhawks routed Texas Tech 79–42 on Senior Night in 2013. Jeff Withey, Kevin Young, Travis Releford, and Elijah

Top Five Senior Day Moments

1997—Jacque Vaughn, Scot Pollard, Jerod Haase, and B.J. Williams

This may have been the most beloved team in the history of Kansas basketball. The squad, including Raef LaFrentz and Paul Pierce, seemed to exemplify all that is good about college basketball— except a national championship. They came up short again in 1997, setting a record for broken hearts and possibly for most flowers on a basketball court. Walk-ons Joel Branstrom and Steve Ransom joined the festivities. "I've got the best group of kids in America," Roy Williams said. "Other coaches can say it. But no coach can say it with the conviction Roy Williams does."

1988—Danny Manning, Chris Piper, and Archie Marshall

Basketball band director Ron McCurdy had his musicians in tuxedos. McCurdy's was all white. The band played "Oh Danny Boy" for Manning, who had 31 points and 10 rebounds.

Marshall had injured his left knee in New York in late December. Before the game Manning suggested the Jayhawks should put Marshall on the floor, and with 1:33 left on the clock, Larry Brown sent Marshall to the scorer's bench. Oklahoma State coach Leonard Hamilton told his defender to back off. Marshall attempted a 40-footer that hit the rim and bounced off. Marshall was given a standing ovation as he returned to the bench. There weren't many dry eyes in the house.

2013—Jeff Withey, Travis Releford, Kevin Young, and Elijah Johnson

Withey made the night truly memorable by swishing a three-pointer with 5:18 left in the first half. It was the first three-pointer in the career of the seven-foot center. Pollard, another California guy, had

Johnson gave their speeches. Self recognized Ben McLemore as well. McLemore was a freshman, but as was widely accepted, he headed to the NBA and played his final home game that night. That was a nice touch, but these moments are for the players who stayed four years. "It was a great way to send those four studs off, and they've been studs the whole time they've been here," Self said.

hit a three during the 1997 Senior Night. "I heard Scot bragging about that," Withey said, "not any more." Withey had 22 points, and Johnson had one of his career-high 12 assists on Withey's three-pointer.

2003—Nick Collison and Kirk Hinrich
The two seniors from Iowa combined for 43 points as the No. 7 Jayhawks beat No. 16 Oklahoma State 79–61. Collison missed seven free throws but had 16 rebounds and seven blocks. Cowboys coach Eddie Sutton rushed over to the KU bench to embrace Collison and Hinrich when they exited the game with 55 seconds left. Both players broke down when talking about their family. "Every time the national anthem plays, I think of Grandpa," Collison said, referring to Arden Collison, a tailgunner whose plane was shot down in World War II. Said Hinrich: "I don't know how I would have gotten up here and given this speech if we would have lost this game."

2008—Sasha Kaun, Darnell Jackson, Russell Robinson, Jeremy Case, and Rodrick Stewart
The Jayhawks improved to 27–3 with a 109–51 Senior Night romp against Texas Tech. KU, of course, was on the way to the national championship, but it was still a journey at that point. This one was memorable for a quote from Robinson, a tough New York City guy, who had to dry his eyes before the game. "Coach told us last week he didn't think the Lakers could come in and beat us on Senior Night," Robinson said. "I agreed with him right away. I don't think Kobe [Bryant] could have guarded me today." KU made 14-of-24 three-pointers, and Robinson scored 15 points. "I don't get emotional publicly that often, but I almost choked up before the game," Self said.

"They've won a lot of games, got their degrees, and been great ambassadors for our university."

Kansas tradition says the seniors start the game whether they are regular starters or not. They might not stay in long—but they start. In 1995 Kansas and Oklahoma State played for the Big 8 Conference title. Even though they were tied with 10–3 conference records, walk-on Scott Novosel was in the lineup. Novosel received a standing ovation as he left the game. Kansas went on to win 78–62 and then took the Big 8 title.

56 The Sunflower Showdown

Maybe you aren't the romantic type. Perhaps your life philosophy includes a mandate that there's no crying in basketball. Maybe you don't enjoy sappy speeches from athletes. If any of those traits describe your personality, Senior Day at Allen Fieldhouse may not be your bag of basketballs. But if hostility is your thing and throwing live chickens or bananas on a basketball court sounds more appealing than a "shower of flowers," then let us suggest the 85-mile trip west on I-70 to Manhattan, home of the Kansas State Wildcats. Seriously, the Sunflower Showdown viewed from a different angle should be on the to-do list of any Jayhawks fan. But it does require courage.

With Missouri bailing out of the Big 12 for dollar signs and life in the Southeastern Conference, Kansas State is now KU's most heated rival. Mizzou certainly was a much more competitive group, and it is hard to define Kansas-Kansas State as a rivalry since the Jayhawks dominate the series so thoroughly.

The Jayhawks went 3–0 against K-State in 2012–13. The Wildcats did tie Kansas for first place in the Big 12 regular season with identical 14–4 records, but any possible bragging rights were settled in the Big 12 tournament when KU crushed K-State 70–54 in the championship game to complete the sweep.

KU leads the series 186–91. The Jayhawks are 75–45 all time in Manhattan, including a 23–2 record in Bramlage Coliseum, the

Scoreboard Sabotage

One theory is that a Kansas State fan, later identified as "Wildcatman," hid in a closet inside Allen Fieldhouse the night before the Sunflower State Showdown game on February 20, 1965. Others say there were multiple perpetrators—perhaps as many as 12—armed with blueprints, 400 feet of cable, and an electric trigger device.

The truth may never be known. But with 8:02 remaining in the first half and KU leading 23–9, a pair of 6-by-12 foot banners were unfurled on the east and west side of the scoreboard. The message on each banner read "Go Cats, Kill Snob Hill Again." And at the bottom was a drawing of a broken peace pact.

Players, fans, coaches, and officials were all stunned. "I couldn't believe my eyes," KU's Al Lopes said. "It was a pretty impressive stunt." The banners had been attached to curtain rods and rolled up in window-shade fashion with weights attached.

KU officials had to wait until halftime to lower the scoreboard and remove the banners. KU was leading 42–26 at the half and won the game 86–66, but the mystery was never solved. Nobody got hurt, and even Jayhawk fans had to admit it was an impressive prank. And all it really did was draw attention to another score K-State would rather forget.

cozy 12,528-seat arena better known to some as "The Octagon of Doom," where there is a certain amount of rhythm required to rock back and forth as the K-State band plays Wabash Cannonball. That has been the unofficial fight song since the 1960s. And according to the band, the song represents the "survival of the underdog in the hearts and minds of all true K-State fans." And that underdog status certainly must be on their minds every time the Jayhawks visit.

But, hey, the Jayhawks need a conference rival. Texas auditioned, but the football school couldn't sustain their basketball success, and things have spun back in the direction of Kansas State. The Wildcats and Jayhawks were solid combatants in the days of the Big 7 and Big 8 conferences. Before the construction of Allen

Fieldhouse, there was a time that Phog Allen actually envied coach Jack Gardner and K-State's 14,000-seat Ahearn Fieldhouse, which opened in 1950.

Later, when talented players such as Bob Boozer, Rolando Blackman, Mitch Richmond, Mike Evans, Lon Kruger, Chuckie Williams, and Curtis Redding wore the purple—and Jack Hartman was coach—the series was both heated and fun. KU's advantage over K-State in Big 8 games was 42–34, but it has shifted to 30–3 since the formation of the Big 12.

The Jayhawks run into hostility everywhere they play. The stature of the program carries a certain level of vitriol reserved for those at the very top, such as Kentucky, North Carolina, Duke, and UCLA. K-State fans have taken that hatred to a different level over the years. Give them credit or charge them with poultry abuse—as some organizations actually have done. It has been a tradition for K-State, originally named Kansas State Agricultural College, to throw live chickens—often painted red and blue—during KU player introductions. It's symbolic of the play on words they use, referring to Jayhawks as Chickenhawks. "One year, I thought I'd be a good guy and I picked a chicken up and rubbed it," former KU coach Ted Owens told the *Lawrence Journal-World*. "I was carrying it back to the bench when I said, 'What if he has a few droppings?' I put it back down pretty quickly."

K-State officials have cracked down on the tradition from time to time. In 2005 a rubber chicken on a noose landed close to KU's Wayne Simien during pregame warm-ups. But in 2007 the Associated Press reported "the chicken toss has been declared off limits at Kansas State." The People for the Ethical Treatment of Animals (PETA) cited at least three chickens thrown on the court at that year's Manhattan game and wrote a protest letter saying the chickens had been subjected to "deafening noise, bright lights, terror, abusive handling, and likely death for the sake of amusement."

In a simpler time back in 1978, the problem was hot dogs and bananas. When the Jayhawks won in Lawrence, KU students launched hot dogs at K-State's Redding, a cocky New York product who had a lot of mustard in his game. Less than a month later in nationally televised game at Ahearn Fieldhouse, students tossed bananas and chickens on the court during introductions. The start of the game was delayed more than 20 minutes to clean the floor. Another K-State fan wore a gorilla costume and was allowed to prance around by the KU bench. "I was fearing for my life," KU guard Darnell Valentine said. "These people were crazy."

Kansas power forward Donnie Von Moore told the *Journal-World* in a 2007 interview that, "It ticked us off because at first we thought it had some racial connotations. They were basically calling us gorillas. Later they said we threw hot dogs so they threw bananas. It's just food. We beat them. So that's what mattered."

Welcome to the Sunflower Showdown—Manhattan-style. Attend at your own risk.

57 All Good Things Must Come to an End

The worst thing about home-court winning streaks is when they end. Kansas basketball enjoys one of the greatest home-court advantages in all of sports. As a result, the Jayhawks have put together 16 winning streaks of 16 games or longer—including the Big 12 Conference record of 69 games and the Big 8 record of 55 games—on its various home courts.

That 69-game streak started February 7, 2007, and ended January 22, 2011, when Texas beat KU 74–63, the day after Thomas Robinson found out his mother had died. It certainly was one of the more stressful and heartbreaking days in KU history. But those emotions were reserved for Robinson's grief much more than the ending of a streak. "It hurts. You don't like to lose," guard Brady Morningstar said. "We're not playing to keep the streak alive. We're playing to get a win. It happens. You've got to bounce back."

That streak led the nation for more than two seasons and ranks 11th all-time in NCAA history. The previous school record had been a 62-game streak from 1994–98 that ended with an 85–81 loss to Iowa.

In Self's first 10 seasons at Kansas, he had more Big 12 regular season conference championships (nine) than home-court losses. Self was 161–8 (95.3 winning percent) in the Phog. In that 10th season, Oklahoma State defeated KU 85–80 on February 2, 2013, to snap a 33-game winning streak at Allen Fieldhouse. The celebration by the Cowboys included a backflip in front of press row by guard Marcus Smart. "We couldn't believe it," Smart said. "We just beat them."

That streak ended up tied for the fourth-longest streak in KU history. Missouri snapped the other 33-game streak back in 1955 at Hoch Auditorium. Sunflower State rival Kansas State holds the distinction of breaking the most streaks in Lawrence. Of those 16 streaks, the Wildcats have ended four of them—two at Robinson Gym (16 games in 1915 and 20 games in 1925) and one at Hoch Auditorium (16 games in 1934).

Most notably, K-State ended that Big 8 record 55-game winning streak in Allen on January 30, 1988, during Danny Manning's senior season and the year the Jayhawks won their second NCAA championship. Again, it was the longest home-court winning streak in the nation at that time. KU had not lost in Allen since a 92–82 overtime loss to Oklahoma in 1984. Manning and fellow senior Chris Piper had never lost on their home court until K-State gave them that rare and humbling experience.

Manning was dueling with K-State's Mitch Richmond, and KU coach Larry Brown, trying to spark his 12–6 team, was tinkering with his starting lineup. He had just moved Kevin Pritchard to the point guard. Richmond had 35 points and 12 rebounds. Manning finished with 21 and eight, but K-State won 72–61.

KU officials started wondering if they might have to print NIT tickets. But Brown viewed it as a turning point. "We've beaten some great teams in this building, and a great team beat us tonight," Brown said. "I'm encouraged with the way we played."

And oddly enough, KU's remarkable streak of 31 consecutive victories over K-State ended at Allen Fieldhouse—not in Manhattan. The Wildcats marched into Lawrence on January 14, 2006 and beat the Jayhawks 59–55. K-State's last previous win against KU had come in 1994. "I underestimated them a little bit," Brandon Rush said. "But that won't happen again. We won't underestimate anybody any more."

58 Brandon Rush

They say everything happens for a reason. In the case of Brandon Rush, that theory certainly has validated itself more than once in his basketball career. In a strange kind of way, that's why another national championship trophy ultimately found its way to Lawrence.

The story begins in March 2005. Coach Bill Self was not a happy camper. KU had been eliminated from the NCAA tournament in embarrassing fashion, falling to Bucknell in a first-round game played in Oklahoma City, Self's old stomping ground.

The tournament went on, and Roy Williams, the man Self replaced and was still being compared to, won the national title at North Carolina. The Tar Heels defeated Illinois, where coach Bruce Weber used many of Self's recruits to reach the Final Four. But on May 19, 2005, Self faced a roster problem he didn't want or need.

Sophomore J.R. Giddens, who had been KU's third-leading scorer, was stabbed in an early-morning knife fight outside a Lawrence bar. Giddens was underage in an over-21 bar and had suffered a severe cut to his calf. Giddens ultimately transferred, but Self didn't like the headlines the incident created for the program. "To me, that was the low point," Self said. "Coaches can deal with losing, but you don't want to deal with defending who you are."

With Giddens off the roster, Self and KU had room for Rush. Kansas fans knew his name because his brother, Kareem Rush, had played at Missouri. The Rush brothers, including another older brother, JaRon, who went to UCLA after considering KU, were from Kansas City, Missouri. The older brothers came under intense media scrutiny for their involvement with AAU coach Myron Piggie, who pleaded guilty to fraud charges involving money paid to JaRon, Kareem, and three other players.

Brandon attended four high schools but eventually established himself at Mount Zion (North Carolina) Academy, a prep school not known for its academic standards. Rush intended to jump directly to the NBA and submitted his name for early entry in 2005. But he changed his mind after a pre-draft workout in Houston, faxed his withdrawal letter before the deadline, and eventually chose KU over Illinois and USC for his college days. Self called the recruiting victory "our energy boost" after the spring of bad news. But academic issues, questions about Rush's transcripts, reviews of his amateur status, and his reputation for not caring about school, made Kansas fans nervous he would be a one-and-done player. He was facing an uphill battle with popularity.

On the court, he became the first freshman in Kansas history to lead his team in scoring and rebounding. And he was the first freshman in Big 12 history to be named first team All-Big 12. He averaged 13.5 points on a team that won 25 games, starting along

Brandon Rush, dunking over Colorado guard Dwight Thorne II during Kansas' 72–59 victory on February 2, 2008, bounced back from an ACL injury to help lead KU to a national championship.

with fellow freshmen Mario Chalmers and Julian Wright and sophomores Russell Robinson and Sasha Kaun. Self blamed youth when the Jayhawks again exited the NCAA Tournament with a first-round loss—this time to Bradley. In the locker room after that game, Rush said he would be back for his sophomore season and he was. He led the Jayhawks in scoring again, averaging 13.8 points as KU won 33 games but lost to UCLA in the San Jose Regional final.

That was the end—or at least that's what everyone expected. Rush had stopped going to classes, making it clear he wasn't planning on staying school. He joined Wright in declaring for the draft, and the Jayhawks suddenly were losing 26 points of production per game. Rush was projected as a late first-round choice, but he never joined Wright in the green room at Madison Square Garden. Before he could hire an agent, Rush tore the anterior cruciate ligament in his right knee while dunking in a pickup game with his older brothers on May 23. He had surgery on June 1 and faced six months of rehabilitation.

Rush withdrew his name from the draft again. Robinson remembers the team meeting Self called when Rush got hurt. "He didn't say hello. He didn't say, 'How are you?'" Robinson said. "He said, 'We just got better.' By that, he meant Brandon was coming back for another year."

Rush asked, "Why me?" But his mother, Glenda, called it a blessing in disguise. The injury made Rush an even better player. His work ethic changed, and he returned to the team ahead of schedule. By February he was able to play without his knee brace. His rehab taught him discipline, and he was a force for the Jayhawks all the way to the national championship, leading KU in scoring for a third consecutive season.

Rush suddenly took pride in playing defense and in the Elite Eight game against Davidson he held super shooter Stephen Curry in check as Curry missed eight consecutive three-pointers in the second half. Rush was MVP of the Big 12 tournament and averaged 15.8 points in six NCAA tournament games. He had 25 points and seven rebounds against North Carolina in the national semifinals, tossing aside his laid-back image and scoring every time the Tar Heels tried to make the game close. He followed that with 12 points and six rebounds in the national championship win against Memphis.

After winning it all as a junior, the time was finally right for Rush to leave. He was selected 13th overall by the Portland Trail Blazers in the 2008 NBA Draft and traded that night to the Indiana Pacers. Playing for the Golden State Warriors on November 2, 2012, Rush tore his left ACL and was lost for the remainder of the season. It was just one more challenge for Rush, who was traded to the Utah Jazz during the 2013 offseason, to overcome. But he seems to be at his best when adversity strikes.

59 Coach Hudy

Got Hudy? Kansas basketball does. And the Jayhawks have made it very clear that she is the program's "secret weapon."

Hudy is Andrea Hudy—or Coach Hudy—as the KU players call her. Hudy's official title is assistant athletics director for sport performance. That's cool, but she's better known as the strength and conditioning coach for the KU men's basketball team—the only female strength coach in Division I basketball.

Surprised to hear that the Jayhawks have a female strength coach? That's okay. Hudy is used to that reaction. And when former Kansas athletic director Lew Perkins suggested in 2004 that Bill Self interview Hudy for the job, the KU coach was a bit reluctant as well. "Lew kept telling me if you just interview her, you're going to hire her," Self said in a video feature on Hudy that ESPN produced in February 2013. "And, I'm like, 'I don't know about having a woman as our strength coach.'"

In 2003, Perkins made the move to Kansas from the University of Connecticut, where Hudy spent nine and a half years and worked with UConn's men's and women's basketball programs. She was part of eight national championships in Storrs—two in men's basketball, five in women's basketball, and one in men's soccer. In that ESPN feature, Hudy said Self asked her what makes her different. "Why would I want you here as a coach?" Self asked. "She convinced me, 'Hey, I've worked with [Geno] Auriemma and I've worked with [Jim] Calhoun. So I don't think really you're going to throw too much at me that I haven't already seen.' I realized then, after talking to her, that she'll have the guys' respect."

Hudy has a small orange cone on her desk inscribed with the words, "IF YOU HAVE NOTHING TO DO, DON'T DO IT HERE!" Next to the cone sits a jar labeled, "Ashes of Wimps & Whiners." After nine Big 12 championships, two Final Fours, and a national championship in 2008, she should have the respect of everyone associated with Kansas basketball. "I don't know where we'd be without her," Self told ESPN.com.

If you are a devoted Kansas fan, you know Hudy when you see her.

If you are in Lawrence and hang around the KU campus, perhaps you've seen the gray T-shirts with the white "got hudy?" lettering on the front that is modeled after the successful "got milk?" ad campaign. On the back of the shirt is a human arm and flexed muscle showing the results of a Hudy workout. When it comes to strength and conditioning, it's all about results. That Hudy checklist includes 16 Jayhawks who have been drafted in the NBA. In all, she has worked with 33 former student-athletes who went on to play in the NBA. That number will reach 35 when Jeff Withey and Ben McLemore suit up this fall.

Hudy's NBA Preparation

Strength coach Andrea Hudy has never worked in the NBA, but her presence in the league is strong. Here's a list of NBA players from KU and Connecticut who have drilled under Hudy's direction in weight rooms at the two universities:

Kansas (16 players): Cole Aldrich, Darrell Arthur, Mario Chalmers, Sherron Collins, Xavier Henry, Darnell Jackson, Keith Langford, Aaron Miles, Marcus Morris, Markieff Morris, Thomas Robinson, Brandon Rush, Josh Selby, Wayne Simien, Tyshawn Taylor, Julian Wright.

UConn (17 players): Ray Allen, Rashad Anderson, Hilton Armstrong, Josh Boone, Denham Brown, Scott Burrell, Caron Butler, Khalid El-Amin, Rudy Gay, Ben Gordon, Richard Hamilton, Travis Knight, Donny Marshall, Emeka Okafor, Charlie Villanueva, Jake Voskuhl, Marcus Williams.

In early January 2013, Hudy was named the National College Strength and Conditioning Coach of the Year by the National Strength and Conditioning Association (NSCA). She received the award at the association's conference in Nashville, Tennessee, and it is given to a coach for "dedication to improving athletic performance with safe and effective science-based programs."

Hudy said she was honored and humbled to receive the award, which Keith Kephart of Kansas also received back in 1981. "There are lots of talented people out there around the country who were also very deserving," she said. "The only reason we can do what we do at Kansas is because of the support we receive from the great alumni, administration, and coaches that we have."

Hudy was a four-year, letter-winner in volleyball at Maryland, where she graduated from in 1994 with a bachelor of science degree in kinesiology. She then earned her master's of art and sport biomechanics degree while at UConn. It didn't take long for Hudy to make an impact at Kansas. She arrived in Lawrence in September 2004. Heading into the 2005–06 season, center Sasha Kaun was asked how he had improved his game in the offseason. "I have improved in the weight room," said Kaun, who was entering his sophomore season. "I feel stronger…Hudy has done a phenomenal job with the entire team."

One season later, a 5'11" point guard from Chicago showed up in Lawrence with his sizable reputation and a big appetite for fast food. Freshman Sherron Collins soon became the poster child for the Hudy approach to conditioning. In December of that season, she put Collins on a supervised, 2,400-calorie diet, and he ultimately lost 28 pounds. After a slow start to the season, Collins gave the Jayhawks a spark in Big 12 play by averaging 11.3 points. "He had to be hungry, he had to have low energy, and he had to struggle," Hudy said as the Jayhawks went into the NCAA tournament that year. "But he stuck with it and he did it. The way he's been performing lately, it's paid off for him."

When we say it was a "supervised" diet, we mean Hudy was at the training table with Collins early in the morning to make sure he got a good, balanced breakfast. And if he tried to sneak out for a late-night fast-food run, she would track him down.

She describes her job as 24/7. And the players know she is always there—even when they've gone on to other things. In May 2013 Collins sent out this tweet: "Love my ku coaching staff so supporting and of course my ku mom @A_Hudy lol #GotHudy" Notice the reference to his "KU mom" in a tweet three years after the former Jayhawks captain departed Lawrence. When Marcus Morris became a lottery pick in the 2011 NBA draft, he didn't mince words. "If it weren't for Hudy," Morris said, "I wouldn't be in the NBA."

And Withey may have been the opposite of Collins. The seven-foot center showed up in Lawrence in 2009 weighing just more than 200 pounds. He wasn't strong enough or bulky enough to get the job done for the Jayhawks in the lane. Hudy used to ban Withey from the weight room until he loaded enough calories. She made Withey his favorite strawberry Muscle Milk shakes and hung out with the San Diego native while he dined on breakfast burritos. "Our secret weapon definitely is Hudy," Withey said.

60 Bond Like the 2008 Team at Henry T's

Check out Henry T's on Sixth Street. It's a great place to watch basketball and enjoy some good food. And you can pay tribute to KU's most recent national championship team. If not for a team meeting held at Henry T's, the Jayhawks might not have won that trophy in 2008.

Heading into Manhattan to play Kansas State on January 30 that season, the Jayhawks were 20–0, had beaten their last six opponents by an average margin of 24.3 points, and were ranked No. 2 by both major national polls. Top-ranked Memphis was the nation's only other undefeated team.

The smooth ride was about to end for Kansas. Kansas State, led by freshman Michael Beasley, was getting national attention as well, and the Wildcats desperately wanted to end a 24-game losing streak to Kansas—*in Manhattan.* There was too much emotion in Bramlage Coliseum that night, and the Jayhawks lost 84–75. K-State fans rushed the floor, but there certainly was no reason to panic. The Jayhawks bounced back and defeated Colorado, Missouri, and Baylor in succession.

The Jayhawks never stumbled into an all-out slump. But that loss at K-State seemed to damage their confidence on the road. KU traveled to Austin and lost to Texas 72–69. On February 16, it was back to Allen Fieldhouse for a 69–45 thrashing of Colorado. The Phog was still Home Sweet Home.

But seven days later, it was time to visit Stillwater, Oklahoma, always one of the toughest road challenges in a Big 12 season. This was no different. Oklahoma State held on for a 61–60 victory that ripped the hearts out of the Jayhawks and their fans. It was the low point of the season, but it wasn't just about basketball. In the week before the Oklahoma State game, Darnell Jackson and Rodrick Stewart had each suffered personal tragedies. Jackson's cousin was shot and killed at an Oklahoma City nightclub. Stewart also lost an adopted brother the same day in Seattle from gun violence. The Jayhawks were distracted and unfocused heading into Gallagher-Iba Arena.

Coach Bill Self knew it would be hard for his team to stay focused on what was happening on the court. "I don't know the coaching manual on that stuff," Self said after the Oklahoma State game. "We've got a lot going on."

The Jayhawks had become a band of brothers long before the occurrences of that week. Several players had experienced tragedies and death at different stages in their lives. They had learned to lean on each other and help during the darkest moments. One year earlier Jackson had been so anguished by the death and pain in his family, he drove home to Midwest City, Oklahoma, determined to quit school and basketball. Like all those other experiences, the Jayhawks understood they couldn't get through this moment individually and without their teammates.

The day after the loss to Oklahoma State, the players gathered at Henry T's Bar and Grill in Lawrence for a dinner/team meeting. No coaches allowed. Just the players, some burgers, and hot wings. Jackson credited freshman big man Cole Aldrich with the idea. "More than anything, it just brought everybody back to the same page," guard Russell Robinson said. "We were all in the same book, but we were on different pages with different concerns."

Reserve guard Tyrel Reed, also a freshman, said the Oklahoma State loss and all the problems off the court made the Jayhawks realize they weren't invincible. In 2011, Reed told *The University Daily Kansan* the meeting has taken on a "legendary quality." He said, "I assume this is at least partially because nobody outside the team knows exactly what happened there—except that we never lost again that season."

That is true. The Jayhawks won their next 13 games and the national championship.

Reed said there was nothing official about the meeting. But everyone showed up and piled into one extra large booth in the corner. "The idea was that if you had something to say, this was the time to say it," Reed told *The UDK*. "If you had some issue with a teammate or a coach, get it off your chest here and now. You could say whatever you wanted to say, no holds barred. In other words what we said mattered less than the fact we were saying things. I think it was a turning point. There might have been a little animosity, and guys were maybe saying stuff to other people instead of coming out in front of everybody and saying how they felt. It was a 45-minute meal, and we were out. I think we grew closer that night."

Henry T's remains a popular destination for KU players and, of course, fans, too. Like any other sports bar, it isn't unusual for KU students to grab a table and sit for hours while watching games. That can cost an establishment some cash. During the NCAA tournament, some Lawrence bars, including Henry T's, have started a reservation system. If you want a table for four, you must agree to spend at least $100. With a table of six, that security blanket increases to $150.

Jeff Hornberger, manager for Henry T's, told KCTV in Kansas City, that it's not hard for four people to spend $100. "I mean one person can spend $25 on a meal, a couple of beers, and a tip," he said. "It adds up pretty quick."

61 Drink and Dine at 23rd Street Brewery

There are many great spots in Lawrence to dine and drink, down a few beers with friends, and watch the Jayhawks play ball, but there's only one place where you can order "The Bill Self" or the "Danny Manning Marsala Chicken." We're talking about 23rd Street Brewery, located at 3512 Clinton Parkway in Lawrence. It gets our nod for the best atmosphere for watching games, the best brewpub, and—without a doubt—the most innovative menu in town.

Tasty Lawrence Eateries

In the interest of fairness, good food, flat screen TVs, and brewpubs, we can't limit our "to do" dining list to 23rd Street Brewery. We must give a tip of our KU hat to these fine establishments as great places to watch a KU game.

The Wheel—This burger restaurant, pizza place, and bar is on 507 West 14th Street and is home of The Wang Burger. Legend has it that the tradition started in the 1970s with the Kappa Burger, a cheeseburger with bacon. At some point a Sigma Chi with the nickname "the Wanger" asked for a fried egg on his Kappa Burger. The Wang Burger was born. Scott Van Pelt and Neil Everett frequently express their desire for a Wang Burger on ESPN, giving it national exposure.

Johnny's Tavern—"Serving Up Tradition Since 1953," Johnny's has nine locations, but the original is at 401 N. 2nd Street. There is a Cajun night and a trivia night. But there should be a "thank goodness the 3.2 (abv) beer is gone" night.

Free State Brewing Company—"Because without beer, things do not seem to go as well" is the motto for the establishment at 636

I recommend ordering "The Bill Self." The menu calls it: "An Amazing Dish inspired by our Amazing Coach! Our Made From Scratch Mac and Cheese baked to perfection and topped with Buffalo Chicken Tenders." This pasta item at 23rd Street is the most popular item and "the most obscure" selection on the menu, according to managing partner Matt Llewellyn.

Llewellyn says it was the first to-go order 23rd Street ever received from the KU basketball team. "Go figure," Llewellyn said. "[Self] ordered mac and cheese and an order of buffalo chicken tenders. We thought that was a cool thing. We tried it out together, loved it, and put it on the menu. It was the same thing with Danny Manning. He ordered chicken marsala. We happened to be changing the menu around, so we thought it was a great opportunity

Massachusetts. Enjoy outstanding food, great people watching on the front patio, and the satisfaction of not being in a slave state. I recommend the Wheat State Golden and the Stormchaser IPA.

Bigg's Barbecue—With the slogan, "Sports, Ribs, and Rock 'N Roll," the joint at 2429 Iowa has the best barbecue in Lawrence; no bones about it. I love the brisket. Get there early for a good spot to watch the game. If you are having a watch party, they cater, too. The decor features old framed *Rolling Stone* magazines on the wall, including a classic Bruce Springsteen cover.

Jefferson's Restaurant—The establishment that serves "wings, burgers, and oysters" is on 743 Massachusetts. In addition to the great wings and burger baskets, Jefferson's has 10 oz. margaritas for $1.50 on Tuesdays. Dollar bills—with personal messages left behind by customers—adorn the walls.

Wayne & Larry's Sports Bar & Grill—"Never a dull moment," as the proprietors say, the place at 933 Iowa is an increasingly popular spot to watch KU games. It has 12 TVs and three 95-inch projection screens, and even if there's no KU game on, hit the billiards and shuffleboard tables.

to put both of those names on it." The menu description reads: "Tender chicken breast cutlets sautéed with red onions and wild mushrooms. Finished in a creamy marsala wine sauce and served over a bed of rice."

Llewellyn said both of those dishes would remain on the menu indefinitely as will Max's Mac & Cheese (for Max Falkenstien), Chris Piper's Pip'n Hot Cajun Pasta (with Andouille sausage), and all the sweets on the Bud Stallworth signature dessert menu. "Bud has the biggest sweet tooth of anyone I know," Llewellyn said.

If you are craving a giant German-style brat, try "The Withey." It is topped with homemade chili, Tex Mex fondue, and Fritos chips. Llewellyn says center Jeff Withey didn't hesitate to approve the menu item. Withey's family stopped in on Senior Night in 2013, and half of the clan ordered Jeff's brat.

Whatever you order, you're going to want one of 23rd Street's brews to wash it down. The Wave The Wheat Ale, a light ale made with Kansas-grown malted wheat is the most popular. But you can also try a Crimson Phog, a Rock Chalk Raspberry, or The Bitter Professor IPA, which honors three KU professors who frequent the brewery.

Llewellyn said menu items are generally spontaneous. There's nothing new planned at the moment, but there has been some discussion of a "One And Done" platter. That sounds like it would be best served with a side dish of national championship trophy.

62 Howard "Rope" Engleman

Basketball players at Kansas are held to a high standard today in large part because of some of the tremendous men who have come before them. One glance at the all-time roster makes that easy to understand. There are numerous examples of players who not only excelled on the court, but also contributed as citizens, businessmen, and with military service to our country.

Howard Engleman, who led KU in scoring in 1939 and 1941, met all that criteria and more, helping to establish that high standard. When Engleman died in 2011 at age 91, Jayhawk Nation felt a deep sense of loss. "Our entire KU family should feel so good and proud of the way he represented us for many years," KU coach Bill Self said.

Engleman, a six-footer, who went on to a 40-year career as an attorney in Salina, Kansas, led Kansas to two Big 6 conference championships and a trip to the Final Four in 1940. He was a consensus first team All-American in 1941 when his 16.1 points per game qualified as the highest average by a KU player to that date. And when Phog Allen was required to take a medical leave from coaching for half a season in 1947, Engleman filled in. Under his leadership the Jayhawks won eight games and lost six, finishing the season 16–11.

When Engleman's No. 5 jersey was retired on March 1, 2003, he had the Allen Fieldhouse crowd in stitches throughout his speech. In addition to his other talents, Engleman had a wonderful sense of humor and was a terrific storyteller. He said he had joked with coach Roy Williams that he was being honored for his coaching record as the man with the fewest losses as coach at Kansas. Engleman also speculated that he was joining Academic All-American Jacque Vaughn, saying he had a 4.0 grade point average like Vaughn. Engleman said he got one point for each year at Kansas—from freshman through senior seasons.

Between his playing days and that short coaching stint, Engleman served in the Navy and was navigation officer on the destroyer *USS England*. His daughter, Mary Engleman Kemmer of Wichita, wrote a biography for the Kansas athletic department, including the fact that the *England* "was credited with sinking six Japanese submarines in the South Pacific, the most of any destroyer in the war, before being sunk by a *kamikaze* suicide plane. Howard was badly injured, hospitalized, and received the Purple Heart. He was released from the Navy to attend law school under the G.I. Bill of Rights and while at KU Law School coached the KU freshman basketball team and was honored to be selected to lay the cornerstone for the KU Memorial Campanile."

What a thrill that must have been for the man who was nicknamed "Rope" for his blond, curly locks of hair. Under those curly locks was an intellect that earned him recognition as a "thinking man's basketball player."

Bill Mayer, longtime sportswriter for the *Lawrence Journal-World*, related one of Engleman's classic stories in a tribute written upon his death. Engleman claimed he coached before the smallest crowd in KU basketball history in 1947. There had been a flu epidemic in Columbia, Missouri, and the only people allowed in old Brewer Fieldhouse that day were the teams, officials, and MU football players who were there to make sure no fans slipped in. "We won the game [48–38], and I remember Otto Schnellbacher getting fouled. He stepped to the line, and an MU footballer [against whom two-sport star Schnellbacher had competed on the gridiron] yelled, 'Hey, Schnelly! Is that your nose or a banana you're eating?' Otto gave him the finger, spitefully made both free throws, and we won. But Otto wasn't out of line because there were no women in the hall."

63 Max Falkenstien

Sixty will always be Max Falkenstien's number. That's the number of years he spent behind the microphone calling University of Kansas basketball and football games. That's the number of years KU fans welcomed his recognizable voice into their living rooms, backyards, and on the car radio.

Sports fans appreciate reliability and familiarity with their favorite teams. Falkenstien was there for multiple generations of KU fans. His voice became comfortable and trusted like that of a close family member. That's why Jayhawks fans simply call him Max. "When Bob [Davis, his broadcast partner] and I were together," he said, "literally thousands of people told us night after night, week after week that 'Whenever a game is on television, we always turn the sound down and listen to you guys on the radio.'"

Maybe that's because Falkenstien is a Lawrence guy, who was born there on April 10, 1924. His first house was at 1332 Massachusetts Street. He went to Lawrence High School and graduated from KU with a degree in mathematics. Straight out of the service and World War II, Max started broadcasting KU games in 1946. He retired at the end of the 2005–06 basketball season, which was just two years shy of KU's third NCAA championship in basketball. But he was there for everything in between—the great, the good, and the disappointing moments in the history of KU athletics.

He handled every aspect of the broadcasting job. He was a play-by-play man, color analyst, storyteller, historian, and occasional singer. He vocalized *Kansas City*, *Way Down Yonder in New Orleans*, and *Georgia On My Mind* when the Jayhawks found their way to those Final Four locations. *Sporting News* named Falkenstien

"Best College Radio Personality in the Country" in 2001, and that seemed the perfect honor for him.

When Falkenstien received the Curt Gowdy Electronic Media Award from the Naismith Memorial Basketball Hall of Fame in September 2004, I asked him about his approach to broadcasting games. By the time he retired two seasons later, he had called roughly 650 football games and 1,750 basketball games. Included in that basketball total was every men's basketball game played at Allen Fieldhouse from the opener in 1955 to Senior Night in 2006. "My philosophy has always been to try to have fun in the broadcast and not take it all that seriously," Falkenstien said. "It's not the end of the world. It's not war. It's just a game."

The man has so many stories that he was able to fill two books, and I'm sure he had plenty left over. *Max and the Jayhawks* covers his first 50 years with KU sports, and *A Good Place To Stop: 60 Seasons with Max and the Jayhawks* puts a wrap on his career. Both are full of tales about the players and coaches he covered as well as their own comments and remembrances. "[The second book] should have been titled *A Bad Place to Stop*," he said. "Right after I quit, we not only won the Orange Bowl but the national basketball championship. Frankly, I would have liked to have still been on the air through 2008."

The first book includes a delightful section at the end called "Max Falkenstien Gallery of Memories" that includes his favorite places to eat in the old Big 8 and "Language Slips and Goofs." (Yes, even Falkenstien made a mistake or two on air.) "The friendships and relationships have been the treasure to it all," Falkenstien said.

Many of those friends and relations showed up for Senior Night on March 1, 2006, with no idea what they were about to witness. At halftime, Falkenstien sat at midcourt with members of his family and watched as his commemorative jersey dropped into place in the rafters. The sellout crowd of 16,300 gave him a standing ovation.

No. 60 took its place next to Nick Collison's No. 4. Falkenstien simply gushed. "As my good friend Larry Brown taught me to say, 'Gosh, this really is special,'" Falkenstien said. "I thought this day would never come, but since it has, I'm glad I was here to enjoy it."

64 Bob Davis

Max Falkenstien and Bob Davis formed a broadcasting partnership in 1984, and they've been having fun with Kansas fans ever since. Falkenstien spent 60 seasons calling Jayhawks basketball and football action until he retired after the 2005–06 season. Davis joined the Jayhawk Radio Network in 1984, taking over the play-by-play duties as Falkenstien moved to the analyst chair. Davis works with Greg Gurley now and just completed his 29th season with Kansas and his 45th season overall in the broadcast booth. Those are impressive numbers all the way around.

Through all those years, it is possible Max and Bob had a disagreement or two—but don't bet on it. They were a dynamic duo who enjoyed spending time with each other. One of Falkenstien's most famous sayings has always been, "Now, don't make me laugh." According to his writings, he has "implored governors, chancellors, athletic directors, coaches, athletes, and countless others not to tickle his funny bone once on the air." But he probably used that line the most on Davis.

"Davis has a great sense of humor," Falkenstien said. "He was always telling funny stories or going through some routine as we'd be driving to a game. And we'd get to laughing, like a couple of seven-year-old kids until I'd get hoarse from laughing. So, I'd say,

'Now don't start telling that story about so and so and don't start making me laugh. I'll be hoarse before the broadcast.'" Davis didn't let up often. "As [Max] has told me many times, fun is fun," Davis said.

Although Davis now is identified with the Jayhawks, he started out broadcasting Fort Hays State University sports from 1968 to 1984. He also was part of the Kansas City Royals broadcast team for 16 seasons. He worked play-by-play for the Royals on television with Royals Hall of Fame pitcher Paul Splittorff for 11 years. And Davis also worked the CBS Radio broadcasts of the NCAA women's Final Four in 1990, 1992, and 1994 through 1997.

Davis, at age 68, left the Royals on February 14, 2013. "I just felt I needed to spend more time at home," Davis told FOXSportsKansasCity.com. "I've had a good run with the Royals, but as you can imagine, doing both the Jayhawks and the Royals doesn't allow you much of an offseason." Davis also wanted more time to spend with his wife, Linda, who has Parkinson's disease. He has a son, Steven, who broadcasts games of the Royals' Double A affiliate in Northwest Arkansas and is also the voice of the UMKC basketball team.

Honored 13 times as Kansas Sportscaster of the Year, Davis is known for his dramatic and emotional style. Of course, his tenure at KU allowed him to call national titles in 1988 and 2008. One of the great pregame thrills at Allen Fieldhouse in recent years has been watching the highlight video before player introductions. Many of the biggest plays in Kansas history are now synched to the radio calls made by Davis, including the three-point shot by Mario Chalmers against Memphis in the 2008 national championship game: "Chalmers shoots…Whoa…A three. The game is tied…2.1…Memphis inbounding…A halfcourt shot. No good… Overtime! Overtime!"

65 How Phog Saved the Final Four

Phog Allen accomplished many things in his Hall of Fame career, but the Kansas coach may not get enough recognition for rescuing the basketball tournament that creates the hysteria now known as March Madness. Believe it or not, the NCAA tournament was not an instant success in 1939. When Oregon defeated Ohio State 46–33 in Evanston, Illinois, there was a chance the tournament that determined the national championship would not last past that first year. There was little to no advance publicity, and the event wasn't yet under the auspices of the NCAA.

The National Association of Basketball Coaches (NABC) had organized the first tournament, and many of those attending the championship game were coaches. The ticket was included in their membership dues. When all the receipts were counted, the tourney had lost $2,531. "That first year when Oregon beat Ohio State, we didn't know anything about [the tournament]," said Howard Engleman, who played for KU in 1939. "Oklahoma did. Oklahoma got the regional bid, and they got beat by Oregon [in the Western Regional finals]. But the [championship] game only drew 5,500 people or something like that."

Engleman had no idea that Allen had plans to turn things around the next year, but Engleman and his teammates ultimately became part of Allen's scheme. Allen was part promoter, part innovator, and part salesman in addition to his historic stature as a coach. He offered his own solution even as the NABC considered dropping the tournament. He approached officials at Municipal Auditorium in Kansas City, Missouri, and secured the building for the 1940 Western Regionals and the championship game.

How Phog Got His Name?

Phog Allen eventually became known as the "father of basketball coaching," but no one called him that. In fact it was rare that anyone referred to him by his given name—Forrest. Around KU and most of the basketball community, Allen was either Phog or Doc. After all, he was a doctor of osteopathy.

Phog? Where did that come from?

Sportswriter Ward Coble tagged Allen with that nickname in 1905 after he heard Allen umpiring a baseball game. When calling balls and strikes, Allen would bellow out the word "B-A-L-L" in a manner that reminded Coble of a foghorn. In his 1947 book, *Phog Allen's Sports Stories for You and Youth,* Allen wrote that the nickname was shortened to Fog "as a time saver." Later, Allen picked up a sports page to find the name spelled "Phog."

Allen contacted Coble and asked about the spelling change. "Oh," Coble said, "Fog was too plain. I thought I would doll it up a little." To that, Allen wrote, "Coble's nickname was 'Pinhead.'"

Maybe so, but let's extend some thanks to Coble. "Beware of the Forrest" never would have intimidated an opponent inside the Allen Fieldhouse.

He repeatedly issued his personal assurance of success. Allen had organized other tournaments in Kansas City, including the 1936 Olympic playoffs and never failed financially.

This time Allen vowed not only to pay back the deficit, but also to make money.

"They lose money on it, and he convinces them to move it to Kansas City," said Allen's grandson, Mark J. Allen, a doctor in Kansas City. "I think he said, 'We'll sell tickets for a dollar and we'll make money.'"

There was no sponsor or broadcast contract, and the NABC had no funds to handle the debt from the 1939 championship. No one wanted to interrupt the momentum basketball was gaining on a national stage, and the NABC ultimately asked for a bailout. The NCAA agreed to a loan to pay the debt. In return the NABC turned over the responsibility of future championships to the NCAA.

But the Jayhawks still had to do their part. Oklahoma appeared to be the team to beat in the Big 6 in 1939–40, but Allen knew his players would derive incentive from the fact the tournament was moving to nearby Kansas City. In his annual summer letter to his players, Phog made them aware. "In order to get there, we had to beat Oklahoma in a three-way playoff in Wichita and then beat Oklahoma A&M on a neutral court," Engleman said.

Kansas tied Oklahoma and Missouri for the Big 6 title. After a coin flip, the Sooners beat Missouri for the right to play Kansas. The Jayhawks won that game in Wichita and then edged Oklahoma A&M (now Oklahoma State) 45–43 in a district playoff in Oklahoma City. A release from the American Press Syndicate predicted the greatest crowds ever for a sporting event in Municipal Auditorium. "Two weeks ago sports experts predicted that the tournament would draw great crowds," the release said. "But when the University of Kansas came through victorious in its playoffs… then the weekend of play was termed a natural."

Kansas beat Rice and then edged Southern California 43–42 to advance to the national championship game against Indiana. The Hurryin' Hoosiers, coached by Branch McCracken, had defeated Springfield (Massachusetts) and Duquesne in the Eastern Regionals. "They beat the hell out of us [60–42]," Engleman said. "We got off to a nice 10–4 lead, and the next thing I knew, we were behind so far we could never catch them. They ran the fast break good. To get there, they beat Duquesne [39–30] and here they were running up 60 points on us."

The Jayhawks and their fans obviously were disappointed. But the most important number of the night was 10,000. That was the attendance for the championship game, though the demand may have been three times that total once the Jayhawks qualified. Total attendance for the tournament's five sessions was 36,880—an improvement of more than 21,000 from the year before. "The tournament was looking for both acceptance and financial stability in 1940," wrote Joe McGuff of *The Kansas City Star*. "It found both in Kansas City…The tournament, which even turned a profit of $9,523, had taken its first steps toward becoming one of the nation's greatest sporting events."

66 Phog's WWII Letters

War impacts a college campus in many ways. Young lives are the common denominator in both, and during World War II, the overlap was especially common, very intense, and often tragic. It was a very different world in the 1940s. Imagine our top college athletes inducted into the service or heading off to war instead of the NBA.

KU's top players in 1943—athletes like Ray Evans, Charlie Black, and Otto Schnellbacher—were called into service. Kansas coach Phog Allen was extremely patriotic and also deeply loyal to the athletes at KU. He served as secretary of the Douglas County Selective Service Board, chairman of the County Red Cross War Fund Drive and chairman for other various bond drives. He saw to it that basketball and baseball uniforms and other equipment were donated when nearby Fort Leavenworth made requests. Allen did something that coaches today wouldn't even consider. He wrote letters—a lot of long ones. He wrote about basketball, rules, and tournaments. He wrote about his ideas and dreams. He wrote to his players about conditioning, preparation, schedules, and recruiting.

In the summer of 1943, he used his typewriter to produce newsletters called *Jayhawk Rebounds*, a series of 18 communications

Phog Allen, watching his team during a 1953 game against Tulane, wrote and distributed a newsletter to stay in contact with his Kansas players in the armed forces.

with his players, alumni, and friends in the armed forces. He kept them updated on KU sports news and other matters he found important. He reprinted replies and developed a mailing list of several hundred by 1945.

The most compelling of these letters had to be the 11th edition, written on September 12, 1944. That's when Allen passed on the emotional news of the death of Marine Lieutenant T.P. "Teep" Hunter, a letter winner for the Jayhawks from 1940–42. Hunter had been part of the 1939–40 team that Phog called "The Pony Express." He came to KU from a broken home and become one of Allen's favorite students.

The first three pages of that 17-page edition were devoted to Hunter, and it started this way: "Somehow this is the most diffi-cult letter that I have ever attempted to write. Over a dozen times, I have begun it and each time I have walked away from my desk because words fail me. I feel such a void. Something has gone from me. Your friend and mine—good, old honest 'Teep,' T.P. Hunter [1st Lt. 9th Marines], was killed on Guam, July 21, 1944. And yet this morning he feels closer to me than at any moment that I have known him. Across the miles that span Lawrence and Guam, it seems so trivial. This thing we call death has brought him closer to me at this very moment than he has been for years.

"The glories of his life are magnified a hundredfold. A Chinese philosopher once said, 'Life seems so unreal at times that I do not know whether I am living dreams or dreaming life.' The life here and the life hereafter seem so much a part of all of us that T.P.'s presence is manifest. He will live forever in our hearts. What more love can a man have that he lay down his life for his friend? He did that."

67 Bob Dole

After the Jayhawks won the national championship in 2008, coach Bill Self, his staff, and the KU players visited the White House and met President George W. Bush. It was assistant coach Danny Manning's second visit to the White House. Back in 1988 the Most Outstanding Player of the Final Four presented President Ronald Reagan with his own Kansas national championship jacket.

Visiting the White House and meeting the president is cool stuff. But there was a former Kansas basketball player who had a chance to become president of the United States. That's right. A Jayhawk almost sat in the oval office. How cool it would have been if the 1997 Jayhawks with Jacque Vaughn, Scot Pollard, Jerod Haase, Paul Pierce, and Raef LaFrentz had gone to the White House to meet President Bob Dole?

That ultimate Kansas moment never happened for two reasons. Dole lost the 1996 presidential election to Bill Clinton, and that Kansas squad lost the NCAA Southeast Regional semifinal to Arizona, a heartbreaking finish to a 34–2 season.

Robert Joseph "Bob" Dole, the pride of Russell, Kansas, was a prominent member of the U.S. Senate from 1969 to 1996. He was the Republican nominee for president in 1996. And he was one of 24 players on the roster of Phog Allen's "Ever-Victorious" team that won the Big 6 championship in 1943. The 1943 team photo shows Dole wearing jersey No. 6, standing two spots from Allen.

Phog had heard of Dole's athletic ability from his son, Mitt, who played on an amateur basketball team in Russell. Phog invited Dole to the 1940 Kansas Relays, one of the nation's top track meets that always served as a recruiting tool for Allen. Dole played freshman football and basketball and dressed for a preseason exhibition basketball game as a sophomore. But when the travel roster was posted for a December 11 game in Kansas City, Dole didn't make the cut.

There was promise for Dole as a Kansas athlete his junior year, but his grades had slipped in the spring of 1943. He had enlisted in the Army in December 1942 and was called into active duty on June 1, 1943. During an April 1945 offensive in Italy, Dole was hit by German machine gun fire in his upper right back. His right arm was badly injured, leaving him handicapped and unable to continue an athletic career. Dole received two Purple Hearts for his injuries and also was decorated with the Bronze Star. When he returned home, he spent six months hospitalized in Topeka. Phog Allen and longtime KU trainer Dean Nesmith were among his first visitors.

It may not have been much of a playing career, but Phog Allen clearly impacted Dole's life. Dole remembered that hospital visit in a September 19, 1974 congressional record tribute to Phog upon his death: "He cleared up many things and helped me get a better perspective on what was ahead. He convinced me there was more to life than football and basketball—a large lesson for a young man with expectations like those I entertained before the war—and he helped me realize that there could be other challenges and other rewards in my future. I felt an immediate sense of personal loss when I learned of his death Monday. I shall always be in his debt."

And Kansans have always been in debt to Bob Dole for a lifetime of service to his country—both as a soldier and as a senator. When President Clinton gave a speech at Allen Fieldhouse in May 2004, Dole was there to greet him and show him around the famous gym. Jayhawks Aaron Miles and Keith Langford presented the two politicians with KU jerseys bearing the No. 1 and their names on the back. Clinton's jersey was blue with red trim. Dole's was white with blue trim.

And there was an April 1997 meeting between Dole and Jayhawks of all types. The event was called "A Tribute to Bob Dole," and he announced he was donating all of his papers to a remarkable building known as the Bob Dole Institute of Politics on KU's West Campus.

68 Ralph Miller

Phog Allen had many prized pupils in his basketball classroom. Adolph Rupp and Dean Smith, who went on to enjoy their own coaching greatness at Kentucky and North Carolina, get most of the attention. But Ralph Miller should not be overlooked.

After going to college at KU, Miller went on to coach college basketball from 1951–89, splitting his time between Wichita State, Iowa, and Oregon State. He retired from Oregon State in 1989 after posting a career record of 674–370. Those wins were the most by any active coach at that time and ranked seventh all time behind Rupp (876), Hank Iba (767), Ed Diddle (759), Allen (746), Ray Meyer (724), and John Wooden (664).

Miller is one of 17 former Jayhawks in the Naismith Basketball Hall of Fame in Springfield, Massachusetts. He was inducted in May 1988 after being named Associated Press Coach of the Year in 1981 and 1982. The Chanute, Kansas, native was a starter for Allen on KU's 1940 NCAA tournament runner-up team, the squad that Allen referred to as "The Pony Express" and included Dick Harp, Bob Allen, and Howard Engleman.

At Chanute High School, Miller displayed his tremendous athleticism and won letters in football, track, basketball, golf, and tennis. He was an All-State basketball player for three years. Bob

Allen, Phog's son, actually scrimmaged against Miller in junior high and reported back to his father that Miller was the best player he had ever seen.

Phog and Stanford coach John Bunn, another former KU player under Allen, actually became embroiled in a significant recruiting battle over Miller—despite the fact Allen had used his osteopathic skills to help Miller through a hip injury at the state tournament in Topeka. When Miller was injured in the first half, Allen, a doctor, was summoned to examine his hip. Allen treated him, Miller scored 26 points in the second half, and Chanute won the state championship. "I knew many schools were angling for Miller's services, but I did not use my advantage to endeavor to entice him to KU," Allen wrote in 1937.

Despite word from Miller's father that he would attend KU, Miller actually changed his mind and decided to attend Stanford. According to Blair Kerkhoff, author of *Phog Allen, The Father of Basketball Coaching*, Miller was initially convinced when a Stanford alum from Wichita flew Miller out for a visit and then promised to take care of Miller's tuition and books.

Phog and Bob Allen changed Miller's mind again during a drive back to Kansas from an All-Star football game in Chicago. Bunn had been in Chanute for two days, waiting to drive Miller back to California. Kerkhoff wrote that the friendship between Phog and Bunn, who played at KU from 1918–20, was "tested" on the front porch of Miller's house. "I own a farm in Kansas and pay taxes," Bunn, a native of Humboldt, Kansas, told the *Topeka Daily Capital*. "Why shouldn't I have a few Kansas boys?"

Kansas hasn't seen many athletes like Miller. He was a star for the Jayhawks in football (as the starting quarterback) and basketball, earning three letters in both sports. And don't feel too bad for Bunn. He coached 42 years and then was a member of the NCAA rules committee. He was inducted into the Basketball Hall of Fame in 1964.

69 Coach Brown vs. Coach Manning

Before Kansas could arrive in New Orleans for Final Four week in 2012, word leaked out that assistant coach Danny Manning had agreed to become the next head coach at Tulsa. After nine years on Bill Self's staff, KU's all-time leading scorer and rebounder was getting his chance to be a head coach. That came as no surprise. As a highly respected assistant coach, it was only a matter of time before Manning got that chance.

A slightly bigger surprise came about three weeks later when Manning's coach at Kansas, 71-year-old Larry Brown, decided to return to coaching at Southern Methodist. After such a long relationship, student and mentor were brought together again as head coaches in the same conference—Conference USA. Facing off as opponents wasn't either man's idea of a good time, but Manning's Golden Hurricane won at SMU 48–47, and SMU returned the favor at Tulsa 71–65 in the rematch. "We split, so I guess it ended up being okay," Manning said.

About a half dozen former Jayhawks were in attendance at the first game in Dallas, the city where Brown and Manning represented KU in the 1986 Final Four. "It was a lot of fun," Manning said. "Whenever you're able to get together and enjoy each other's company, talk about your kids, different things that are going on, the experience we had, and how it impacted your life, it's pretty cool. It's very hard to believe [25 years have gone by]."

The one-point loss in the first game made it hard on Brown, and going against Manning was even more difficult. "Then you look at the way the game ended, it's a terrible feeling," Brown said. "I'm happy for Danny. I didn't like the idea of playing against him. Once the game went on, I wasn't thinking about

Danny. I think we were thinking about our team and how we could win the game."

The former Jayhawks had a quick reunion with Brown outside the locker room after the game. "We're all pulling for Danny because he's the underdog in a sense," said Milt Newton, a starting guard on the 1988 team and now vice president of player personnel with the Washington Wizards, to The Associated Press. "At the end of the day, we can't lose because if coach wins, that's our coach, and if Danny wins, that's our teammate."

The Mustangs struggled to a 15–17 record (5–11 in C-USA) in Brown's first season, but he put together one of the top recruiting classes in the nation. Manning was 17–16 (8–8 in conference) in his first season as a head coach. "I enjoyed it. It was a lot of fun," Manning said. "The kids bought into our system, and they played extremely hard for us. Obviously we need to get better and we will. But we got our foundation down and we're moving in the right direction."

Brown was attracted to the SMU job, in part, by the prospect of joining the Big East Conference. But with the split of the Big East, SMU joined the American Athletic Conference in July of 2013. That, though, doesn't mean the meetings between Brown and Manning are over. Tulsa joins the AAC in 2014.

70 Turgeon and Boyle: A Tale of Two Point Guards

You can come home again. You really can. It's just not that easy for former Jayhawks required to sit on the opposing bench at Allen Fieldhouse—especially that first time. "I was excited. I really love being in this building and I wasn't really emotional at all," Mark

Turgeon told *The Topeka Capital-Journal* in January 2009 when he was coach at Texas A&M. "When I walked in for shootaround, I got a little emotional then."

Colorado coach Tad Boyle endured a similar experience. "What's neat about coming back to a place like this where you spent four years of your life is all the memories," Boyle told the *Lawrence Journal-World* in December 2012. "[The Fieldhouse] does look the same—absolutely. They've still got the bleachers. The colors are the same, still got the same chairbacks, still got that clock. I remember playing for Coach [Larry] Brown. When he would say, 'One more time, guys, one more rep,' that meant another half hour. You looked right up there at the clock."

This is a tale of two former Kansas point guards, two former teammates, two Jayhawks who have gone on to successful coaching careers in college basketball. That is what brought them back to the enemy bench. Boyle wore the Kansas uniform from 1981 to 1985, playing two seasons for Ted Owens and two more for Larry Brown. Turgeon arrived in 1983, Brown's first season after replacing Owens as KU's coach. Now Boyle is head coach at Colorado, giving the Buffaloes an infusion of winning seasons that has attracted some fresh Top 25 attention. And Turgeon is continuing the basketball tradition at Maryland, his latest step as he climbs the coaching ladder.

They were teammates for two years and then reunited on the coaching staffs at Oregon, Jacksonville State, and Wichita State. Boyle was Turgeon's assistant at Wichita State for six years. When the Colorado job came open in 2010, Turgeon gave his endorsement and support. Mike Bohn, a 1983 Kansas graduate who was Colorado athletic director at the time, hired Boyle. "Quite frankly, [Mark and I] weren't real close as teammates at Kansas," Boyle said. "We certainly liked each other, had a mutual respect for each other. But it's not like we hung out together. Our relationship really grew after I graduated and Mark got done playing. It was one of those friendships that just kind of evolved."

Boyle, who was 6'4" when he joined the Jayhawks, played behind Turgeon and Cedric Hunter. Turgeon, a 5'10" guard out of Topeka Hayden High, was the first KU player to play in four consecutive NCAA tournaments and remains among the all-time leaders in career assists at Kansas with 437. But he decided coaching should become his career path when Brown called him in one day and told him he had no future in the NBA.

After graduating in 1985, Boyle worked nine years as a stockbroker before returning to the game as a high school coach. Said Boyle: "When I got into coaching, Coach Brown's exact words to me were, 'Tad, make sure that your teams defend and rebound every night, and if you do that, you give yourself a chance to win.' And he's exactly right."

71 Ted Owens Relives the 1971 Final Four

For most Final Four fans streaming into Houston's Reliant Stadium in April 2011, the building across the parking lot was a novelty, a shrine to domed stadiums and that artificial surface known as AstroTurf. Perhaps younger fans didn't even know about the facility known as the Astrodome. Older fans may have thought a wrecking ball had long ago destroyed the evidence and didn't realize this wonder of the world was still standing.

But former Kansas coach Ted Owens took one look at the site of the 1971 Final Four and was overcome by memories. With Owens guiding the way, Dave Robisch, Bud Stallworth, Roger Brown, Pierre Russell, Aubrey Nash, and the rest of the Jayhawks traveled to Houston that year with a 27–1 record. Kansas lost to UCLA in a national semifinal and then fell to Western Kentucky in the consolation round that is no longer a part of the Final Four experience.

It was the first of two Final Four appearances for Owens at KU. And even though he never won a national championship, Owens takes great pride in those Final Four teams and the players who produced so many victories. It made the 2011 Final Four in Houston an emotional experience for him. "That was the 40th anniversary of that [1971 team], and it brought back a lot of memories," Owens said. "When I was outside the Astrodome on the way over to the game, I was so moved by it that I called a couple of our players, and we talked about those times. I talked to Bud and I talked to Robo. I had both of their phone numbers. I would have called them all if I had had their numbers with me."

When Owens talks to those players, there are wonderful basketball memories to share. But the off-the-court experiences may have been even more moving. Owens was in charge of the Kansas basketball program during perhaps the most turbulent time in campus history. The late '60s and early '70s were a period that featured racial unrest, protests of the Vietnam War, campus shootings, and demonstrations.

That team that reached the 1971 Final Four is remembered not only for winning, but also for unifying a campus that had come unhinged. Political activist Abbie Hoffman spoke at Allen Fieldhouse in April 1970, and 12 days later an arsonist's firebomb caused nearly $1 million damage to the Kansas Union. Owens remembers Dan Rather of CBS News and other national reporters descending on the Lawrence campus. In July 1970, two KU students were killed in separate shooting incidents. "That team in '71 really brought the campus together," Owens said. "The players had such a great love for another. They demonstrated to the campus that people of all colors could work together. The year before [KU] had eliminated final exams and sent everybody home because things were so bad. They emptied the campus. We had two shooting incidents that resulted in deaths on campus. The National Guard had to come in, and it was a rough time. We had a recruit in, and the National Guard had to take over the campus. There was a curfew, and we lost the kid."

Chancellor E. Laurence Chalmers told Owens that the team gave the student body something to rally around. The tension could be felt every day. Owens was a member of Lawrence's human relations commission and understood all the issues. He chose not to make it a topic of discussion with the team. "That team had a special friendship and trust, and their success just set a great example," Owens said. "Pierre and a bunch of the guys were up at the Student Union trying to put out the fire."

It required a special type of coach to keep his team focused with so many distractions. Owens was a great fit. It also demanded attention to strange details in other areas, especially recruiting. "I had calls from parents, worried about the campus," Owens said. "I had calls all the time. And it just [destroyed] recruiting. When two people are killed, there's obviously some danger. I just tried to let them know the authorities were in control. The National Guard came in and handled it very well."

Owens occupied the chair of head basketball coach at KU from 1964–83. His 19-year tenure as coach is second longest in school history, trailing only the 39-year stint recorded by the legendary Phog Allen. With a record of 348–182 (.657), Owens ranks third in victories at Kansas behind Allen and Roy Williams.

That 1971 Final Four was significant in NCAA history because it was the first one in a domed stadium. The championship game between UCLA and Villanova was played before a crowd of 31,765, and total attendance for the tournament soared over 200,000 for the first time. Because of the seating configuration, the court was raised higher over the regular floor. "They tried to build our bench up," Owens said. "Today coaches walk the sidelines. We would have had hernia problems getting off our bench to the court.

Pierre Russell was notorious for diving for loose balls. The drop-off at Allen Fieldhouse was only a few inches. We get to Houston, and the drop-off was about eight feet. Even as gutty as Pierre was, he wasn't going after a loose ball there."

The Jayhawks fell behind by 13, rallied to tie the game at 39, but then lost their momentum when a traveling call against Robisch negated the go-ahead basket. Henry Bibby and Sidney Wicks led UCLA to victory. The 77–75 loss to Western Kentucky in the consolation game ended KU's terrific season with a 27–3 record.

72 John McLendon

The 1979 enshrinement ceremony at the Naismith Memorial Basketball Hall of Fame in Springfield, Massachusetts, was a great day for Kansas basketball. Jayhawks great Wilt Chamberlain was the star of that Hall of Fame class along with legendary coaches Pete Newell and Ray Meyer. Coach John McLendon, from Hiawatha, Kansas, and the first African American college coach elected to the Hall of Fame, was in that class, too. McLendon didn't play at Kansas or coach at Kansas, but he was the first African American to graduate from KU with a bachelors' degree in physical education in 1936.

McLendon's accomplishments in coaching were beyond significant. He was the first coach in history to win three consecutive national championships. Those NAIA titles came at Tennessee State from 1957–59. His Hall of Fame biography lauds him as a "spokesman for heightened awareness of basketball at all-black colleges" and credits him with initiating "an era of integrated basketball."

His direct ties to Dr. James Naismith gave added meaning to his enshrinement. Naismith mentored McLendon at Kansas—not just in basketball and physical education activities—but also in life. And before McLendon died in 1999, he made it clear how much Naismith meant to him. "Dr. Naismith taught me far more than was found in textbooks," McLendon wrote in an essay for *The Kansas Century: 100 Years of Jayhawk Championship Basketball.* "Very often he would put aside his books and teach us lessons in life from his world experiences."

McLendon's father told him he would encounter problems as a black student at KU in 1933. He also told him, according to that essay, to find Naismith and "tell him that he's to be your adviser." When McLendon did that, Naismith wanted to know who told him that. "My father," McLendon said.

"Fathers are always right," Naismith replied.

Naismith came to Lawrence in 1898 and stayed until his death in 1939, but he almost left town in 1933 because of the level of racism on the campus. That racism was brought to light by McLendon's presence and the swimming pool at Robinson Gymnasium, a whites-only bastion in 1933. Swimming was an important part of the physical education curriculum, but the school offered to waive the requirements for McLendon, a former life-guard. Black students were given an automatic A, but McLendon would not accept the grade without doing the work.

The details of the incident are described by Milton S. Katz in his book *Breaking Through: John B. McLendon, Basketball Legend and Civil Rights Pioneer.* McLendon went to take a swimming test one day, and the pool had been drained. The attendant told him the pool was drained every Wednesday, but McLendon knew that wasn't true. McLendon told the attendant, "He was going to have a big water bill because I was going swimming every day." He came back the next day. The pool was drained, and McLendon was told not to return.

But he went back with white classmates from the P.E. department who swam with him in support. Naismith sent football players to guard the pool. Racist signs started to appear around campus. McLendon gathered the signs, and Naismith took them to the chancellor and president at KU. Naismith told them that the next sign he saw would lead to his resignation. "He deplored any form of discrimination, segregation, or prejudice, and helped me to surmount glaring institutional discriminatory practices during my junior and senior years," McLendon wrote in his essay. "There's no question that my life would not have been anywhere near what it has become if I had not met Dr. Naismith. He never looked at life as black and white. One thing he taught me in the adjustment to adversity is that no matter what kind of problem you had, never let it defeat you."

McLendon was a true pioneer. When hired at Cleveland State in 1966, he became the first African American basketball coach at a predominantly white university. George Steinbrenner hired him as head coach of the Cleveland Pipers of the American Basketball League in 1961, making him the first African American head coach in pro basketball. In 1958, McLendon was named NAIA National Coach of the Year. He retired in 1969 with a 25-year college coaching record of 523–165. His teams, according to his Hall of Fame bio, "featured superior conditioning, a patented fast break offense, and an aggressive in-your-face defensive attitude." All of that was a reflection of Naismith's philosophy.

In 1979 the KU administration awarded McLendon a citation of merit for "integration of swimming and swimming pool programs at the University of Kansas."

That was the same year McLendon entered the Basketball Hall of Fame. And by that time, he had accomplished so much, in great part because he followed his father's advice on that first trip to KU and pursued the mentoring of Dr. Naismith.

73 LaVannes Squires

When Wilt Chamberlain was being recruited out of high school in Philadelphia, he made it clear he wanted to experience life away from home and avoid the segregated South. He also wanted to play basketball at the highest level and for the best coach. Kansas met all of Chamberlain's qualifications, but it's only fair to wonder if Chamberlain would have become a Jayhawk if not for LaVannes Squires. That player never started a game for Kansas, but his impact was immeasurable.

By the time Chamberlain became the object of Phog Allen's desire in 1952, the Kansas coach had already unknowingly laid the groundwork for Wilt by integrating his team in 1951. That's when he accepted Squires of Wichita onto his Kansas roster. The color line in the Big 7 Conference had been broken in 1949 with Kansas State football player Harold Robinson, but Chamberlain had made it clear he didn't want to be the first black player in the program he chose. A big supporter of the Olympics and a fan of Jesse Owens, Allen had struggled with the issue of integrating athletics for years.

Yet future Hall of Fame basketball coach John McLendon was a KU student around Owens' time and did not play on Allen's team. "It was Dr. Allen's job to resist integration then," McLendon said in Blair Kerkhoff's book *Phog Allen: The Father of Basketball Coaching*. "He was the AD, and the whole school knew it was an area where he'd be challenged. He practically apologized to me. But as quickly as he could, he got black players on his team."

Jerry Waugh, who played for Allen from 1948–51, remembers the team voting against integration in either 1947 or 1948. In a way Allen encouraged his players to vote that way. He explained the difficulties an African American player would encounter at that time and in that society. "He didn't do it in a biased way," Waugh said. "He said we were going to have problems traveling because black people aren't accepted in certain places particularly in the South. No one was going to stand up and tell Doc that was wrong."

There are photos of Squires with the 1952 national championship team, but he did not travel that season. The son of Arthur and Charlotte Squires, he was born in Hartdale, Missouri, the eighth of 12 children. Arthur died when LaVannes was three. His mother was only educated through the fifth grade, but she became his role model due to her hard work ethic. Squires became the first in his family to attend college. Small but a good athlete, he became the captain of the basketball team at Wichita East, playing guard and forward for former KU player and future Hall of Famer Ralph Miller. At KU he played guard and earned the respect of Allen, who said he had "a lot of fire, enthusiasm, and ability."

Of course race relations were still extremely tense at the time of Squires' debut, and Lawrence was not exactly a liberal hotbed at the time. When Allen first inserted Squires into a game, many KU fans walked out of Hoch Auditorium in a huff.

Maurice King, a 6'2" guard who would be Chamberlain's teammate in 1956–57, became the first African American starter for a Big 7 team. By the time Chamberlain arrived at KU, Squires and King had set the stage and absorbed much of the negativity.

74 Pay Your Respects to Dr. Naismith and Phog

Two things you need to understand about former Kansas coach Roy Williams: He was enthusiastic about his daily runs during his 15 years in Lawrence and he is a very superstitious man. Put those together, and Williams arrived at a unique ritual—one that no other college basketball coach could entertain the thought of matching. As part of his daily run, Williams would head east along 15th Street to Lawrence Memorial Park Cemetery, where Dr. James Naismith is buried. Across the street is Oak Hill Cemetery, the final resting place of Phog Allen.

That's right. The inventor of basketball and the Kansas basketball coaching legend are buried across the street from one another. It could only happen in Lawrence. On gamedays Williams and his staff would often stop at both locations. "We'd make sure we tapped the headstone and then said, 'We need some luck tonight,'" Williams said. "When you can go to the founder of the game and the father of basketball coaching…I'm a little wacko, and I try things like that. We won a lot of games when I patted those tombstones."

Memorial Park Cemetery is at 1517 E. 15th Street. A simple stone marks Naismith's burial place, but a monument near the entrance includes a short biography and an engraved portrait of the game's inventor with a basketball in his right hand and books in his left. Under the biography is a Jayhawk logo. "In 1898 he accepted a position at the University of Kansas," the bio states. "His goal was to develop the University's Physical Education Department. He also agreed to accept the coaching position of KU's first basketball team." True to form, the idea of coaching basketball was secondary in detailing Naismith's life.

Oak Hill Cemetery is off 15th Street at 1605 Oak Hill Avenue. There is a plot with a large stone simply bearing the "ALLEN" name. In front of that are smaller markers, including one that reads, "Forrest C. "Phog" Allen, Nov. 18, 1885–Sept. 16, 1974, Treasured Husband, Father, Friend."

No mention of basketball.

People do not line up to visit either gravesite. Some basketball fans consider showing their respects to Naismith among their bucket list and have posted YouTube videos proving they were there. In 2003, *Sports Illustrated On Campus* compiled a cover story list of "100 Things You Gotta Do Before You Graduate (Whatever The Cost)." No. 64 was "Pay homage to the man who gave us basketball by visiting the grave of Dr. James Naismith in Lawrence." But for the most part, showing respect to the inventor and the coach can be done in privacy.

Rebecca Phipps, director of the Watkins Community Museum of History, told the *Lawrence Journal-World* in 2003 that more should be done to celebrate Naismith's accomplishments. "Basketball is a worldwide event," Phipps said. "We need to make an awareness of it by continuing to emphasize that the man, who invented the game, lived and died here."

75 Wilt's Speech

He showed up wearing his Kansas letter jacket. That simple gesture made everyone in Allen Fieldhouse feel so much better.

Wilt Chamberlain—without a doubt the greatest Jayhawk of them all—returned to Lawrence on January 17, 1998, to see his No. 13 game jersey officially retired by the university. It was part of the 100th anniversary celebration of basketball at KU, and you might say it was the icing on the cake.

The Big Dipper had not been back to Lawrence since the 1970s. Every effort to get him back had failed. Only those closest to him realized that he had stayed away because he still blamed himself for the triple-overtime loss to North Carolina in the 1957 NCAA championship game. That's a long time to carry a heavy burden inside.

But in a brief halftime ceremony during a game against Kansas State, the fans at Allen Fieldhouse seemed to wrap their arms around Chamberlain to give him a hug. In return Chamberlain gave an emotional speech that will forever be one of the highlights in the building's history. Standing there in his well-preserved letter jacket, Chamberlain finished his speech with three words. "Rock Chalk Jayhawk," he said in his magnificent deep, booming voice. It triggered a thunderous round of applause. Fans wiped away tears.

To everyone's surprise, Chamberlain spent over an hour at a press conference, then took time for some one-on-one interviews. Coach Roy Williams asked him to stop by practice to talk to the team. The KU players were reportedly awestruck, and that's easy to understand. Chamberlain could command a room just by walking through the doors.

Kansas beat Kansas State that day 69–62. At KU, things often happen that defy explanation. Paul Pierce scored exactly 11 points that day to tie Chamberlain for 12th on the all-time scoring list at Kansas. Chamberlain reached that point total in just 48 games, and it took Pierce 93.

After the game, Chamberlain pulled up a folding chair and sat at a table signing autographs for fans for more than two hours. Just before he left town, Chamberlain told athletic director Bob Frederick and former KU teammate Monte Johnson that it was one of the most meaningful days of his life. Chamberlain made the trip despite enormous health problems afflicting his heart and his

Scoring two of his 42 points during his freshman team's 81–71 victory against the KU varsity squad in 1955, Wilt Chamberlain would return to Kansas in 1998 to have his No. 13 jersey retired.

hip. His sister, Barbara, later told KU officials he had no business making the trip. Wilt died less than two years later, on October 12, 1999. Those who love Kansas basketball are forever grateful he traveled back to Lawrence one last time.

If you've never seen Wilt's speech, check it out on YouTube. It's worth a viewing. These are the words Wilt spoke:

> A little over 40 years ago, I lost the toughest battle in sports in losing to the North Carolina Tar Heels by one point in triple-overtime [of the national championship]. It was a devastating thing to me because I let the University of Kansas down and my teammates down.
>
> But when I come back here today and realize not a simple loss of a game, but how many people have shown such appreciation and warmth, I'm humbled and deeply honored. I've learned in life that you have to take the bitter with the sweet, and how sweet this is, right here! I'm a Jayhawk and I know now why there is so much tradition here and why so many wonderful things have come from here. And I am now very much a part of it by being there [pointing to his retired jersey in the rafters] and very proud of it.
>
> Rock Chalk Jayhawk.

76 The 1922 and 1923 National Champions

The national championship banners hanging in Allen Fieldhouse include two that were not products of the NCAA tournament, which began in 1939. In 1936, the Helms Athletic Foundation in Los Angeles put together a group of experts charged with the task of choosing national champions in college basketball, retroactively to 1901.

Phog Allen's Jayhawk teams got the nod in 1922 and 1923. Thus, those are the first two of five banners displayed in the fieldhouse named for Allen. The players on those two teams were some of the brightest stars of the early period of Kansas basketball, including Paul Endacott, Charlie Black, and Tus Ackerman. Future Kentucky coach Adolph Rupp was a member of both teams, but he played limited minutes.

Those two banners are as special to Kansas history as the NCAA titles from 1952, 1988, and 2008, and they reflect two other important ingredients in the recipe for basketball tradition at KU. First, conference championships have always been important to Kansas coaches. It had been stressed from Allen to Bill Self. Second, the 1923 championship may have saved Phog's coaching career.

It certainly didn't hurt Allen's cause that the primary opposition in 1922 and 1923 was Missouri. It's hard to believe—given what we know now about Allen—but Phog envied Coach Walter Meanwell's success in Columbia. Missouri had become the team to beat in the Missouri Valley Conference, and the Jayhawks had gone six years without a conference title. After Allen came back for his second tour with Kansas, he lost his first nine games to Missouri, including four to Meanwell. To top it off, Meanwell was flamboyant, had five nicknames (including Doc and the Wizard), and eventually wrote a book called *The Science of Basketball*.

Meanwell didn't stay long. He was back coaching at Wisconsin and had been replaced by Craig Ruby by 1921. Missouri was undefeated in 1922 and appeared headed to a third straight outright title before the Jayhawks visited Columbia on February 21. The Jayhawks were forced to play without starting forward Armin

Woestermeyer, who learned at 5 PM on the day of the game that he was academically ineligible for the final four games of the season.

Forward George Rody scored 12 points, and center "Long John" Wulf provided the defense as KU upset the Tigers 26–16. It was Phog's first win against his rivals. The two teams shared the Missouri Valley title at 15–1, but KU's 16–2 overall record, combined with the late-season win over Missouri, proved to be the tiebreaker for the Helms Foundation—when it got around to voting more than a decade later.

The Jayhawks were loaded the next season. Endacott was back from the previous team, and Allen added freshman Tus Ackerman, also from Lawrence. Ackerman would be the leading scorer in 1923 and then a first team All-American in 1924. He captained the 1925 team and averaged 10.2 points a game.

Charlie T. Black—not to be confused with Charlie B. Black from the 1940s—played intense defense, was a two-time all-conference and All-America selection, and helped KU compile a 49–6 record from 1922–24. Endacott was the 1923 Player of the Year and a two-time All-American. All three have had their jerseys retired by the Jayhawks.

Allen didn't want to share the conference championship again. He was ready to reverse the dominance enjoyed by Missouri and direct the Jayhawks back to the top. He put together a vigorous training program and held intense practices with the intent of climbing into first place—alone.

The two games against Missouri in 1923 meant everything to Allen and the Jayhawks. The first on January 16 was in Columbia. Coming off three games in three in nights in Iowa, the Jayhawks embarked on what would become an arduous, two-day journey to Columbia. There was an overnight stay in Sedalia, Missouri, a train to Columbia that never showed, altered breakfast plans, another train that broke down, and a six-mile hike before the final three miles were completed in a truck.

Allen still managed to have his team ready to go. Ackerman scored 11 points as KU went back to Lawrence after a 21–19 victory. More than a month later, on February 28, the Tigers played at KU. Ackerman again was KU's leading scorer with seven points as the Jayhawks won 23–20 before a record crowd of 3,000. Reportedly 2,000 more were turned away from the doors at Robinson Gym.

For the first time, Kansas had recorded a perfect record in conference play. The Jayhawks were 16–0 in the Missouri Valley and 17–1 overall. The Helms Foundation eventually awarded another national championship, but Allen was in business.

No one knows what might have happened if the Jayhawks and Tigers had split those two games. Endacott later revealed that Allen might have considered retirement from coaching if he had been unable to overcome Missouri. Allen had told his wife, Bessie, if he couldn't beat Missouri twice he would "abandon coaching" to concentrate on his duties as athletic director. "I don't know if he would have gone through with it," Endacott said. "But that's what Bessie Allen told me, and I believe it."

The 1923 team photo included four future Hall of Famers—Naismith, Allen, Endacott, and Rupp. Allen labeled the team "Ever Victorious" for that 16–0 record. It was the second of six consecutive conference championships for the Jayhawks. The foundation for basketball greatness had been laid at Kansas.

77 The Loss That Left a Scar

Time simply does not heal the pain of some losses. For Kansas players, coaches, and fans, the Jayhawks could win the national championship every year, and the empty feeling from March 21, 1997 still would never fade. That's the day Arizona built a 13-point lead and held on for an 85–82 Sweet 16 victory over one of the most talented and most loved Kansas teams of all time, a team that was ranked No. 1, lost only twice, and rode around town together in a green 1964 Cadillac named Marvin.

Ten years later, as he addressed about two dozen of his best players from Kansas and North Carolina, coach Roy Williams revealed his most honest and heart-felt emotions regarding that loss during his Basketball Hall of Fame induction speech in Springfield, Massachusetts. "Paul Pierce, Raef LaFrentz, and Jacque Vaughn, the leaders of great teams that I feel I failed because I didn't get you to the Final Four," Williams said. "Jacque, the best student-athlete I've ever known, winning the NBA championship this year with the Spurs brought tears to my eyes. It didn't make me forget not getting you to the Final Four, but it gave me a great smile to see you in that celebration."

After the ceremony, Vaughn approached Williams and said, "Coach, I've never felt that way one second in my entire life." Pierce and LaFrentz called the apology unexpected and unnecessary. "He feels like he let down his players. That tells you what type of person he is," Pierce said. "But I feel like I failed him because we didn't win more." Said LaFrentz, "That's him in a nutshell. He's always thinking about the players. He was the biggest aid I can think of. He got me to where I am at."

Where Williams and the Jayhawks took each other in 1997 was remarkable. It started with a road win against Santa Clara and victories against LSU, Cal, and Virginia to win the Maui Invitational. December brought wins against Cincinnati, UCLA, and North Carolina State. In the midst of the Big 12 schedule, Williams took the Jayhawks on the road and beat a Connecticut team that had won 46 consecutive non-conference games in Hartford.

Kansas was ranked No. 2 in the preseason poll, moved to No. 1 by the season's third week, and never dropped down again. The Jayhawks set a school record with a 22–0 start. The only loss other than the season-ending defeat to Arizona came February 4 in Columbia, Missouri, where Missouri pulled out a 96–94 double-overtime decision.

And they were a combination of academic All-Americans, NBA draft picks, and crazy characters. Vaughn, the point guard who wrote poetry in his spare time, and Jerod Haase received the academic honors that season. Ryan Robertson followed in their footsteps in 1999. Pierce, LaFrentz, Vaughn, and Scot Pollard all went on to play at least 10 years in the NBA. Pollard was the seven-foot center who owned Marvin, painted his nails, shaved his head, and didn't care if people thought he was entirely nuts. The five starters averaged between 10.2 points (Vaughn) and 18.5 (LaFrentz).

None of them ever played in the Final Four. Williams took Kansas to the final weekend in 1991, 1993, 2002, and 2003, but as the regular season progressed, there was growing confidence that this would be Williams' first championship team and the first KU team to win it all since 1988. "I thought the '97 team was the best team," Williams said in 2008. "That's a void that I will always have. Like I said in my Hall of Fame speech, I felt like I let those guys down and I failed them. If I die tomorrow or die 20 years from now, that will still be the one thing that bothers me more than anything in my coaching career."

How good was this team? The players from 1997 dominate the all-time career rankings at Kansas. LaFrentz ranks third in scoring. Pierce, Haase, Vaughn, Billy Thomas, and Robertson all rank in the top 45. LaFrentz is second in rebounds with Pollard and Pierce in the top 18. Thomas is second in three-pointers made and attempted, trailing only Jeff Boschee in both. LaFrentz is first in double-doubles with 56. Vaughn is second in assists with Robertson 11th and Haase 17th. Haase, Vaughn, Pierce, Robertson, and Thomas are all in the top 25 for steals. Pollard, LaFrentz, and B.J. Williams rank in the top 14 in blocked shots. And yet, only Robertson ranks among the top 10 in games played with 142.

Arizona beat North Carolina and Kentucky, two other No. 1 seeds, on the way to the national championship. But that came as no consolation to the Kansas players and coaching staff who exited in the Sweet 16 after beating Jackson State and Purdue in the first two rounds. "To me, it will never go away," Robertson told *The Kansas City Star* in 2007. "It's only been 10 years, but it will be the most painful basketball loss or feeling I'll ever have. To this day, it sours my feeling about the NCAA tournament as a whole."

The Jayhawks trailed early and were still down 75–62 with three and a half minutes remaining. Thomas made pressure three-pointers to climb back within one with 21 seconds left. Two free throws by Mike Bibby gave Arizona an 85–82 lead, and then the Jayhawks missed three 3-point attempts on their final possession.

Vaughn, who had eight points and was 0-for-4 from three-point range in his final game, turned down an open three in the final sequence because he thought his foot was on the line. He passed to Robertson, who missed an off-balance leaner. LaFrentz rebounded that miss, dribbled into the corner, and missed a prayer. "Sometimes, the best teams do not win," Vaughn told reporters in a quiet locker room. "We will be all right. Families have to overcome heartache." But it doesn't go away. Pierce, who led KU with 27 points, wishes Vaughn had taken the shot he turned down. Haase says the loss will always haunt him. Robertson calls it a scar on his career and 10 years later told *The Star*, "I have my demons."

As for Williams, he will never, ever stray from what he told his team in the locker room after the game. "I told them, 'Life isn't always necessarily fair, and they've had a fantastic, fantastic year,'" Williams told reporters with tears running down his face. "It's been a dream season, but we didn't reach our final dream. That happens sometimes in life."

78 Indiana Roadblock

Missouri and Kansas State have provided intense rivalries within conference play for Kansas. The tangled ties between North Carolina and the Jayhawks have been well documented. Kentucky, Duke, and Texas have been formidable foes for KU over the years.

But only one school—Indiana—has defeated KU twice in national championship games. The Jayhawks are 6–1 in games against the Hoosiers since 1981, so Indiana might not seem to be an intimidating opponent for recent KU fans. But Kansas lost its first six meetings with the Hoosiers, including those title games in 1940 and 1953—both in Kansas City's Municipal Auditorium.

Phog Allen had Howard Engleman, Ralph Miller, Bob Allen, Dick Harp, and John Kline on the 1939–40 team he called "The Pony Express" because they "delivered the mail." The NCAA had held its first national championship tournament the year before, but it still wasn't as well known as the National Invitation Tournament in New York and was on the verge of failure. "That first year when Oregon beat Ohio State, we didn't know anything about it," said Engleman, KU's All-American who would become the leading scorer in the 1940 tournament. Phog was aware of the tournament and he knew poor attendance in Evanston, Illinois, had resulted in a financial disaster. That's when Phog put his reputation on the line, promising sellout crowds and a financial turnaround if the 1940 tournament ended in Kansas City.

The Jayhawks unexpectedly reached the semifinals and finals in Kansas City. Even though they didn't win the championship, it has been written that their presence in the title game may have saved the tournament from extinction. Led by Engleman, Kansas beat Oklahoma A&M 45–43 in the district playoff in Oklahoma City to move on to Kansas City. The Jayhawks defeated Rice 50–44 to win the Western Regional, and Engleman hit a 12-footer to lift KU past Southern California in the national semifinals.

Joe McGuff of *The Kansas City Star* wrote that Indiana was "considered something of a wonder team because of its offensive ability. Indiana was known as the Hurryin' Hoosiers because of its fiery fast break, and as the point-a-minute team because of its prolific scoring."

The Jayhawks got a taste of that as coach Branch McCracken's team led 32–19 and then beat KU 60–42 for the championship. Engleman said the Jayhawks had no idea Indiana had been running a wide-open attack. The Jayhawks hadn't seen Indiana play, and there were no television tapes or scouting reports. "They ran the fast break good," Engleman said years later. "To get there, they beat Duquesne [39–30], and here they were running up 60 points on us."

The teams didn't meet again on the court until 1953, but Allen and McCracken had their own recruiting feud in 1948. That's when Allen was finalizing plans for a championship team in 1952. The final piece in the puzzle was a big man, and Allen wanted 6'9" Clyde Lovellette from Terre Haute, Indiana. Lovellette had already told McCracken he was attending Indiana. That didn't stop Allen from driving to Terre Haute and talking Lovellette into a ride back to Lawrence to check out the KU campus.

Lovellette liked what he saw and changed his mind. With "Cumulus Clyde" leading the way, KU won its first NCAA title in 1952, defeating St. John's 80–63 in Seattle. Even after replacing Lovellete and three other starters the next season, Allen had a chance to repeat as champions. The Jayhawks marched past Oklahoma City and Oklahoma State in the NCAA tournament, went back to Kansas City, and defeated Washington 79–63 in a NCAA semifinal.

Forced to watch Kansas dominate St. John's the year before with Lovellette, McCracken got his shot at sweet revenge in the 1953 championship game and made the most of it. An emotional game came down to one play. Allen wanted guard Al Kelley to take the shot to make the Jayhawks repeat champions, but he was closely guarded. Kelley passed to reserve Jerry Alberts deep in the corner. Alberts' desperation shot banged against the rim, and Indiana grabbed the rebound to win 69–68.

Despite the painful loss, the Jayhawks were greeted by 2,500 fans well after midnight after bussing back to Lawrence. "I have received more cheer from this team than any other in my 43 years of coaching," Allen told the crowd.

79 KU and the Olympics

Phog Allen was buried in his USA Olympic sweat suit. That tells you how strongly he felt about his country and his belief in the global basketball movement. Allen was instrumental in getting basketball included as part of the official Olympic competition in 1936. It should come as no surprise that his inspiration was Dr. James Naismith, the inventor of the game and Allen's mentor at Kansas. And it may have been Allen's proudest achievement.

Several of Naismith's friends from the YMCA in Springfield, Massachusetts, had gone overseas and taken the concept of basketball with them. The game was introduced in France before the turn of the century and then spread to Italy. One of Naismith's former students took the game to Japan. Allied soldiers in Europe increased the popularity of the game during World War I.

Phog's Olympic idea was met with resistance at first. He had hoped to get basketball into the 1932 Games at Los Angeles. As host the United States could introduce two new sports. In 1930 Allen was told it was too late to consider basketball, but it might become a demonstration sport. Even though basketball was gaining interest coast to coast, college football was growing at a fast rate, and the organizing committee wanted to attract a big gate. Football became the exhibition sport.

But Allen still attended the Los Angeles games and while there he met with Carl Diem, secretary for the Organizing Committee in Berlin in 1936. On October 25, 1934, Diem telegraphed Allen with notification of a resolution to include basketball.

Despite a series of organizational battles between Allen and the Amateur Athletic Union, basketball did make its debut in the Berlin Olympics. Allen led a nationwide fund-raising drive to collect money to send Naismith to Berlin. He was the first inventor of a game to see his sport played at the Olympics. Naismith called it "the proudest moment" of his life and tossed the opening tip of the opening game between France and Estonia. He watched as his adopted U.S. squad defeated his native Canada for the gold medal.

The 1936 U.S. team was put together through an eight-team playoff in New York that included five college teams. Despite an 18–0 regular season record, KU fell short of the New York playoff when the Jayhawks lost two of three to Utah State. Allen and his Jayhawks would have to wait until 1952 for their big Olympic moment. Charles Hoag, Bill Hougland, John Keller, Dean Kelley, Robert Kenney, Bill Lienhard, and Clyde Lovellette all made the Olympic team that year after winning the NCAA championship. Allen was there, too, as assistant coach.

That was all according to Allen's plan. He recruited Lienhard, Hougland, and Kenney—all three from Kansas—with the promise that they would not only win the national championship in 1952, but they also would go on to Helsinki and win the gold medal in the Olympics. Assistant coach Dick Harp delivered the message

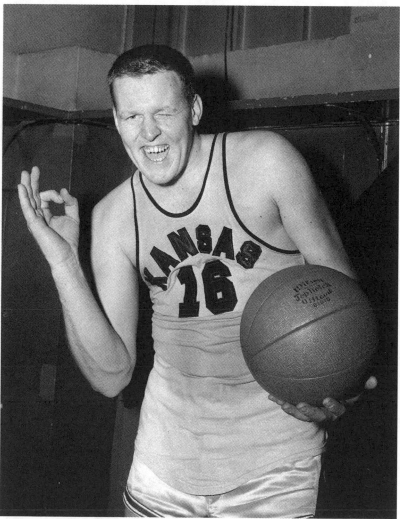

A jokester despite being a rugged big man, Clyde Lovellette led all Olympic players in scoring average (14.1) en route to winning the 1952 gold medal.

to those three. Allen drove to Terre Haute, Indiana, to personally lure Clyde Lovellette, a 6'9" center, who would become the key to everything. "He recruited all of us with that thought in mind," Lovellette said. "It turned out to be his prophecy. It all turned out the right way."

Four days after beating St. John's in Seattle for the NCAA championship, the 1952 team was back in Kansas City, Missouri, playing in the eight-team Olympic playoff. The Jayhawks defeated NAIA champion Southwest Missouri State to advance to New York, where Kansas defeated a talented LaSalle team that won the NIT championship and included Tom Gola.

The Olympic Committee wanted only five Kansas players, but Allen battled to get seven, and the LaSalle victory secured that. The only part of the dream plan that didn't come true involved Allen. When the Jayhawks lost to the AAU champions—the Peoria Caterpillar Diesels—Warren Womble became head coach, and Allen was an assistant. The seven Jayhawks easily led the United States team to the gold medal game. Lovellette led all scorers at the Olympics with a 14.1 average, and the U.S. won the gold medal game 36–25. Lovellette called it the "cherry on the cake." It was the last time that one college team provided half of the U.S. team.

In the library of his Lawrence home, Hougland proudly displays a picture of his KU teammates on the medal stand. "I'm corny about this, but the thing that always impressed me most was playing for your country," said Hougland, who also won gold in Melbourne, Australia in 1956. "My best memory of anything that happened in my time is when we got our gold medal, they raised the flag, played the 'Stars and Stripes,' and all of us were standing at attention."

Jo Jo White was the next Jayhawk to play in the Olympics. He averaged 11.7 points and helped the Americans win the gold in

1968. Darnell Valentine was selected in 1980, but the U.S. boycotted the Games in Moscow. Danny Manning was on the 1988 team coached by Georgetown's John Thompson that settled for a bronze. They are the only two Jayhawks not to win the gold in Olympic basketball.

80 B.H. Born

The population of Medicine Lodge, Kansas, was 2,288 in 1950 when Bert H. Born graduated from high school and headed to the University of Kansas in Lawrence. He was a 6'9" center who had been an All-State selection and averaged 25.1 points per game in the 1A state tournament.

Born, who would simply become known as B.H. Born at KU, had to wait his turn behind the legendary Clyde Lovellette. But after Lovellette and the Jayhawks won the 1952 NCAA championship, Born would be named the Most Outstanding Player of the 1953 NCAA tournament. And he accomplished that, even though the Jayhawks lost the national championship game. How's that for the story of a small town boy making good?

It must have been rewarding for Born to enjoy so much success after a difficult youth. Thanks to his tall and thin frame, he absorbed the insults of being called "Christmas Tree," "Beanpole," or "Broom Handle," while growing up in Medicine Lodge. He had been born in Osawatomie, Kansas, during the Great Depression, so he was tough enough to handle adversity. Playing with a weight disadvantage against Lovellette in practice his first two seasons just added another layer of grit and intelligence.

Retired Jerseys

Kansas started retiring jerseys of outstanding men's basketball players prior to the 1991–92 season when banners honoring Clyde Lovellette, Danny Manning, B.H. Born, Charlie B. Black, Charlie T. Black, Paul Endacott, and Wilt Chamberlain were unveiled in the south end of Allen Fieldhouse.

The original criteria for a retired jersey included being named Player of the Year, Most Valuable Player of the NCAA tournament, or a four-time All-American. The list was expanded in 1997 to include Ray Evans, an All-American in both football and basketball.

The criteria was changed again prior to the 2002–03 season to include consensus first team All-Americans, two-time first team All-America selections, and Academic All-American of the Year. And longtime broadcaster Max Falkenstien was added in 2006 for his 60 years of calling KU games.

The following figures have had their jerseys retired: Tus Ackerman, Charlie B. Black, Charlie T. Black, Born, Bill Bridges, Chamberlain, Nick Collison, Endacott, Howard Engleman, Evans, Falkenstien, Drew Gooden, Gale Gordon, Kirk Hinrich, Raef LaFrentz, Lovellette, Manning, Al Peterson, Paul Pierce, Fred Pralle, David Robisch, Wayne Simien, Bud Stallworth, Darnell Valentine, Jacque Vaughn, Walter Wesley, and Jo Jo White.

Born was Lovellete's backup during the 1952 title season and averaged 1.6 points per game. But with Lovellete off to the pros, Born averaged 18.9 points as a junior and led the Jayhawks back to the NCAA title game the next season. Although Indiana defeated Kansas 69–68 at Municipal Auditorium in Kansas City, Born enjoyed his finest moment. With 26 points, 15 rebounds, and 13 blocked shots, Born became the first player from a losing team to be selected the Most Outstanding Player. And with those incredible numbers, Born had an unofficial triple-double—the first in Kansas history. (Blocked shots, assists, and steals were not officially recorded at Kansas until the 1970s.)

In both his junior and senior seasons, Born led the Big 7 in rebounds and scoring. In 1953 he was an All-American in addition to making the All-Big 7 team.

Born finished his career with three conference titles and a career record of 63–14. Few players from the state of Kansas have gone on to such an illustrious career with the Jayhawks. He also represented the USA on the way to winning a gold medal at the 1954 world championships. Born then turned down a NBA contract offer and played for Peoria in the popular AAU league.

KU retired Born's jersey on February 15, 1992. He died February 3, 2013, at age 80. "He was certainly a gentleman and a great ambassador for KU through the years," Kansas coach Bill Self said. "Our sympathies certainly go out to his family as they go through this difficult time. I'm sure our KU family is saddened today but also very proud of the legacy that he left as a faithful Jayhawk."

81 Nine Straight Big 12 Titles

There are times to celebrate and there are times for quiet introspection. Ordinarily a conference championship at Kansas prompts jubilation. It wasn't quite like that on March 9, 2013, in Waco, Texas. The Jayhawks won their ninth consecutive Big 12 championship that day, a remarkable achievement on so many levels. But an 81–58 blowout loss at Baylor meant the Jayhawks shared the conference crown with Kansas State instead of winning the title outright. No one in the KU locker room was happy about that. "It doesn't feel like we won it at all, really," senior center Jeff Withey told the *Lawrence Journal-World* after the game. "It's cool to win nine in a row, but it just stinks to lose."

Hours earlier Kansas State had lost to Oklahoma State, guaranteeing KU a share of its ninth straight conference crown. All the Jayhawks had to do was beat Baylor to win the title outright. But Baylor was playing for its NCAA tournament life, needing a win over a highly-ranked team to add to its resume, and the Jayhawks didn't seem motivated.

The end result was KU's second-worst loss in the 10-year Bill Self era. (Texas defeated KU 80–55 in Austin, Texas, on February 25, 2006.) Self said the Jayhawks had "the golden opportunity" but didn't jump through the hoop. Both teams from the Sunflower State finished 14–4. "I went in and told my team, 'Hey, bad job, but congratulations,' one of those deals," Self said. "I'm happy we got a ninth. I will never apologize for winning a league championship. It's not entirely the way we scripted it, which is obvious."

Enough negativity. The streak of conference titles that so many programs envy remained alive. The Jayhawks went on to defeat Kansas State 70–54 in the Big 12 tournament championship game, emphatically breaking the tie in the eyes of most observers. But conference championships are a big thing at Kansas. Phog Allen established that tradition, winning 24. Through 2013, Kansas had 56 regular-season conference titles, the most of any team in Division I. By conference affiliation, it breaks down this way: Missouri Valley (13), Big 6 (12), Big 7 (5), Big 8 (13), and Big 12 (13). Kentucky was second in the nation with 51.

Under Self the question has become, "Is this the year someone can knock the Jayhawks off the top perch?" Nine times, the answer has been a firm no. In Self's first season at KU in 2003–04, the Jayhawks were 12–4 in league play and tied for second. Over the next nine seasons, Kansas shared the title four times and won the Big 12 outright five times.

The sweetest of those outright titles came on March 3, 2007, a 90–86, come-from-behind victory against Texas at Allen Fieldhouse that gave the Jayhawks their 50th conference title and victory No. 1,900 in school history. Self and his players cut down the nets, there was a highlight reel shown immediately on the videoboard, and Big 12 commissioner Kevin Weiberg presented the Big 12 trophy.

Texas freshman Kevin Durant scored 25 of his 32 points in the first half as the Longhorns built a 16-point lead and led 54–42 at the half. But the Jayhawks didn't panic. They defended Durant better and went on a 24–7 run to take the lead four minutes into the second half. When it was over, athletic director Lew Perkins strolled the floor with an unlit victory cigar, shaking hands with players and coaches. It was a moment with historical impact, but it had simply been a great college basketball game. "It was a great stage, a perfect setup," KU's Russell Robinson said. "We had to take advantage. No way we could let it slide and share it." Said Brandon Rush: "It's a special day for us. We won it in our own home with the fans going crazy."

82 Jerry Waugh

The first time I sat down to talk Kansas basketball with Jerry Waugh, I was a bit skeptical. Several KU officials had told me Waugh was one of the first people I should interview. But when I was attending KU, Waugh was the golf coach and a special assistant to athletic director Clyde Walker. I didn't associate him with Kansas basketball at all—just another example that college students aren't always as smart as they think.

Jerry and I met at a popular breakfast spot in Lawrence. We ordered some coffee, and I pushed the record button on my digital voice recorder. I never met Phog Allen, so I wanted to know much more about the legendary coach—from someone who actually knew him. Two hours later, the available space on my recorder was about to run out. I had this strong desire to cancel all my other appointments that day. I could have listened to Jerry Waugh until sundown and beyond.

Waugh grew up in Wellington, Kansas, and enrolled at KU in the spring of 1947 after serving two years in the Army during World War II. He became a freshman guard for Allen in 1947–48 and was a team captain as a senior in 1950–51. He played with juniors Clyde Lovellette, Bob Kenney, Bill Lienhard, and Bill Hougland on a team that tied for second in the Big 7 Conference. "I missed 1952 by a year," he said, referring to Allen's NCAA championship team.

Waugh's nickname was the "Sheriff of Sumner County," and that offers a reasonable image of how he locked up opponents on defense. Waugh left Lawrence a few times to teach, coach, and to join the business world in other locales. But he always found his way back, returning as an assistant coach under Dick Harp, assistant AD, golf coach, administrator, and mentor to many KU athletes.

Retirement is a word Waugh doesn't understand. The resident storyteller in Lawrence, he still works with young people. Waugh pays tribute to an era of Kansas basketball that most of us can't remember by bringing it to life through words. It would take another book to share them all, but here's a sampling.

On Allen as a father figure: "He would tell the same stories over and over. He could paint the picture. He was like the Indian chief sitting around the fire at night, telling of great victories, great games, and great players."

On Allen's teaching technique: "Doc did a lot of teaching. He described how animals used their bodies and how they moved. He said as a defensive player I needed to be furtive like a squirrel. Then he would explain to us that furtive means fearful for your life. He would get into the position of a squirrel coming down from a tree.

He was talking about screens and seeing everything when you were playing defense. He had a movie of the mongoose and the cobra because the mongoose could kill a cobra. The mongoose would move closely, and then the cobra would strike, but the mongoose would just drop away. Then he'd get closer. Then the mongoose would have him. Then he would talk about defensive position. He'd talk about dogs. He said if you've ever chased your dog, did you ever notice when you come up close, he'll drop to the ground? He said your dog is lowering his center of gravity so he can move any direction. And then he will dart away."

On Wilt Chamberlain: "Wilt was politely disobedient, hard to coach. There's nobody playing the game today who is as physical as he was. Here's a seven-foot guy who could jump. I mean jump. He was a long jumper, a high jumper. Then he had stamina. He could run forever."

On Clyde Lovellette: "He was a great player. He was a great scorer. He was not a rebounder. He couldn't jump. He didn't have foot speed. I was asked to pick my all-time [KU] team—10 players. I didn't have Clyde on it. I picked the players I could coach. I want to know did they work hard in practice? Clyde didn't work as hard. He was a natural scorer. He was a good person. I think he matured in his junior and senior year. When he came he was very selfish as a player. Points were important to him—not whether we won or lost. We complained to Doc, and he did bear down."

83 Gale Gordon and Al Peterson

The championship seasons in 1922 and 1923 signaled a shift of power from Missouri to Kansas in the Missouri Valley Conference.

Phog Allen's teams finished first in the conference for six consecutive seasons (from 1922 to 1927).

The Jayhawks posted a 16–2 record after finishing the season on a 14-game winning streak in 1926. That was the fifth consecutive conference title, and in recognition of that accomplishment, the *Lawrence Journal-World* asked James Naismith to select an "All-Modern KU Basketball Team" from those five squads. Naismith's choices were Paul Endacott, Tus Ackerman, Charlie T. Black, Gale Gordon, and Al Peterson. It was hard to argue those selections. Each of the players earned All-America honors twice at KU. Endacott, Ackerman, and Black had played on the "Ever Victorious" team. Gordon and Peterson, both from Kansas City, Kansas, took the baton from 1925–27 and seamlessly continued the championship relay for Jayhawks basketball.

The Jayhawks were 17–1 in 1925 with the only loss coming on January 14 to Kansas State. KU then began the 1926 season 2–2, losing both the season opener to Washington (Missouri) and then falling to Oklahoma 29–21 at home in Lawrence. One game, according to *Kansas Jayhawks History-making basketball*, was "a neat Dr. Jekyll-Mr. Hyde stunt, playing the Sooners off their feet in the first half and being just as badly outclassed in the second frame."

Allen may have been in agreement. Before the Jayhawks played Missouri next, Allen changed his lineup, putting Glenn Burton in Gordon's spot and moving Gordon to forward. The Jayhawks won 24–15 and never lost the rest of the season. When the season was over, the *Jayhawker* yearbook heaped praise on KU's best players. "Peterson, Gordon, and [George] Schmidt were too strong a combination for the opposing teams to overcome in the offensive part of the game," the *Jayhawker* said. "Without question, this trio is one of the smoothest and fastest scoring combinations ever unleashed on a college basket ball (sic) floor."

Gordon and Peterson experienced defeat only five times in three seasons at KU, and they were part of the program's 300th victory in 1925 when the Jayhawks defeated Iowa State 33–18. Gordon won All-Missouri Valley Conference in 1926 and 1927 while Peterson accomplished that during all three seasons. Peterson also led KU in scoring back-to-back seasons, averaging 10.3 points his final season. The pair had their jerseys retired on January 15, 2003.

84 Two Bs, UNI, and VCU

Kansas fans would rather forget these initials. They symbolize NCAA disappointment, tournament shockers, and appearing on the cover of *Sports Illustrated* in such a way that you want to throw out the issue as soon as it arrives in the mail. The letters stand for Bucknell, Bradley, University of Northern Iowa (UNI), and Virginia Commonwealth University (VCU)—four teams that stunned the Jayhawks in the NCAA tournament this past decade.

We apologize for bringing up bad memories, but the Kansas basketball story isn't complete without a decent dose of heartache. Some tournament losses are hard to forget. Phog lost two national championship games to Indiana. Wilt lost to North Carolina in triple overtime in 1957. Jo Jo stepped out of bounds—or so the official said—against Texas Western. Roy had UTEP, Virginia, Syracuse, Rhode Island, Syracuse again, *and* Arizona in 1997.

That brings us to the decade of Bill Self. It has been amazing. Heading into the 2013 season, Self is 300–59 and has won nine consecutive regular season Big 12 championships in his 10 years at

KU. He led the Jayhawks to the NCAA championship in 2008 and returned to the Final Four in 2012. Self has taken KU to the Elite Eight three times and the Sweet 16 twice.

Then there's Bucknell, Bradley, UNI, and VCU. The Killer Bs toppled Kansas in consecutive first-round NCAA games in 2005 and 2006. Prior to that KU hadn't lost an opening round NCAA game since 1978 when Darnell Valentine, Paul Mokeski, Ken Koenigs, John Douglas, and Donnie Von Moore fell to UCLA. UNI ended the careers of Sherron Collins and Cole Aldrich in an NCAA second round game in 2010. And the Morris twins could only watch the clock run down in 2011 as VCU defeated the Jayhawks for a trip to the Final Four in Houston. Reliving those moments is painful around KU. Jayhawk fans dream of the Final Four every March. It goes with the territory. And these were good teams. Kansas was a No. 3 seed in 2005 and a 4 seed in 2006. The Jayhawks were a No. 1 seed in 2010 and 2011. Ouch.

When the Jayhawks reached the Elite Eight to play Davidson in 2008, it was Self's fifth trip to that stage in his career. The players felt the pressure, and so did Self. "It's something that I think about all the time," Self said of the past disappointments, "and a lot of times, many times a day."

Here are four players from those games that Self would rather not think about again. The rest of you can either give these guys credit for rising above the Jayhawks or construct their voodoo dolls and insert a few pins.

Kevin Bettencourt, Bucknell—He had 19 points, five three-pointers, and four steals in Bucknell's 64–63 win on March 18, 2005. It was Bucknell's first NCAA victory. The Bison band was on spring break, so the band from *Northern Iowa* filled in. You can't make up this stuff.

Marcellus Sommerville, Bradley—He had 21 points and five three-pointers in Bradley's 77–73 win on March 17, 2006. The

Braves made 11 three-pointers for their first NCAA victory in 20 years while KU had 18 turnovers.

Ali Farokhmanesh, Northern Iowa—He had 16 points, including four three-pointers in Northern Iowa's 69–67 win on March 20, 2010. Northern Iowa became the first Missouri Valley team to reach the Sweet 16 since Larry Bird led Indiana State there in 1979.

Jamie Skeen, VCU—He had 26 points, 10 rebounds, 2 steals, and four three-pointers in VCU's 71–61 victory on March 27, 2011. The Rams became just the third No. 11 seed to reach the Final Four. KU trailed by 18 with three and a half minutes left in the first half.

85 Wayne Simien

The final 10 seconds of Wayne Simien's basketball career at Kansas did not play out the way he had dreamed. Losing to the Bucknell Bison in the first round of the 2005 NCAA tournament was enough of a nightmare. But Simien missed an open 15-foot jumper at the buzzer that could have saved the Jayhawks. Instead, the preseason No. 1 team went home much earlier than expected. And Bucknell, the No. 14 seed from the Patriot League, had its first NCAA victory in three tournament tries. "I don't know how many game-winning shots I hit in my backyard dreaming I was a Jayhawk," Simien said after his four years in the KU program ended so abruptly. "The ball was in my hands. It didn't work out."

Kansas fans desperately wanted it to work out for Simien as well. The 6'9" forward essentially was a hometown hero, growing up about 40 miles away in Leavenworth, Kansas. Simien was recruited by Roy Williams, the Hall of Fame coach who departed for North

Carolina after trips to the Final Four in Simien's first two seasons. Then Simien shifted gears and played for Bill Self as a junior and a senior. The Jayhawks hadn't lost in the opening round of the NCAA since being eliminated by UCLA in 1978, and it simply didn't seem possible for a team that included Simien, Keith Langford, Aaron Miles, J.R. Giddens, and Christian Moody. But KU lost consecutive conference games to Texas Tech, Iowa State, and Oklahoma in February; fell at Missouri in the final regular season game; and lost to Oklahoma State in the Big 12 tournament. As Bucknell celebrated, Simien walked to the KU locker room for the last time. "There's no need to go into words about it," he said.

It certainly was a difficult ending for a player who accomplished so much. Simien ranks 13th in career scoring (1,593 points) and seventh in rebounds (884) at KU. He had 38 double-doubles and 39 games with double-figure rebounds. His four teams combined for a 110–28 record, three Big 12 championships, four NCAA tournaments, two Final Fours, and an Elite Eight.

Simien's scoring average increased from 8.1 points as a freshman, to 14.8 as a sophomore, 17.8 as a junior, and 20.3 as a senior. His popularity soared as well as a Kansas guy who gave a total effort and was a role model off the court as well. Simien won the 2005 Lowe's Senior CLASS Award and was a consensus first team All-American and Big 12 Player of the Year the same season.

The Miami Heat selected him with the 29th pick in the first round of the 2005 NBA Draft, and he won the NBA championship there in 2006. But at age 26, Simien retired from pro basketball in 2009 to pursue work in the Christian ministry. He started Called to Greatness, a Christian-based sports organization, and continues to follow that calling in the Lawrence area. "There was a time when I was in college where I basically had everything the world says should make you happy," Simien told the *Lawrence Journal-World*. "I was big man on campus, I had a measure of fame, I was headed

Wayne Simien, a native Kansan who grew up in Leavenworth, shoots over Kansas State's Cartier Martin during the 2005 Big 12 tournament.
(Getty Images)

to the NBA, I had access to all the drugs and alcohol you could ever want, all the girls, popularity, and things like that, but I just wasn't fulfilled deep down in my heart."

Now that he has found that fulfillment, he still stays active in the basketball world, has contact with the KU program, and is a community leader. When the Jayhawks had their rare three-game losing streak in 2012–13, Simien talked to the team and gave his perspective from that difficult ending to his senior season. "It gave us a lot of hope," KU senior Kevin Young told the *Journal-World*. "We knew we'd be all right if we kept working hard."

The Morris Twins

It was never easy to distinguish Marcus Morris from Markieff Morris at KU. The twin big men from Philadelphia arrived in Lawrence in the summer of 2008, immediately creating confusion over their strikingly similar resemblance. They kept it identical down to the details such as beards and tattoos, which included biceps ink that declared "FOE"—Family Over Everything.

Marcus, 6'9", came to KU more touted, but the 6'10" Markieff made drastic improvement especially in his junior season. The twins led KU in scoring in 2010–11 with Marcus at 17.2 points per game and Markieff second at 13.6.

They came in together and left together, exiting early for the NBA. On draft night in 2011 they were selected with back-to-back picks. Markieff was first as the Phoenix Suns used the 13th pick to take him. On the next selection, Houston scooped up Marcus. "It's just amazing how things played out," Marcus said. "It played out exactly the way we wanted."

In February 2013, Phoenix traded to acquire Marcus, and the twins were together again. "It's not an accident that these two guys are here," Lon Babby, the Suns' president for basketball operations told *The New York Times*. "We believe their bond is special and is going to make each of them better and therefore make our team better." The only other set of twins to play for the same NBA team—Dick and Tom Van Arsdale—also played for the Suns.

86 NCAA Probation

Kansas fans barely had a chance to celebrate the 1988 national championship before coach Larry Brown left for the NBA. And Brown's replacement, Roy Williams, barely had a chance to introduce himself before informing his players they would not get a chance to defend their title.

Before Williams could coach a regular season game at KU, the NCAA slapped a three-year probation on Kansas for recruiting violations committed under Brown's watch and banned the Jayhawks from defending their title. The NCAA found Kansas guilty of "improper recruiting inducements" in connection with Vincent Askew, a guard at Memphis State who had considered transferring to Kansas but never played for the Jayhawks. The rules violation that received the most attention in the media was a $364 plane ticket Brown bought for Askew to return home to see his dying grandmother.

Kansas became the first NCAA basketball champion not allowed to defend its title, a distinction no school wanted attached to its program. Athletic director Bob Frederick had informed Williams during the interview process that Kansas was under NCAA investigation. KU had been given the impression the violations would be considered secondary and that the penalties would not be severe. But in addition to the tournament ban, the Jayhawks were not allowed to pay for campus recruiting visits in 1989 and were stripped of one scholarship during the first year of the probation.

News of the penalties was delivered to Williams on Halloween, while he was trick-or-treating with his children. "I was dumbfounded and very scared to be honest with you," Williams said in an interview 20 years later. "I didn't know if we were going to be able to get it done."

It could have been worse. The Associated Press reported that the NCAA seriously considered shutting down the Kansas program for an entire year. The KU football program had served a two-year probation from 1983–85, and this was at a time when the NCAA was cracking down on schools. The so-called death penalty specified that when a school was charged with two major violations within five years, the second program would be subject to suspension. "Kansas was on the bubble, so to speak," an unnamed NCAA assistant director for enforcement told the Associated Press.

KU did not appeal the decision. "I gave him exactly $364," Brown said in a press conference in San Antonio, "which was the price for the round-trip ticket, and we told the NCAA about it. The kid's grandmother, who raised him, passed away a short time later." Brown said payment for the ticket wasn't something he was trying to hide. "I'd give it to anybody if they told me his grandmother was passing away," Brown said.

Despite the sanctions KU finished 19–12 during the 1988–89 season. Two years later, Williams led KU to the national championship game.

87 Bob Frederick

Bob Frederick had an impressive resume in athletics, but when you stripped away all the titles and all the responsibilities he was really just one thing—a Jayhawk.

Frederick was a basketball player, an assistant coach, and athletic director. He was a KU graduate with three degrees, a teacher, a professor, and a department head. Frederick served as chairman of the NCAA men's basketball committee and the NCAA committee on sportsmanship and ethical conduct. He was a husband, a father, a grandfather, a competitive bike rider, and a friend. Bob Frederick became Dr. Bob on campus, and Dr. Bob tried to help anybody and everybody.

Frederick was the athletic director who hired an unknown North Carolina assistant coach named Roy Williams to become head basketball coach at the University of Kansas. "Bob had a belief and gave me a chance," Williams said. Many would say the hiring of Williams was a risk, but it worked out pretty well. Some might say that hire defined Frederick's legacy, but he said it was nothing more than luck.

Frederick had just a few hours to enjoy KU's national championship victory against Oklahoma in 1988. He stayed overnight in Kansas City, Missouri, where the game had been played in Kemper Arena, but returned to his office at 10:30 AM the next day. "My secretary said, 'You're supposed to call [athletic director] Peter Dalis at UCLA,'" Frederick said. "And I said to her, 'Wouldn't you think he could let us celebrate one day?'"

UCLA wanted former Bruins coach Larry Brown to leave Kansas and return to the West Coast. The coaching nomad was on the run once again. Brown interviewed in Los Angeles, returned to Lawrence, and then surprised everyone by saying he had decided to stay at KU. But just a few weeks later, on June 13, Brown said yes to a "once-in-a-lifetime" chance to coach the NBA San Antonio Spurs.

Now KU needed a coach.

Frederick had never heard of Williams until a couple of months earlier when he attended induction ceremonies for former Kansas players Clyde Lovellette and Ralph Miller at the Naismith Basketball Hall of Fame in Springfield, Massachusetts. Seated at the Kansas table was Dick Harp, who had coached Frederick at

KU, and at that time was on Dean Smith's staff at North Carolina. "He just talked to me all night about Roy," Frederick said.

When Brown left, Frederick called Smith first and offered the former KU player the job. But Smith, just like Harp, wanted to talk about the man who had been a full-time assistant at North Carolina for just four years. Williams thought Smith "had lost his mind" when he was told Frederick wanted a meeting at the Atlanta airport. "There was no way I was going to be coach at Kansas," Williams said.

Frederick was instantly impressed with Williams, his ability to organize, and his understanding for what was required to be a head coach. "But the thing that really stuck out for me about Roy was his great appreciation of the Kansas basketball tradition," Frederick said. "He had gotten that from Dean and Dick."

Kansas fans doubted Frederick and his decision at first, but Williams led the Jayhawks to the Final Four in his third season, and the critics were silenced. Many in the KU athletic community credit Williams with bringing tradition and pride back to the program, echoing what Frederick saw in his candidate during that interview.

Frederick became a force himself, working on the NCAA men's basketball committee and then becoming the voice of college basketball as committee chair. The national media found him approachable, fair, and helpful. In 2010 the NCAA created the Bob Frederick Sportsmanship Award and recognized Frederick as the inaugural recipient. The honor is open to Division I, II, and III administrators.

More than anything else, Frederick enjoyed his time with KU's athletes and talking to them about their academics. Maryland coach Mark Turgeon, who played at Kansas and was an assistant coach with the Jayhawks, went to Frederick for advice as a senior when he was considering a career in coaching. "He went out of his way and gathered information for me," Turgeon said.

After stepping down as athletic director in 2001, Frederick returned to his teaching roots. He taught classes in sports management, sports law, and sports facilities and served as interim chair of the department. Frederick became a favorite of students who took his classes and others that he simply counseled.

Frederick touched a lot of people before a tragic bicycling accident took his life on June 12, 2009 in Lawrence. He was 69. Hundreds of people filled the Lied Center on campus for a memorial service, including Williams, who made the trip from North Carolina to honor the man who gave him his big break in coaching. "As fine a man as could possibly be, that was Bob Frederick," Williams told The Associated Press.

In *What It Means To Be A Jayhawk*, Frederick said he was always amazed at the emotional attachment people have to KU. "From my observation, it's tied to both the athletic and academic traditions," Frederick wrote. "I believe they are unique and set us apart from most other public universities. People don't forget about this place. It becomes part of their life forever."

88 Archie Marshall

Over the years, Kansas fans have found a variety of reasons to open their hearts to Jayhawk players. Archie Marshall found his way there through adversity and injuries. His spot in the scrapbook of memories is secure. Marshall was a member of the 1986 and 1988 Final Four teams. He started only 12 games in his career and scored just 377 points. But if you are searching for the inspiration that helped carry the Jayhawks to the 1988 NCAA championship, Marshall must be included.

It's hard enough to watch a teammate fall to the floor with a devastating knee injury once. But Danny Manning, coach Larry Brown, and the Jayhawks saw Marshall go down twice. The first time was in Dallas as the Jayhawks lost to Duke in a 1986 national semifinal game when he tore the anterior cruciate ligament in his right knee. The injury was so bad he needed a medical redshirt and missed the entire 1986–87 season. He made it back, and his role changed from super-sub to starter when he rejoined the Jayhawks for the start of the 1987–88 season. That was the good part of the story.

The gut-wrenching part came on December 30, 1987, when the 6'6" small forward tore the ACL in his left knee in a game against St. John's. Marshall had surgery, and his career was over. It was just one slice of the overall adversity the Jayhawks had to overcome that season. But that didn't keep the senior from Tulsa, Oklahoma, from contributing in a major way to KU's championship season.

Brown wept on the bench when Marshall was injured against St. John's. Marshall had become one of the coach's favorites after he transferred from Seminole (Oklahoma) Junior College. "He's never asked for anything and he's been so receptive to coaching," Brown said. "I've never heard one person say anything bad about him...Life isn't fair."

Manning put Marshall's uniform number 23 on his wrist bands and wore them the rest of the season. During an emotional Senior Night, Brown decided late in the game to send Marshall on the floor. Still in the early stages of rehab, Marshall hobbled out, took a pass, and attempted a long three-point shot that missed. Whether or not the shot went in didn't matter. Marshall got a standing ovation from the Allen Fieldhouse crowd.

There were few—if any—dry eyes when Marshall took the first snip as the Jayhawks cut down the nets after defeating Kansas State in the regional final and again at Kemper Arena in Kansas City after the Jayhawks defeated Oklahoma in the national championship game. As one final stroke of inspiration, Marshall got into uniform for the championship game and went through pregame warm-ups despite a noticeable limp. "Sure, it gave us a lift," he said. "You can't give me credit. Give it to the players and Larry Brown."

When the team was greeted at Memorial Stadium the next day, he smiled and posed with the NCAA trophy just like any other member of the team. His biggest honor, though, may have come in 2005 when Marshall graduated with a bachelor's degree in communication studies at age 40. "It's haunted me for a long time," Marshall told the *Lawrence Journal-World.* "Now I'm able to put it behind me. Now I'm officially a University of Kansas alumnus."

89 Wonderful Walter Wesley

"Wonderful." That was Walter Wesley's nickname during his playing career at Kansas, and all things considered, he certainly lived up to the label. "Wonderful Walt" was a two-time All-American and a two time All-Big 8 selection. Back in the days when freshmen weren't eligible for varsity play, Wesley averaged 19.3 points in his three seasons with the Jayhawks. Through 2012–13, that still ranks sixth among career scoring averages in KU history with a minimum of 45 games played. He's not far behind Danny Manning's 20.1 average from 1984–88.

Wesley's All-American and All-Big 8 honors followed his junior and senior seasons in 1965 and 1966. The 6'11" center from Fort Myers, Florida, was a scoring machine. He was blessed with a soft shot and a great pair of hands. Wesley could hit the mid-range jumper—a lost art in college basketball. And he came to KU from Lee County's all-black high school at a time when segregation was a way of life, and Florida colleges were not admitting black athletes.

As a sophomore, Wesley was KU's second leading scorer on the 1963–64 Jayhawks. He averaged 10.5 points as George Unseld led the squad with an 18.4 average. That was Dick Harp's final season as Kansas coach. Wesley really flourished under Ted Owens and assistant coach Sam Miranda. "Sam was the taskmaster and he got you ready to be coached," Wesley said. "And without a doubt, he pushed you to your limits. He was the one during conditioning and training that tested your limits. And Ted was the glue that kept it all together."

Wesley, who could run the floor as well as any big man who ever played at KU, averaged 23.5 points overall and led the Big 8 Conference with a 26.9 average in 1965. That was the highest scoring average in the conference since Wilt Chamberlain's 28.3 mark in 1958. Wesley averaged 20.7 points as a senior in 1966. That 1966 team lost just four games, including the controversial Texas Western game in the NCAA Midwest Regional when Jo Jo White's game-winning jumper was negated by an official's call that White stepped out of bounds.

Despite Wesley's impressive numbers, *Lawrence Journal-World* columnist Chuck Woodling wrote in 2009 that if he walked Lawrence's Massachusetts Street asking pedestrians if they had heard of Walt Wesley, he would want to do that on a warm day. "I couldn't stand on Mass that long in cold weather," Woodling wrote.

Woodling also wrote that Wesley was the original nomad, playing for eight teams during his 10-year NBA career after leaving Kansas. Since his retirement from the NBA, he has worked as a Police Athletic League executive in Fort Myers, Florida. Wesley often returns to Lawrence for basketball anniversary celebrations and strolled San Antonio's Riverwalk with KU fans when the Jayhawks won the 2008 national championship.

90 David Robisch

Kansas retired David Robisch's jersey during a ceremony at Allen Fieldhouse on February 27, 2005, so the case could be made that he has been rightfully recognized as one of the greats. But maybe that's not enough. Maybe Robisch should be in the discussion of the best Jayhawks ever, which includes Wilt Chamberlain, Clyde Lovellette, Danny Manning, and Paul Pierce.

The Springfield, Illinois, native wore the Kansas uniform for coach Ted Owens from 1969–71 and was an All-Big 8 selection all three seasons. The Helms Foundation honored him as an All-American after his last two seasons. The Jayhawks were 64–19 during his career, including a 14–0 record to win the Big 8 in 1971 when KU advanced to the Final Four.

Flip through the pages of the Kansas record book, and Robisch's fingerprints can be found everywhere. Robisch averaged 21.1 points in his Kansas career, and that still ranks fourth in school history behind Chamberlain (29.9), Lovellette (24.7), and Wayne Hightower (21.3). He scored 1,754 points, and that's ninth all-time—just behind Paul Pierce, who scored 1,768 from 1996–98.

In addition to those stats, Robisch was an extraordinary shooter, and the Jayhawks relied on him time after time to hit the biggest shot of the game. "Dave was about the finest competitive shooter I've been around," Owens told Gary Bedore of the

Lawrence Journal-World. "He did something I don't think I've seen anybody else master. He could bank in a shot straight out. Down the stretch if you needed a basket, Dave would find a way to get the ball in there."

He was left-handed and didn't exactly have textbook form. But Robisch always got results. "For some reason growing up and learning the game, I knew the angles on the backboard and used the board to shoot a ton of shots," Robisch told Bedore. "Within seven or eight feet, I'd use the bank shot."

Robisch averaged 26.5 points a game in 1969–70, the fourth-highest single-season mark in KU history. He led KU in scoring all three of his seasons and in rebounding in 1969 and 1970. Robisch ranks 12ᵗʰ in career rebounds with 815 and had 26 rebounds against Iowa State on January 10, 1970, the sixth highest single-game total in KU history—and the most in one game by anyone not named Chamberlain or Bill Bridges. His 9.8 career rebounding average ranks fifth, behind Chamberlain, Bridges, Hightower, and Lovellette.

One of Robisch's career highlights came March 8, 1971 when he helped the Jayhawks close Missouri's Brewer Field House with a 71–69 overtime victory against the rival Tigers. Missouri had 75 former letter winners in the house they had called home for 42 years. Robisch had four points, two rebounds, and an assist in the final two minutes of overtime, and the fourth-ranked Jayhawks moved to 13–0 in the Big 8 on the way to the first perfect league record since Kansas State in 1958.

The Jayhawks went on to the 1971 NCAA tournament on a 19-game winning streak. Their only loss had come December 21 at Louisville. Kansas slipped past Houston 78–77 in the first round of the Midwest Region as Robisch finished with 29 points, 16 rebounds, six blocks, and four steals.

The final win of Robisch's career came two days later when he scored 27 points in a 73–71 victory against Drake. The Jayhawks were on their way to the Final Four for the first time since 1957, but the dream of a national championship ended with a 68–60 loss to UCLA at the Astrodome in Houston. Kansas fell behind by 13, rallied to tie the game at 39, but a traveling violation called against Robisch negated the go-ahead basket and turned the game in UCLA's favor. "As I look back, I think we had a great season," Robisch said. "Obviously, there is disappointment. I have told a lot of people what sticks in the brain all the time…the one shot I remember the most was one I made to put us ahead in the second half against UCLA, but they called me for traveling. I just wonder what would have happened if I hadn't been called for traveling."

91 Drew Gooden

Drew Gooden became known as Mr. Unpredictable to his teammates and coaches on the Kansas basketball team. It had nothing to do with his performance on the court. He was consistently outstanding while wearing the Kansas uniform. No, it was all about Gooden's gift of the gab—or lack thereof. Coach Roy Williams used to say the one sure thing about Gooden was you never knew what he would say next. Those of us lucky enough to interview Gooden—whether it was once or 1,000 times—understood exactly what Williams meant

There are plenty of examples.

When Gooden helped the Jayhawks defeat Oregon 104–86 for the Midwest Regional championship in the 2002 NCAA tournament, he was asked on national television about the fast pace of the game. Gooden explained that he had clipped his toenails the night before the game. "I wanted to be ready to run up and down the floor," he said. Williams laughed and said he probably would not have made the same confession on national television. "If Drew feels comfortable with that," Williams said, "it's all right with me."

One year earlier when Kansas traveled to San Antonio to play Illinois, then coached by Bill Self, in the NCAA tournament, Drew was asked what he knew about the Alamo. "All I know about the Alamo is that Ozzy Osbourne got kicked out of the state for urinating on it," Gooden replied. When Gooden was drafted by the Memphis Grizzlies in 2002, he was asked if he would visit Graceland, Elvis Presley's home. Gooden said: "I didn't know Elvis was from Memphis. I thought he was from Tennessee."

Gooden grew up in the state of California—Richmond to be exact—just outside Oakland. By his junior season, it was obvious he had studied a little history of Lawrence, not to mention the border battles between Kansas and Missouri. Before No. 18 Missouri visited No. 2 KU on January 28, 2002, Gooden was asked about the tension between the two schools and the history of the rivalry. "Once again, it's people from Missouri coming into a little a town in Kansas and trying to cause chaos," Gooden said, referencing William Clark Quantrill, the pro-slavery Missourian, who rode into Lawrence in 1863 with his band of guerrillas and looted, murdered, and burned Lawrence to the ground.

Just a few days later in that Big Monday game at Allen Fieldhouse, Gooden scored 26 points and grabbed 10 rebounds as the Jayhawks defeated the Tigers 105–73. It was not yet February, and that already marked the 16th double-double of the season for Gooden. He went on to earn first team All-America status and was named Big 12 Player of the Year. After that victory against Mizzou, Gooden was so enthusiastic he seemed willing to talk to reporters until early the next morning. Gooden made his first six shots that night and scored 17 points in the first half of his first start against Missouri. "Just look out there on the court and you can see how much fun I'm having," Gooden said. "I knew going in I was going to be hot. I wanted the ball on every possession and I was going to put it up until I missed."

The hype for that game—combined with the performances by Gooden and Kirk Hinrich (23 points on 8-of-11 shooting)—created one of the great atmospheres ever in Allen Fieldhouse. Many longtime observers said it was the loudest crowd they had every heard. "It was unbelievably loud for 40 minutes," Missouri center Arthur Johnson said. "I couldn't even hear myself think."

That season, Gooden led the Jayhawks to their first Final Four since 1993, averaging a team-high 19.8 points on a squad that included Nick Collison, Jeff Boschee, Wayne Simien, and Hinrich. Gooden's leadership as a junior was a testament to how much a player could improve under the tutelage of Williams. The coach benched Gooden as a freshman and repeatedly scolded him at practice for his lack of focus and streetball mentality. "They pay me enough money to ship your ass back to Oakland on a bus," Williams screamed at one practice.

Fortunately, Williams never did. Gooden, whose jersey was retired in 2003 in what would've been his senior year after he turned pro, became just the second player in Kansas history to record at least 1,500 points, 900 rebounds, 100 blocks, and 100 steals in a career. Danny Manning was the other. Gooden ranks 18th on KU's all-time scoring list with 1,526 points; sixth in rebounding with 905; and third with 44 career double-doubles.

92 The Forgotten Coach

Most conversations about the coaching lineage at Kansas focus on the seven men most responsible for combining to accumulate more than 2,000 victories in program history. It's an amazing group, consisting of James Naismith, Phog Allen, Dick Harp, Ted Owens, Larry Brown, Roy Williams, and Bill Self. That's unfair to William O. Hamilton, the third head coach of the Jayhawks and a man who actually logged more seasons in that position than either Naismith or Harp.

Hamilton is KU's forgotten coach because his tour of duty was from 1909 to 1919 and, as the Kansas media guide points out, he "bridged the gap between Phog Allen's two tenures" as coach. In those 10 years, Hamilton had a 125–59 record for a .679 winning percentage. Those numbers are better than Naismith (55–60, .478, nine years) or Harp (121–82, .596, eight years).

Before arriving in Lawrence, Hamilton had been director of physical education at Central High School in Kansas City,

Two Other Unknown Coaches

What do Karl Schlademan and Howard Engleman have in common with Phog Allen, Larry Brown, and Bill Self? They are in the record book as coaches of the Kansas basketball team.

Schlademan won the only game he coached in 1920 before Allen began his second stint as KU coach. Engleman was 8–6 as he finished the 1947 season for Allen, who was ordered to take a rest following the 13th game that season. Allen had suffered a concussion working with his players in practice.

After W.O. Hamilton left in 1919, there were financial issues within the athletic department, and several coaches were asked to handle more than one sport. Schlademan was track coach and he was assigned the men's basketball team just as Allen was returning to Lawrence as athletic director. Schlademan won the season opener against Emporia State and then resigned to focus on his track squad.

Allen was already coaching the freshman team, so he signed up for the varsity as well. You could say it all worked out for the best. Allen stuck around until 1956 and had 590 wins when he finally left the Kansas bench for good.

Missouri, before taking the same title at William Jewell College in Liberty, Missouri.

Hamilton couldn't have had a much better debut season at KU. Tommy Johnson, who became KU's first All-American selection in 1909, and Vern "Shorty" Long led the Jayhawks to a remarkable 18–1 record. The only loss came to Washington University of St. Louis, a team the Jayhawks had defeated three other times that season. Kansas won or shared five Missouri Valley Conference championships in Hamilton's first six seasons. Conference titles and beating rivals had already become a big thing in Lawrence. Hamilton's teams won 23 of 36 against Missouri, and Kansas State was the only opponent to beat Kansas in 1914 and 1915.

Hamilton had a philosophy of substituting freely and using many players. But much of KU's success from 1913–15 could be attributed to Ralph "Lefty" Sproull, who became the first player to lead the Missouri Valley in scoring three straight years. Sproull had a 40-point game against Washington in 1913, and when you consider the entire Kansas team scored fewer than 40 points in 13 of 22 games that season, it really was a magnificent individual effort. That remained the KU individual game scoring record until Clyde Lovellette scored 44 against St. Louis in the 1952 NCAA tournament.

Hamilton also coached John Bunn, who went on to coach 42 years, and Dutch Lonborg, who coached at Northwestern for 23 seasons before returning as athletic director at KU. Both Bunn and Lonborg have been inducted into the Naismith Hall of Fame.

Hamilton had accepted athletic director duties in addition to coaching. But on June 10, 1919, he stepped down from both positions. He entered the business world, devoting more time to his Chevrolet dealership and stayed in Lawrence as a strong supporter of KU athletics until his death in 1951.

93 The Wild 2008 NBA Draft

One of the traditions associated with the NBA Draft involves the baseball cap handed to each player after he is selected. That hat is emblazoned with the logo of the player's new team, the franchise for which he will commence his professional future. But in 2008 perhaps the NBA should have bypassed this tradition.

Just weeks after Kansas won the 2008 NCAA championship, a record-setting five Jayhawks heard their names called in two rounds at New York's Madison Square Garden on June 26. All five were traded before the night was over. Darrell Arthur was swapped three times.

To say it was a wild night in the Big Apple would be putting it mildly. There was plenty of drama as more than two Jayhawks were selected in a single draft for the first time since the draft was trimmed to two rounds in 1989. The five players taken in two rounds of the draft tied the record for one school. Connecticut had five in 2006, and Florida matched that in 2007.

Brandon Rush, a lottery pick, was the first one taken. Arthur (27th overall) became the sympathetic figure who dropped lower than expected, and Mario Chalmers (34th) went early in the second round. Darnell Jackson was selected by the Miami Heat with the 52nd overall pick and Sasha Kaun, who already had signed with a team in his native Russia, became selection No. 56 when the Seattle SuperSonics called his name.

Rush, the No. 13 pick, wore a Portland Trail Blazers cap for about 30 minutes. He never seemed too concerned about the fit. Rush, who helped lead the Jayhawks to the NCAA title after coming back from ACL surgery, was dealt to the Indiana Pacers in a five-player deal. Rush answered questions with the gathered media with his Trail Blazers cap on before the deal was announced. But he didn't seem surprised by the trade. He had gotten word before he walked across the stage. "My reaction is the same," Rush said. "I'm going to do the same things to help Indiana win. Their coach [Jim O'Brien] is a defensive-minded coach and shoots the three. I didn't enjoy going through rehab, but winning a national championship and coming to the green room and being a lottery pick is a big blessing."

The roller-coaster ride for Rush was quick and harmless compared to what Arthur endured. Rush had to wait just one hour and 15 minutes before commissioner David Stern called his name. Arthur's wait was closer to two hours, and as the last player in the green room, he became one of the major story lines of the night. Rumors of a mysterious and unspecified kidney condition helped account for Arthur's tumble to the No. 27 pick. When the New

Jayhawks Draft History

Most KU sports fans associate Otto Schnellbacher with football, but the "Double Threat from Sublette" was the first Kansas basketball player taken in a pro basketball draft. Schnellbacher, an All-American receiver for the 1947 Jayhawks football team, was drafted by the Providence Steam Rollers in 1948 and played one season in the Basketball Association of America, the forerunner of the NBA.

Clyde Lovellette became KU's first NBA first-round draft pick in 1952. Lovellette, who earned titles with the Minneapolis Lakers and Boston Celtics, also was the first KU alum to play on a NBA championship team. The next first-round draft pick for KU was Wilt Chamberlain in 1958, and through 2013 there have been 29 Jayhawks selected in the first round. Through 2013, when Mario Chalmers got his second ring with the Miami Heat, 10 Jayhawks have played for an NBA champion.

Three Jayhawks who were first-round picks—Chamberlain, Jo Jo White, and Paul Pierce—have been named Most Valuable Player of the NBA Finals.

Orleans Hornets finally ended the wait and made the sophomore forward a first-round pick, he let out a sigh of relief and then hugged his mother and grandmother. "I was just waiting there anxiously and just nervous because I didn't know who was going to pick me up," Arthur said.

In the end, Arthur was traded three times—first from New Orleans to Portland. The Trail Blazers then dealt him to the Houston Rockets, who passed Arthur on to the Memphis Grizzlies. The crowd in the theater gave a big cheer for Arthur when he was selected. Even Stern applauded at the podium when the wait was finally over for the former Jayhawk. Arthur's mother, Sandra, said she was "overwhelmed" when she heard her son's name called. "We expected him to go sooner, so it was difficult to see the anticipation and the hurt that he might not go in the first round," she said. "But we got through this."

The Miami Heat drafted Jackson and then traded him to the Cleveland Cavaliers. (Call it the bizarro path of LeBron James.) The SuperSonics drafted Kaun and then sent him to the Cavaliers. The Minnesota Timberwolves took Chalmers and then traded him to Miami. Chalmers was asked to compare his famous shot against Memphis in the 2008 national championship game to being drafted. "Right now, that's a tough decision, but I'd definitely have to say being drafted in the NBA [is bigger]," he said. "It's a dream come true. It was a long wait for me, but it was a great accomplishment. After the national championship, we all talked about going in the first round together. Congratulations to [Rush and Arthur] for making it. Now I just have to make the best of my opportunity."

Chalmers has certainly accomplished that, having starting for a Heat team that won the NBA championship with James in 2012 and 2013.

94 Sherron and Cole

They were the guys left behind after the 2008 national championship. They were the guys who had to be leaders and help coach Bill Self put the pieces back together after Mario Chalmers, Brandon Rush, Russell Robinson, Darnell Jackson, Darrell Arthur, and Sasha Kaun departed. Two years later, in the final 30 seconds of their own KU careers, they wrapped their arms around one another in the type of embrace only teammates can understand. It was Senior Night 2010 in Allen Fieldhouse, and this was their moment.

Sherron Collins, the senior guard from the tough streets of Chicago, and Cole Aldrich, the shot-blocking center from Bloomington, Minnesota, did not arrive in Lawrence together. But they did walk away together, and on the night of March 3, as KU disposed of Kansas State 82–65 in another of those incredibly emotional goodbye scenes, that seemed so right.

When the 6'11" center released the 5'11" guard from his grasp, Collins made his way to the bench where Self was waiting. "I love ya," Self told Collins. Collins later told reporters: "He's told me that a few times. It meant more tonight."

Collins, who battled his weight constantly and got plenty of tough love from Self in his four years at KU, spent days stressing over his Senior Night speech. As he walked onto the floor with his mother, Stacey, and was presented his No. 4 jersey in the pregame ceremony, he sobbed constantly. Self gave him a little loving slap to the face, and then Collins went out and missed eight of his first nine shots. "I was a little jittery," Collins said. "I wanted to do well. I got out of my character a bit."

That had to be a first during his four years at KU. The second half was a different story. Collins had nine points, two assists, and

Sherron Collins, a 5'11" guard from Chicago, and Cole Aldrich, a 6'11" center from Minnesota, demonstrate their kinship during a 2009 NCAA tournament practice session.

two rebounds and combined with Aldrich on an 18–4 run that put the game away. Allen Fieldhouse was rocking. Aldrich, a perfect 55–0 in his career at Allen Fieldhouse, had seven points, three rebounds, and three blocks in the second half. It wasn't his Senior Night, but it was a well-known fact he was leaving for the NBA.

"We didn't talk about that because it's Senior Night—not Junior Night," Self said. "But it was emotional for Cole."

Even though they weren't the team's primetime players in 2008, they contributed to the NCAA run and both had huge Final Four moments. In the national semifinal against North Carolina, Aldrich had eight points, seven rebounds, and four blocks in 16 minutes. In the championship game against Memphis, Collins had six assists including the flip pass as he was falling down to Mario Chalmers for the transcendent three-pointer that sent the game into overtime.

Asked to show the way as Tyshawn Taylor, Marcus Morris, Brady Morningstar, and Xavier Henry surrounded them the next two years, the Jayhawks won 60 games and lost 11 and were 29–3 on the way to two Big 12 regular-season championships.

Collins and Aldrich fell short of a return to the Final Four and did so in painful fashion with a stunning loss to Northern Iowa in the 2010 NCAA tournament. But only Danny Manning and Tyshawn Taylor played more games at KU than Collins' 143. He ranks eight all-time in assists (552) and fifth in scoring (1,888 points). Aldrich's 253 blocks are third behind Jeff Withey and Greg Ostertag, and he ranks 48th in scoring with 1,038 points in three seasons.

After the game, Collins gave his senior speech surrounded by seven trophies—four from Big 12 regular season titles, two conference tournament titles, and, of course, the 2008 national championship trophy. At the end of the game, he spoke to the Fieldhouse crowd, which included 26 family members, for 10 minutes. "I didn't want to get off the court," Collins said. "I wish the game could have gone on all night."

95 Allen Kelley

Allen Kelley stood at center court in the Naismith Memorial Basketball Hall of Fame and had his picture taken with Oscar Robertson, Jerry West, and John Lucas. Kelley was obviously thrilled, and the smile on his face wasn't the only giveaway. Kelley was wearing a Hall of Fame jacket just like those other guys with the legendary basketball names.

Kelley's teammates from the 1960 USA men's Olympic basketball squad couldn't possibly imagine what that moment meant to the three-year letterman from Kansas. For a man who spent 45 years working in parts distribution for Caterpillar, Inc., the world-renowned manufacturer of construction equipment, it truly felt as if he was living the American dream.

He was on the NCAA championship team at Kansas in 1952, won an Olympic gold medal in 1960, and topped it all off by becoming a Hall of Famer during enshrinement ceremonies in Springfield, Massachusetts, on August 13, 2010. Kelley and his teammates on the 1960 Olympic team were inducted as a team that day as were the members of the more famous 1992 USA Basketball Dream Team. "This is the highlight of your life to be with a group like this," Kelley said. "[Playing in the Olympics] was more than a basketball game. It was a representation of America, our way of life, our economic system, and the fact we have our comfort. There's nothing like getting a gold medal and hearing the national anthem. I'm still reminded of it today when I go to a game at the University of Kansas, and you hear the Star Spangled Banner. It's a passion for your country that really sticks with you every day of your life."

In those days, the U.S. Olympic team was a collection of college All-Stars and the top players from corporately sponsored amateur teams in the National Industrial Basketball League. Kelley was a 5'11" guard for coach Warren Womble's Peoria Caterpillars, one of the ruling amateur teams from 1945–60. Robertson, Lucas, West, and Terry Dischinger were the leading scorers. Kelley played in five of the eight Olympic games and scored just four points. But he will tell you nothing could ever replace his Olympic experience. "It was kind of nice to have a front-row seat and watch the boys perform," Kelley said.

Kelley's older brother, Dean, also played at Kansas and then won Olympic gold in 1952. Allen was drafted by the NBA's Milwaukee Hawks in 1954 after his KU career ended, but pay was low and there were no benefits. "I've still got the letter, and the offer was $5,000," Kelley said. "They wanted me to pay my way out there, and then I had to make the team. I decided Caterpillar was more stability, so I went to Peoria and visited there. AAU was the place to be. But you went to work every day, and we practiced after work. When we were gone on [game] trips, somebody had to cover your job. Your salary was based on your job, and you were reviewed every year by your boss. Basketball had nothing to do with it."

On the day of his induction in Springfield, it was all about basketball. As he posed for pictures with some of the greatest players of all time, Kelley didn't look one bit out of place. Fifty years after winning gold, Kelley was a Hall of Famer.

96 Ray Evans

Before Clyde Lovellette, before Wilt Chamberlain, and long before Danny Manning, Kansas produced an athlete who has been described as "a true Jayhawk immortal." Most of the honors and stories about Ray Evans come from the football field, but in many ways he was an early day Bo Jackson—as one of the greatest two-sport athletes in NCAA history and an All-American in both football and basketball at Kansas.

He accomplished that and so much more despite the fact that World War II interrupted his career. Evans came to KU after graduating from Wyandotte High School in Kansas City, Kansas. After playing both sports in 1942 and 1943, he served in the Air Corps and then returned for the 1946 and 1947 seasons. Evans is the only athlete in KU history to have both his football jersey (42) and basketball jersey (15) retired. He was KU's first All-America selection in football (along with Otto Schnellbacher) and was a two-time selection as a Helms Foundation All-American for Phog Allen in basketball.

When his basketball jersey was hung from the rafters of Allen Fieldhouse on February 22, 1997, Evans told the sellout crowd of 16,300, "I always look to the right and see the 'Beware of the Phog' banner. Now I'll have to look to the left also." When the Jayhawks shared the Big 6 title in 1942, it marked the 19th time KU had won or shared a crown in Allen's 25 seasons as coach.

The next season Evans was part of Allen's "Iron Five" lineup that included Charlie B. Black, John Buescher, Otto Schnellbacher, and Armand Dixon. On February 26, 1943, a crowd of 3,384 packed Hoch Auditorium to see the Jayhawks defeat Oklahoma 42–35 for a fourth consecutive Big 6 title. Black and Dixon were out with injuries. That meant the starters played almost every minute of the game. Evans, a 6'1" guard, played an important role with stingy defense, and the crowd gave him a standing ovation when he fouled out.

Dixon was the only starter who was not named All-Conference. Evans and Black were All-Americans. But Allen turned down the chance to play in the district playoff because Black, Evans, and Schnellbacher were heading into the service immediately after the regular season. Allen wanted them to have time with their families. With those three back home for the 1945–46 season, the Jayhawks posted a 19–2 record, went 10–0, won the Big 6, and qualified for the NCAA tournament. The season ended there with a 49–38 loss to Oklahoma A&M (now Oklahoma State).

Evans averaged 8.3 points that season and 5.7 points as a senior when the Jayhawks were 16–11 overall and tied for third in the Big 6. That was the same season Allen suffered a concussion in early January, leading Howard Engleman to complete the season as coach.

Evans has been called the "Pied Piper" for KU football and basketball. During his days in the service, he made friends and recruited top athletes who arrived in Lawrence after the war. One of those was Don Fambrough, perhaps the most beloved figure in KU football history as a player, assistant coach, and head coach. "He was just an exceptional individual," Fambrough told *The Topeka Capital-Journal* when Evans died in 1999.

Evans had already made college football history before he left for the war. He is the only player in NCAA history to lead the nation in both passing (1,117 yards) and interceptions (10) in the same season. He did that in 1942. Evans continued to do a little of everything when he returned. He played quarterback and halfback and set a KU total offense record that stood for 20 years.

In 1947 he ran and passed for 1,018 yards and was named an All-American. He was the star of the 1948 Orange Bowl, scoring both of KU's touchdowns, even though Georgia Tech won

20–14. Evans played one professional season with the Pittsburgh Steelers before a rib injury ended his career. "Ray was one of those persons who took a football program from nothing to excellence," Schnellbacher told *The Capital-Journal.*

Evans followed that up with a remarkable career in business and public service in Kansas City. He became president of Traders National Bank, played a role in bringing the Chiefs football team to Kansas City, and was part owner of the NBA's Kansas City Kings. He spent 12 years on the Kansas Board of Regents and was president of the KU Alumni Association. "He was loyal to the University of Kansas," Fambrough told *The Capital-Journal.* "Football, basketball, whatever—they knew they had Ray Evans' backing. He was true, blue KU."

97 An Unexpected Collapse

Add Mitch McGary to the long list of NCAA tournament villains in Kansas basketball history. Rank Trey Burke among the players who broke Jayhawk hearts with improbable clutch shots. The former had 25 points and 14 rebounds, and the latter had all 23 of his points after halftime and added 10 assists. It all happened on March 29, 2013 at Cowboys Stadium in Arlington, Texas, as Michigan won 87–85 in overtime.

There's no shame in losing in the Sweet 16 to a team as talented as the 2013 Wolverines. Michigan went onto the NCAA title game before losing to Louisville. But allowing a 14-point lead to get away in the final seven minutes and losing a five-point lead in the final 21 seconds is an excruciating way to end a season. "Well, this will certainly go down as one of the toughest games that obviously we've been a part of and certainly I've been a part of," Kansas coach Bill Self said. "But props to Michigan for making all the plays late."

Self's summary couldn't have been more accurate. This was a collapse of epic proportions. Kansas had its largest lead of the game—up 14 with 6:50 remaining in the second half. But then Michigan outscored KU 33–17 in the final 11:30 of the game. Burke, the consensus Player of the Year in college basketball, had 15 points in that stretch. The Jayhawks? They had as many turnovers (five) as field goals. "We had a chance to seal the game," senior Travis Releford said. "But we made some bonehead plays late."

In a strange kind of way, Releford's comment applied to the entire season. The Jayhawks were put together in a way we don't often see these days in college basketball. Self started four seniors—Releford, Jeff Withey, Kevin Young, and Elijah Johnson—and a remarkable freshman named Ben McLemore, who would head to the NBA after one record-breaking season. They will be remembered for a 31–6 record, including a 14–4 Big 12 mark that earned Kansas a share of a ninth consecutive regular-season conference title. It was the fourth straight season of 30 or more wins, tying a NCAA record set by Memphis (2006–09), which later vacated the 2007–08 season as part of its NCAA penalties.

The Jayhawks won their ninth Big 12 tournament championship and sixth under Self and climbed as high as No. 1 in the *USA TODAY* rankings and No. 2 in the Associated Press poll. They lost to Michigan State 67–64 in the second game of the season and then rattled off 18 consecutive victories to establish themselves as a national title contender.

McLemore led the way in scoring, Withey elevated the art of shot blocking to new heights, and Releford, the master of self-sacrifice, continued to be a lockdown defender and also discovered his three-point touch. Young, with his Fear the Fro persona, rebounded, defended, and provided energy. In the conference portion of the schedule, freshman Perry Ellis emerged as a key contributor and offered hope for the future.

And then there was Johnson. A combo guard trying to fill the role of point guard, Johnson could thrill one moment and confound the next. More than once, Self said the Jayhawks didn't have a point guard. And when the Jayhawks lost consecutive games to Oklahoma State, TCU, and Oklahoma in February—the first three-game losing streak at KU since 2005—Johnson absorbed much of the heat.

A 62–55 loss at TCU on February 6 was the NCAA tournament equivalent of a No. 16 seed knocking off a No. 1 seed. The Jayhawks were 3-for-22 from the field in the first half when they managed just 13 points. "It's the worst team Kansas has ever put on the floor since Dr. Naismith was here," Self said. "I think he had some bad teams when he lost to Topeka YMCA in his first couple years. The first half...there hasn't been a team play worse than that offensively."

The Jayhawks returned to Allen Fieldhouse, routed Kansas State and Texas in consecutive games, and rediscovered their groove. KU won seven straight before losing the regular season finale at Baylor. The Jayhawks passed NCAA tests against Western Kentucky and North Carolina and were on their way to a third consecutive regional final before the bottom dropped out against the Wolverines.

Michigan was down five with 35 seconds left when Tim Hardaway Jr. missed a three-pointer, but Glenn Robinson III won a scramble for the ball and hit a reverse layup to force Kansas to win the game at the line. Johnson, though, missed a free throw, and the Wolverines snared the rebound and raced down the floor. McGary put Johnson on the floor with a hard screen, and Burke stepped behind it to nail a three-pointer from well beyond the arc with 4.2

seconds left. "[Burke's shot] was from 27 to 30 feet," Self said. "But still it was a great play by a big-time player."

The lead changed hands five times in overtime until McGary hit a short jumper over Johnson to put Michigan ahead for good. KU's season ended on its final possession—an out-of-control drive by Johnson and a missed three-point, game-winning attempt by Naadir Tharpe. "We just didn't get it done," Self said.

98 A Matter of Life and Death

No one would ever question the dedication of Kansas basketball fans. When the Jayhawks are playing, the streets of Lawrence grow quiet and still. At times, events must be rescheduled. The latest example—and perhaps one of the most extreme—came in March 2013 when the Jayhawks played Michigan in the Sweet 16 of the NCAA tournament. Donald J. "Don" Shoulberg, 76, who received a PhD from KU and taught in the School of Social Welfare, died four days before the game. His family clearly understood the importance of Kansas basketball in his life—and perhaps in the lives of those closest to him.

Shoulberg's obituary was ordinary except for this information regarding visitation on March 29, the date of the game against Michigan: "A Prayer Service will be held at 5 PM at the mortuary followed by a visitation until tip-off time for the KU basketball game (approximately 6:30 PM)."

A visitor to Shoulberg's mortuary guestbook suggested that his late friend would be watching as the Jayhawks continued their pursuit of another national championship. "Most of our interaction occurred on the office elevator, and our conversations almost always focused on KU basketball. I understand why the visitation will end before our tip-off against Michigan. Don's steadying hand will be a significant factor in our attempt to knock off Michigan in continuing our quest."

Another entry, simply from "Jayhawk Fan," said, "Although I didn't know Don, I saw the obituary on Yahoo! Sports. I am sorry for your loss, but hope that Don will be able to celebrate in heaven a Hawk win tonight."

Memorial services were scheduled for the following morning at St. John the Evangelist Catholic Church in Lawrence. Those in attendance mourned not only the passing of Shoulberg, but also the end of another Kansas basketball season. Michigan launched a late-game comeback to defeat the Jayhawks 87–85 in overtime.

But the sun did come up again.

99 Legends of the Phog

The movie version could have been called *Fieldhouse of Dreams*. An exhibition basketball game was played in Allen Fieldhouse on September 24, 2011—a game unlike any other held in the Phog before or after. The starting lineup for one team was Mario Chalmers, Wayne Simien, Brandon Rush, Julian Wright, and Cole Aldrich. The other squad started with Darnell Valentine, Marcus Morris, Paul Pierce, Nick Collison, and Markieff Morris.

Was this heaven? Was this an Iowa cornfield near Collison's hometown? No, it was Kansas. *Lawrence, Kansas.* They jammed 16,300 fans into Allen Fieldhouse for this Blue-White game and called it "Legends of the Phog." With the NBA in a work stoppage, many of the pro players from the Roy Williams and Bill Self eras were available, and that set the stage for a very special event. "Not very often can you spin a negative into a positive, but we get an opportunity to do so with the NBA lockout," Self said. "We are going to have a KU alumni game, which is basically a legends game in which many of our most recent KU greats are going to come back, allowing them a chance to run out of the tunnel one more time and play a game hopefully in front of a packed house."

Self had the right idea but he couldn't have imagined the way this exhibition game ended. Pierce, back in the Phog for the first time since his jersey had been retired eight years earlier, broke a 108–108 tie by hitting a three-point basket over the hands of defender Brandon Rush with five seconds remaining. Making that shot even better was the fact Pierce had bolted over to public address announcer Max Falkenstein just seconds earlier to remind the KU broadcasting legend that he never lost a game in Allen Fieldhouse during his three-year Kansas career.

As much as the crowd loved Pierce's shot, it simply set the stage for Mario Chalmers to re-enact his three-point shot from the 2008 national championship game. Chalmers, who capped KU's furious comeback in San Antonio to force overtime and give the Jayhawks a chance to defeat Memphis, made his three again. This time it tied the game as Chalmers scored over defender Ryan Robertson with one second left.

Pierce came up behind the Miami Heat's Chalmers and gave a bear hug to his Eastern Conference rival. Then Self informed officials that the game would end in a 111–111 tie. "I said to Mario, 'That's the way it's supposed to end,'" Pierce said. "Everybody remembers his championship shot. It was just a replay of it tonight."

Allen Fieldhouse rocked the night of the 2008 championship game. It rocks before every game when the videotape of Chalmers' shot against Memphis is shown. And it rocked again for the Legends of the Phog as the crowd chanted "Mario, Mario" during a timeout called by coach Ted Owens, who had Chalmers on his White team.

Legends of the Phog Box Score

WHITE 111, BLUE 111

WHITE (111)—Chalmers 7–15 0–0 17, Simien 2–8 0–0 4, Rush 8–19 1–2 18, Wright 7–7 0–0 14, Aldrich 7–11 0–0 14, Hawkins 2–5 0–0 5, Thomas 3–8 0–0 8, Jackson 5–7 0–2 11, Graves 4–7 0–0 9, Arthur 4–11 0–0 9, Moody 1–1 0–0 2. Totals 50–99 1–4 111.

BLUE (111)—Valentine 0–0 0–0 0, Marcus Morris 5–12 0–0 11, Pierce 6–14 0–0 16, Collison 6–8 0–0 14, Markieff Morris 4–9 0–0 10, Ostertag 1–2 0–0 2, Robertson 6–8 0–0 15, Bradford 1–3 0–0 2, Pollard 4–6 0–0 8, Kellogg 0–4 0–0 0, Henry 8–13 4–5 23, Selby 5–9 0–1 10. Totals 46–88 4–6 111.

Halftime—White 63, Blue 61. 3-point goals—White 10–37 (Chalmers 3–9, Thomas 2–6, Rush 1–6, Arthur 1–6, Graves 1–4, Hawkins 1–3, Jackson 1–3); Blue 15–44 (Pierce 4–10, Henry 3–6, Robertson 3–5, Markieff Morris 2–6, Collison 2–4, Marcus Morris 1–5, Kellogg 0–3, Selby 0–3, Bradford 0–2). Fouled out—none. Rebounds— White 51 (Aldrich 19), Blue 43 (Pierce 8). Assists—White 24 (Chalmers 10), Blue 30 (Collison 10). Total fouls—White 5, Blue 2. Attendance—16,300.

Courtesy: *The Topeka Capital-Journal*

"I heard it," said Chalmers, who had 17 points, 10 assists, and five steals in 26 minutes. "It's something I've done before and something I'm accustomed to doing. This type of atmosphere was great to go out to have fun and be with the older guys and the coaches."

Xavier Henry led the Blue team coached by Larry Brown with 23 points. Pierce had 16. Nick Collison came close to a triple-double for the Blue with 14 points, 10 assists, and seven rebounds. Rush led the White team with 18 points while Cole Aldrich had 14 points and 19 rebounds. The Morris twins and Josh Selby, all NBA draft picks earlier in 2011, were the freshest alums in the game. Valentine, 52, was the oldest Jayhawk to play in the exhibition. The former Wichita star had one assist and one steal in four minutes.

The majority of game's proceeds went to charities, including the Boys & Girls Club of Lawrence, in memory of former KU assistant coach Neil Dougherty, who passed away from a heart attack in the summer of 2011. It was a day for legends, a day for emotions, but most of all, it was an opportunity for generations of Jayhawks to come together and share the deep bond created by Kansas basketball. Gary Bedore of the *Lawrence Journal-World* wrote that Self "noticed Pierce wipe away a tear during the pregame video introductions of all the players."

Pierce laughed and told Self if Allen Fieldhouse had been that loud when he played, he would have stayed in school "four or five years." "This is a family type program," Pierce said. "We have that relationship because we are Jayhawks. It's beautiful…This is a special place. Coach said any time we can, come back. I plan on coming back a lot more than I have in the past. You don't realize how special this place is until you step back away from it and you see it again. It's unbelievable."

100 Andrew Wiggins

If you have a Twitter account and were logged on just after noon on May 14, 2013, you probably glanced at the list of what was trending and saw this at the top: "Andrew Wiggins to Kansas."

That's how much of the college basketball world got the news that the consensus top prospect in the class of 2013 had decided to sign with coach Bill Self and the Jayhawks. Wiggins, a 6'8" wing player with a wingspan around seven feet long, waited until the next to last day of the spring signing period to announce he had picked KU over Kentucky, North Carolina, and Florida State.

Wiggins isn't just the top prospect in his class; he's the kind of recruit who comes along just once in many years. He has drawn comparisons to LeBron James, Kobe Bryant, Scottie Pippen, Kevin Durant, Carmelo Anthony, and other great players who went on to rank among the best players ever in the NBA. Most scouts agree he would have been the No. 1 pick in the 2013 NBA Draft if he had been eligible.

Evan Daniels, a recruiting analyst for Scout.com, broke down Wiggins' game: "On the court, Wiggins has blossomed as a player. He's the best defender in the 2013 class, handles the ball well for his size, and is great scorer in transition and attacking the basket. What stands out about Wiggins is he's just scratching the surface of his potential. He's yet to develop a mid-range game and is just an okay shooter to the three-point stripe. With reps and development, he has the potential to be a future NBA All-Star."

Months before he would even wear the Kansas jersey for the first time, longtime observers of KU basketball were ranking Wiggins with Clyde Lovellette, Wilt Chamberlain, and Danny Manning as the most significant recruits in the history of the program. In a world where secrets no longer exist, this signing went against what has become the standard. The Canadian export—who announced his signing at Huntington Prep in West Virginia, where he averaged 23.4 points, 11.2 rebounds, 2.6 blocks, and 2.5 assists while leading his team to a 30–3 record—had told no one. In fact he hadn't talked to Self in more than a week.

Wiggins opted against nationally televising his press conference or picking from one of four hats on the table in front of him like recruits often do. He arranged it that Grant Traylor, a sportswriter for *The (Huntington) Herald-Dispatch*, would break the news on Twitter as soon as he gave his decision. "I just followed my heart," Wiggins said.

Just like that, Kansas climbed from a borderline top 25 preseason pick to a team projected as Final Four and national championship contender. "I'm looking forward to getting there and just doing my thing," Wiggins said.

Self and KU assistant coach Kurtis Townsend didn't know until a reporter called with the news. Suddenly, Self said, his telephone "blew up" with congratulatory text messages. "Obviously, everyone in Jayhawk-land is overwhelmed and excited today," Self said in a statement. "This was a pleasant surprise because we never had an idea which way he was leaning."

Heading into the 2013–14 season, Self faced the task of replacing all five starters from a team that lost to Michigan in the Sweet 16. But Wiggins joined an already outstanding recruiting class that included center Joel Embiid, forward Brannen Greene, and guards Conner Frankamp, Frank Mason, and Wayne Selden. Sophomore Perry Ellis, who played so well for the Jayhawks down the stretch last season, joins Selden and Wiggins to give KU three McDonald's All-Americans on the roster. After Wiggins signed, Memphis transfer Tarik Black also chose the Jayhawks.

Signing Wiggins, though, was the major coup for Self. "The competition [for Wiggins] was very stiff, and we were fortunate that we were able to ink him," Self said. "He's a tremendous talent and a terrific kid. Probably an even better kid than he is a talent. We think he has a chance to be about as good a prospect as we've ever had."

Acknowledgments

I was halfway through this book project, already on a deadline extension, and terribly behind when I pushed away from my laptop computer for one day and took a break. I attended the induction ceremony of the New England Basketball Hall of Fame in June because I was one of the honorees. Not sure how that happened. I never played the game with any skill, let alone in New England, but I have written a lot of words about the hoops in this region, especially about the Connecticut Huskies. Needless to say, I was humbled and honored by the award.

As part of the induction ceremony there was a seminar on writing basketball books. Two of my favorite writers and respected friends, Bob Ryan and Bill Reynolds, were on the panel. When asked to explain the process of writing a book they answered there are three stages to success: inspiration, perspiration, and desperation. I had to laugh. It was good to know I had reached the third stage. I begin by thanking Bob and Bill for the push I needed to reach the finish line.

This is my second book on the University of Kansas basketball program. The first was a visually oriented coffee table book, and I provided text covering the complete history of the Jayhawks. Given the research I did for that book and my knowledge of Kansas basketball, I accepted this project with little reservation. That doesn't mean the writing came easy. Real life and full-time jobs have a tendency to get in the way—more often than not. I want to thank everyone at Triumph Books for their patience.

Why write this book? Well, there's something special about KU. Once the Crimson and Blue gets in your blood, life is never the same. And there is a connection between Jayhawks that doesn't exist anywhere else. Covering college basketball on a national scale,

I've observed other fanbases, alumni organizations, students, and athletic competition at every level. They simply don't size up to KU. People say KU's enrollment is too big, and students get lost in the crowd. I never found that to be true, at least based on the experience of the four Jayhawks in my family and countless friends.

My wife and I graduated in 1980, but we return to Lawrence and talk to professors who are still at KU. Most of my journalism teachers have left or passed away, but I will never forget learning valuable lessons from Calder Pickett, Lee Young, and Dr. John Bremner, the best editing coach in the world. I took a photojournalism class from Rich Clarkson, the most famous photographer in NCAA basketball history. I have had Lawrence reunions with Susanne Shaw, former associate dean of the school, and stay in touch with former dean Del Brinkman through social media.

To me, Kansas means still corresponding with Tom Stidham, associate director of bands and the best KU basketball band director ever. Tom treats me like a star, even though I was an alternate in marching band in 1976. And he still remembers my wife came to KU from Chittenango, New York. What a truly amazing memory that man has. Kansas means reuniting with a fellow band member after 30 years. Curt Ramm and I played in a KU pep band, covering fight songs for every conference team during the 1976 Big 8 holiday tournament at Kemper Arena in Kansas City. We both live in Connecticut now. I put away my clarinet a long time ago, but Curt still manages to play a little trumpet, touring with Bruce Springsteen and The E Street Band when he is between other gigs. The Boss only settles for the best.

Kansas is English professor James Carothers stopping by your youngest son's graduation party because you and both of your sons took courses taught by him. How cool is that? Kansas means lifelong friendships with quality human beings such as the late Bob Frederick, Floyd Temple, and Don Fambrough—three Jayhawks I miss very much when I visit Lawrence these days. The first Kansas basketball player I ever interviewed was Dr. Ken Koenigs back on media day in 1977. Now we are both New Englanders, and our families have been reunited through KU basketball watch parties in our area.

The best part of my job is interviewing players, both old and new. The national championship team in 2008 was delightful to cover because the players were good people, a real pleasure to be around. Kansas fans can rest assured that the vast majority of Jayhawks are good citizens and well-rounded human beings. They represent well.

Clyde Lovellette is entertaining and engaging, a great storyteller, and a Jayhawks treasure. Interviewing Clyde, Bill Hougland, Bill Lienhard, and Al Kelley about their experiences with Phog Allen and the 1952 championship was a tremendous thrill. I can't thank Jerry Waugh enough for his perspective on Phog and Wilt all the way through Roy and Bill. Spending time with Jo Jo White, Bud Stallworth, and Danny Manning has been a dream come true. I thank all the KU players who have cooperated over the years.

I regret I never had the chance to meet Phog Allen, a truly fascinating man. But coaches Ted Owens, Roy Williams, and Bill Self have been absolutely wonderful to me. They have always responded when I needed something, and I appreciate it more than I can say. Kansas is very fortunate to have had those three men occupy the head coach's office.

Associate athletic directors Jim Marchiony and Chris Theisen were extremely helpful on this project. They answered questions, looked up facts, contacted their sources to factcheck stories, and always responded quickly. While many college media guides around the country have abandoned history to increasingly serve as a recruiting tool, the guides produced by Chris and his staff respect the entire KU story and keep vital stats at your fingertips. Thanks to Candace Dunback of KU athletics, university archivist Rebecca Schulte, and Lisa Eitner of KU Bookstores for all your help over the years. And thanks to KU broadcasters Max Falkenstien and Bob Davis for greeting me with smiles—and lots of great stories—whenever I cover KU games.

I can't forget my writing buddies. Blair Kerkhoff is my source on all things Phog. You could say Blair wrote the book on Phog because he actually did. It's one my of all-time favorite sports books. Chuck Woodling and Gary Bedore have preserved the history of Kansas basketball at the *Lawrence Journal-World* for a long, long time, and I will always call them friends. Gary and I worked together on the *University Daily Kansan*, along with Rob Rains, who recently wrote the definitive book on James Naismith. Rob and I could never have guessed our sons, B.J. Rains and Joe Davis, would later become friends covering KU sports.

A special thanks goes out to Doug Vance, who provided the connection to Triumph Books and made it possible for me to write this book. Doug started out as a professional contact during his time in the KU athletic department. Now I consider him a close friend. His books with Jeff Bollig are so well done and were tremendous resources. I thank you both for your friendship and hard work.

I would be remiss if I didn't thank my professional mentors, Jon Pessah and Arthur Pincus. They always believe in me. They have been there for me during some difficult times the past 10 years, and I am forever grateful. My parents, Don and Loretta Davis, got this whole thing started by taking me to KU games as a child. I'm sure they had no idea it would lead to this. Neither did I. It's a shame my dad isn't still with us to read this book, but I think he would be proud.

Most of all thanks to my faithful family. I begin with our cats, Jake and Ella, who are indeed members of the family. They are my daytime companions when I'm writing at home, furry bosses who keep me on task. Ella unexpectedly became ill and passed away while I was writing this book—on my birthday. She was a sweetheart; we remain heartbroken, and Jake misses her very much.

Contrary to popular belief my sons, Pat and Joe, were not forced to attend KU. They made the choice themselves, but there were no complaints from Mom and Dad. It allowed us to reconnect with many of the friends I've already mentioned and others. During this project they offered their help and support whenever I hit speed bumps. You have grown into fine young men, and I love you very much.

I met my wife, Nancy, in the KU marching band. We both played clarinet, and since I was an alternate, she got me through some tough last-minute assignments on the football fields at K-State and Missouri. She still has me marching in the right direction after 33 years of marriage. In recent months when I screamed out, "I can't do this," she simply replied, "Yes, you can." She was right. When I read chapters out loud, she listened. When I needed editing, she grabbed a pen and went to work. We have an excellent partnership. Thanks for pulling me through the desperation stage. Love you, baby.

Sources

Books

Bollig, Jeff and Vance, Doug. *What It Means To Be A Jayhawk.* Chicago, Illinois: Triumph Books, 2008.

Clarkson, Rich. *The Kansas Century: 100 Years of Jayhawk Championship Basketball.* Kansas City, Missouri: Andrews McMeel Publishing, 1997.

Davis, Ken. *The University of Kansas Basketball Vault: The History of the Jayhawks.* Atlanta, Georgia: Whitman Publishing, LLC, 2008.

Falkenstien, Max; Vance, Doug. *Max and the Jayhawks.* Wichita, Kansas: The Wichita Eagle & Beacon Publishing Company, Inc., 1996.

Hendel, John. *Kansas Jayhawks History-making basketball.* Kansas City, Missouri: Walsworth Publishing Company, 1991.

Kerkhoff, Blair. *Phog Allen: The Father of Basketball Coaching.* Indianapolis, Indiana: Masters Press, 1996.

Kerkhoff, Blair. *A Century of Jayhawk Triumphs.* Lenexa, Kansas: Addax Publishing Group, 1997.

Rains, Rob with Carpenter, Helen. *James Naismith: The Man Who Invented Basketball.* Philadelphia, Pennsylvania: Temple University Press, 2009.

Self, Bill with Rohde, John. *Bill Self: At Home In the Phog.* Overland Park, Kansas: Ascend Media, LLC, 2008.

Smith, Dean with Kilgo, John and Jenkins, Sally. *A Coach's Life.* New York: Random House, 1999.

Sports Illustrated. *100 Years of Hoops.* Birmingham, Alabama: Oxmoor House, 1991.

Vance, Doug and Bollig, Jeff. *Beware of the Phog.* Champaign, Illinois: Sports Publishing L.L.C., 2004.

Newspapers
Lawrence Journal-World
The Kansas City Star
The Topeka Capital-Journal
The Hartford Courant
The New York Times
The Washington Post
Los Angeles Times
USA TODAY

Magazines
Sports Illustrated, Kansas Jayhawks National Champions 2008
Jayhawk Tip-Off, Maple Street Press

Websites
KUSports.com
KUAthletics.com
Scout.com
FoxSports.com
NBCSports.com
ASAPSports.com

Videos and other sources
Louderback scrapbook. Kenneth Spencer Research Library. 1951–1952.
The Golden Jubilee of Basketball Souvenir Magazine. Kenneth Spencer Research Library. 1941.
Phog Allen's letters. Kenneth Spencer Research Library. Multiple years.
University of Kansas Basketball Media and NCAA Tournament Guides, 1951–2013.

Basketball Man: The Amazing True Story of Dr. Naismith and His Invention. Kansas City: Double Dog Sports & Entertainment, 2007.

Hardwood Heavens: Allen Fieldhouse. INHD.com. and Collegiate Images, 2006.

Personal interviews